D1601340

GLOBALIZING INSTITUTIONS

Globalizing Institutions

Case studies in regulation and innovation

Edited by

JANE JENSON
Department of Political Science
University of Montreal, Canada

BOAVENTURA DE SOUSA SANTOS
School of Economics
University of Coimbra, Portugal

Ashgate

Aldershot • Burlington USA • Singapore • Sydney

Published by
Ashgate Publishing Limited
Gower House
Croft Road
Aldershot
Hampshire GU11 3HR
England

Ashgate Publishing Company
131 Main Street
Burlington
Vermont 05401
USA

Ashgate website: http://www.ashgate.com

British Library Cataloguing in Publication Data
Jenson, Jane
  Globalizing institutions : case studies in social
  regulation and innovation
  1. Social institutions 2. Social change 3. International
  relations - Social aspects
  I. Title II. Santos, Boaventura de Sousa
  303.4'82

Library of Congress Control Number: 00-132594

ISBN 0 7546 1404 2

Printed and bound in Great Britain by MPG Books Ltd, Bodmin, Cornwall

Contents

Contributing Authors

Harry W. Arthurs
Osgoode Hall Law School and Department of Political Science
York University, Canada

Ruth Buchanan
Faculty of Law
University of British Columbia, Canada

Jane Jenson
Department of Political Science
University of Montreal, Canada

E. Fuat Keyman
Department of Political Science and Public Administration
Bilkent University, Turkey

Sally Engle Merry
Department of Anthropology
Wellesley College, USA

Maria Celia Paoli
Department of Sociology
University of São Paulo, Brazil

Boaventura de Sousa Santos
School of Economics
University of Coimbra, Portugal

Gay W. Seidman
Department of Sociology
University of Wisconsin-Madison, USA

Lucie White
Law School
Harvard University, USA

Barbara Yngvesson
School of Social Science
Hampshire College, USA

Acknowledgements

This book has its origins in a project sponsored by the Canadian Institute for Advanced Research, through its Programme on Law and the Determinants of Social Ordering. The progamme was formally concluded in July, 1996. However, a number of members of the programme – with several scholars recruited specifically as contributors to this book – continued the work thereafter with the financial support of the Institute. The editors wish to express their appreciation for the support provided, and for the efforts of Liora Salter, the last Director of the Program.

Introduction: Case Studies and Common Trends in Globalizations

JANE JENSON AND BOAVENTURA DE SOUSA SANTOS

Globalization is a word which trips easily off many lips. It is commonplace for everyone from journalists, business people and political leaders to ecologists and other social movement activists to frame their behaviour in terms of global events and processes. Despite, or perhaps because of, the term being so prevalent, globalization as both a popular idea and a concept lacking specificity. Moreover, its influences are usually asserted rather than analysed.

The starting point of this volume is not to dismiss the notion of globalization. We do not share the predisposition of those who, in the face of complexity and lack of specificity, choose to emphasize continuities in social relations and the on-going central role played by the national state, for example (Hirst and Thompson 1996). Rather, all the authors in this volume share two premises which place global processes at the heart of their analyses. One premise is that profound reconfigurations and adjustments in social relations are occurring as a result of a shifting of spatial relations. A variety of social relations now stretch across space in novel ways (Giddens 1990; Robertson 1992; Castells 1996; Featherstone, Lash, and Robertson 1997). Because social relations always involve the deployment of power, a second premise is that such shifts will provoke changes in the patterning of unequal power relations. Globalization means, in other words, that there are losers as well as winners, just as there have been at every other moment in history. If any consensus exists about the proper responses to current conditions, this agreement is often no more than the expression of the hegemony of the winners.

If all the authors in this volume accept that we are experiencing changes that go under the label of globalization, they do not conceptualize the phenomenon as a single thing or single process. A starting point for our analysis is that there are many globalizations, and the noun should most properly be used in the plural. Moreover, as will be elaborated upon in detail below, globalizations are not "global" things; they are no more than the spread of particular localisms. They are, in other words, **globalized localisms**. In addition, the process of making the global always involves the remaking of **localized globalisms**.[1]

In order to grasp these processes in concrete, historical analyses, this volume focuses on a series of case studies. In doing so it highlights the actions of many agents, both hegemonic and counter-hegemonic, engaged in globalizing the local and localizing the global. The privileged method for achieving such concrete analysis is to foreground institutions, by which we mean the point at which agents encounter social structures. All of the chapters focus on the ways in which globalizations are being institutionalized, both by promoting a particular localism to the status of a global phenomenon and by embedding new social relations and their patterns of unequal power in concrete local spaces.

Thinking in the Plural: from Globalization to Globalizations

Most definitions of globalization centre on the economic, focusing on the new world economy that has emerged in the last decades as the result of the trans-nationalization of the production of goods and services and of markets, especially financial markets (Boyer and Drache 1996). New information technologies allow a sub-national state, for example a Canadian province such as New Brunswick, to package its territory as an attractive site for the production of consumer services, as Ruth Buchanan's chapter recounts. This production occurs far distant in space not only from corporate headquarters but even from the consumers of the services. Personalized service no longer requires that provider and consumer share the same geographical space; technology and labour processes can shrink distances so as to generate the appearance of intimate knowledge and proximity of provider and consumer.

With this shift, certain transnational firms producing goods or providing services have achieved the status of global actors. Regional agreements that render much less relevant the borders of national sovereignty, such as the North American Free Trade Agreement (NAFTA) and the European Union, also contribute to the construction of, if not a borderless world, one in which border crossings have different meanings than previously. As economic crises – for example, the 1998 "meltdowns" in Asia, Russia and Latin America – and especially efforts to manage them make abundantly clear, markets for capital and investment stretch around the world. If, at the end of the 19th century, "the sun never set on the British Empire," at the end of our century there is always a major stock exchange open and ready to do business with buyers and sellers located anywhere in the world.

Despite the importance of the restructured economic practices and institutions which have generated such global economic flows, the understanding of globalization used in this volume is never confined to the economic realm. This is because much more than trade and production relations are transnational. Persons also traverse – and transgress – borders, whether as the – sometimes illegal – immigrants from Latin America whom Lucie White locates in child care centres in Los Angeles or as the senior executives of transnational corporations whose migration from regional cities hollows out community capacity, as Harry Arthurs finds. Negotiations for constitutional reform in the early 1990s in South Africa, for example, were profoundly marked by trans-border exchanges of feminist ideas and practices. Such exchanges, stretching from Cape Town to Beijing, from Johannesburg to London, injected new claims into struggles to define a post-apartheid, democratic and more egalitarian South Africa, as Gay Seidman recounts here. Conversely, other types of trans-border exchanges, such as the global diffusion and imposition of the neoliberal crusade in favour of free markets everywhere, have killed Brazil's pioneering institutional innovations in the field of capital and labour relations, as shown by Maria Celia Paoli. In her chapter, Barbara Yngvesson describes how inter-country adoption refashions family forms and definitions of nationality, as well as contacts among adoption agencies widely separated geographically.

Indeed, a wide range of social relations are being restructured as individuals and collective actors make and remake social, political and cultural institutions. State institutions in general are being subjected to strong globalized pressures which, in some cases, call for the weakening of state power (in economic regulation or welfare policies) while in others, call for the strengthening of state power (in the fight against crime and illegal immigration). Illustrative of this is the emerging prominence of courts in the last decade, as analyzed by Boaventura Santos. Another example is the retrenched definition of citizenship and citizen rights described by Maria Celia Paoli and by Jane Jenson. The latter's chapter describes the shrinking of T. H. Marshall's tripartite categorization of citizenship to a set of two, as social rights are reduced and political struggles limited to narrower political goals.

Our understanding of globalization in the plural, as multidimensional, and located in the unequal power relations of social relations, leads to the following definition that serves to organize this volume: globalization is the process by which a given local condition or entity succeeds in traversing borders and extending its reach over the globe and, in doing so, develops the capacity to designate a rival social condition or entity as local.[2]

Two components of this definition merit further attention. One is the relationship between that which is termed global and that termed local, while the second is the notion of power.

Thinking of globalizations as the extension of particular localisms means directing analysis toward a search for the specific processes which render one condition or entity the manifestation of the global and another the simple expression of the local. Such processes are not new, of course. In the 19th and first half of the 20th century, the model of European modernity and its practices – economic, political, religious, familial – of "civilization" extended its reach around the globe. This frequently led states, rising modernizing elites, and other social forces to manifest their "will to civilization" (Ferro, 1995) via a displacement of local beliefs, identities and social forces. The latter were thereby laboriously localized as "traditional" or "backward," in the name of an alternative localism attaining then a global reach, that of Western modernity. Early 19th century restructuring of political-legal authority in Hawaii (analyzed here by Sally Merry) and 20th century Kemalist nationalism in Turkey (presented by Fuat Keyman) provide two examples among many of the elevation of a specific localism – the European – to the status of global truth that is then labeled civilized behaviour.

However, as the latter case also illustrates, the previous waves of globalization are being displaced by more recent ones and, in light of the latter, recodified as localisms blocking the high road of globalization. Thus the Kemalist model of modern Turkish national identity is currently being challenged, if not displaced completely, by new forces and a consensus which use the contemporary discourses of globalization to conceptualize the modern in much less statist and much more market-oriented terms. One result, as the case studies of Turkey, Canada and Brazil illustrate in detail in this volume, is a hollowing out of the previously hegemonic form of global politics – the discourse and practices of the national – carried on a massive restructuring of class, ethnic, gender and other social relations.

Globalizations are also about unequal power relations. Most frequently, the story of globalization is that of the winners, as told by the winners. The victory of their vision of the future is recounted as an inevitability. In the last two decades globalizations follow – to hear the victors tell it – not only from heavy tendencies of economic structures but also from the lucky escape from misguided political visions which sought to achieve social justice and equality via state action and mobilization of the economically and socially disadvantaged after 1945. Neo-liberalism's assault on the Keynesian welfare state now provides a central trope for hegemonic visions of globalization. The view expressed in this volume is that such a reading itself is an expression of power relations, and therefore not inevitable. It is best understood as the intensification of cross-border interactions and social relations promoted by dominant social groups and institutions acting in their own interest.

In the shifting spatial and social relations of globalizations, the less powerful cannot be conceived of as passive bystanders. The rise of globalized localisms, be they the English language, fast food, the Hollywood star system, or the new intellectual property rights, and their specific impact upon the rival local conditions across the globe generate resistances. So, too, do localized globalisms, be they free-trade zones, deforestation to pay the foreign debt, or vernacularization of historical religious sites for tourists.

Thinking in relational terms requires attention to counter-hegemonic globalizations. These are the cross-border interactions and social relations promoted by subordinate social groups or institutions to further their own interests, oftentimes to offset the detrimental effects of hegemonic globalization upon them. South-South dialogues, transnational advocacy NGOs, international consultation among labour unions and women's movements, indigenous peoples' movements throughout the Americas – these are all potential agents of counter-hegemonic globalizations.

Hegemonic and counter-hegemonic globalizations represent different and antagonistic interests, perspectives or positions in the same bundle of globalized and localized social relations. In view of the complexity or ambiguity of the interests involved and of the heterogeneous composition of political, economic and social forces, it is not always easy to distinguish between hegemonic and counter-hegemonic struggles, nor between progressive and reactionary resistance. Indeed, a given institutional innovation may start out as a hegemonic initiative and eventually be appropriated by counter-hegemonic forces. For example, in the United States, Project Head Start began as a childcare program intended to overcome the disadvantages of poor and especially African-American children. Over the years it has nevertheless been transformed, via use by parents and educators, into a real space and place of safety and enpowerment for women as well as children caught up in the population flows and transitions of globalizations. Similarly, in the 1980s, certain sectors in the Brazilian labour movement were able to appropriate to their benefit an institutional innovation originally proposed by the state and business to divide and weaken their movement. Thirdly, although a global interest in the rule of law and in court reform is a distinctive form of hegemonic globalization, subaltern groups and human rights activists may use these institutions to pursue progressive causes.

Of course, the inverse may equally occur. The transnational advocacy of labour standards is certainly a progressive and counter-hegemonic form of globalization when designed and pursued by labour unions and their allies in core countries. However it is likely to be viewed by labour movements of peripheral countries as a form of self-protectionism by the rich, and thus as a form of hegemonic globalization. In the same way, the pursuit of gender parity in electoral institutions may emerge as a demand of progressive women's movements but then be transformed into a much more limited and elitist claim, as the case of France demonstrates.

In part this difficulty of distinguishing the counter-hegemonic from the hegemonic arises from the always inherently complex nature of strategic political action. Any action in favour of a particular policy or outcome is of necessity hostage to unintended consequences, as well as those anticipated by strategists. An even more serious difficulty arises, however, from the fact that the lines of politicized cleavages have become blurred. Those social forces which throughout the 20th century organized claims for social transformation have lost their ideological anchors. They have difficulty mobilizing alternatives. Their resulting weakness allows the story as told by the winners often to appear to be the only story available.

The 20th century in Europe and North America began with two great paradigms of social transformation that challenged the ways liberalism sought to fashion the future. The paradigms of revolution and of reform were alternative, albeit related, responses to the liberal conceptualization of individual rights and *laisser-faire*. Currently these paradigms command much less loyalty than they once did: the collapse of the Soviet Union was the final blow to the revolutionary paradigm; the fiscal problems of states experiencing the crisis of Fordism undermined social democratic reformism. Parties which continue to bear the labels of the progressive Left have become much less recognizable as such. Indeed, some – such as Britain's New Labour and several former Communist Parties in Western as well as Eastern Europe – have changed their names so as to signal their move toward new conceptualizations of state-society relations and the desirable mix of public and private.

Despite being real alternatives to it, the 20th century's two counter-hegemonic paradigms shared much with liberalism when it came to envisaging modernity. Nonetheless, carried by political parties devoted to internationalism as well as development, and committed to equality of classes (as well as, if less stridently, of the sexes and ethnic minorities) these paradigms represented powerful counterpoles in representations of, and conflicts within, social relations for most of this century. They could encompass alliances uniting workers and national bourgeoisie, state managers and business interests, labour and other social movements. The themes of redistribution of economic well-being, of democratic rights and of guaranteed civil rights provided the basic platform, albeit with quite different specifications within each paradigm.

The demobilization of such vehicles for challenging liberalism leaves a void. Counter-hegemonic social forces must, and are, rethinking basic positions about social transformation, seeking to make sense of the new and the unfamiliar. There is room for innovation and creativity, but in the meantime the void is being filled by the triumphalism of hegemonic social forces. Since 1945, and most intensively since 1989, they have promoted the idea that European-style modernity equals progress, and therefore should be everyone's goal. They make several claims. One is that "democracy" has triumphed and we are at the end of history (Fukuyama 1992). Another is the claim that we must learn from the past, with the lesson being that market regulation is superior to political intervention. And there are those who seek to identify the replacement for Cold War conflicts in the clash of civilizations, pitting the West against the "Confucian-Islamic connection" (Huntington 1993). The former is again upheld as the incarnation of modernity, while the latter is characterized as the manifestation of dangerous traditionalism. This danger is not only located at a distance (that is, elsewhere) but supposedly also present at the heart of the centre where disputes over "difference" challenge the "universal values" of Western civilization.

Such visions become both global and hegemonic because they rest upon a widespread consensus about their inevitability and the fact that counter-hegemonic initiatives, in order to be intelligible, credible and effective must be framed in terms of, and with reference to, this consensus. Local resistances and their transnational networking cannot but address the seemingly evident and unassailable claims of those who share the consensus. This consensus has four dimensions: a neo-liberal economic consensus; a weak state consensus; a liberal-democratic consensus; and a consensus about the rule of law and the role of courts.

The Four Dimensions of Consensus

The Neo-liberal Economic Consensus

Consensus on the economic dimension was sealed by the twin electoral victories of Margaret Thatcher's Conservatives in 1979 and the Reagan Republicans in 1980. In each case neo-liberalism was initially and primarily designed for domestic consumption. In the United States the election of Ronald Reagan consecrated the shift away from political compromises between North and South, international and domestic business interests, and internationalists and isolationists which had shaped the American political economy since the 1930s (Ferguson and Rogers 1986). In the United Kingdom, Margaret Thatcher dislodged from the leadership of her party those Tories who had participated with the Labour Party in creating the postwar political economy that was, by 1979, plagued by inflation, work stoppages, and fiscal disarray (Leys 1986). Enthusiasm for these two specific and local reactions to new economic and political circumstances provided support for and contributed to generating a broad – indeed global – consensus that the road to successful economic growth no longer passed by either Keynesianism or national development strategies based on protecting a strong domestic market.

Governments which attempted – even briefly – to hold out for an alternative, such as the French Socialists after the victory of François Mitterrand in 1981, soon fell into line. Within two years the Socialists had joined the consensus (Jenson and Ross 1985). Moreover, if domestic politics did not produce the necessary discipline, an international agency, such as the World Bank or International Monetary Fund, was ready to impose it. This was the experience of countries ranging from Africa to Latin America and Asia. Wandering World Bank officials and their IMF counterparts with briefcases full of structural adjustment plans and agreements, guaranteed that neo-liberal economics spread from the North to the farthest reaches of the South.

Neo-liberal economics envisages a global economy, characterized by global production and global markets for goods, services and finance. The institutional underpinnings of such a stretching of the social relations of production and commerce are international free trade, deregulation (especially of labour markets), refusal to regulate (especially the environment), privatization, macro-economic policies which favour control of inflation over employment creation, and an export-oriented development strategy. The major consequences for state economic activities are a withdrawal from many areas of regulation and reduced social expenditures.

There are three institutional innovations upon which hegemonic globalization depends that merit more detailed attention. These are: 1) new legal restrictions on state regulation; 2) new international property rights for foreign investors and intellectual creations; and 3) new subordination of state sovereignty in economic areas to multilateral or supranational agencies. The sites in which such institutional innovation have occurred are varied. Sometimes national states have given life to this consensus by binding their own hands, inflicting discipline on themselves. They have created new institutions, such as the very liberal NAFTA and World Trade Organization (WTO), which set limits on their capacity to regulate, protect national producers, or take decisions freely. Other national states have agreed to strengthen the disciplinary hand of existing institutions, such as the European Union, whose treaties impose constraints on members' spending decisions as well as regulatory behaviour. Sometimes, however, national states have had little choice. Rather than designing their own institutions, they have been subjected to adjustment by others, such as the IMF or World Bank.

Whatever the route by which the discipline arrives – from within or from the outside – a consensus now exists among elites, even those who have had the least choice, that this institutionalization of neo-liberal economic policies is the only road to follow. As the examples of the campaign for North American Free Trade and for the strengthening of the European Union via the Treaties of Maastricht and Amsterdam demonstrated, support for new arrangements is concentrated among economic and political elites. Opposition was found more in the middle and working classes, among state employees, among women, and in the ranks of cultural elites. In each of these cases, moreover, the hegemonic position prevailed, despite challenges mounted by such oppositional forces. Repeating this same pattern of class-based and social opposition is the current campaign – thus far successful – against the Organization of Economic and Cultural Development's (OECD) orchestration of a Multilateral Agreement on Investment (MAI). This struggle, still being played out, provides one of the few examples of counter-hegemonic mobilization against the neo-liberal consensus which stretches widely around the world rather than remaining regionally, and usually even nationally, concentrated. Whether such mobilizations will be sufficiently powerful to counter neo-liberal economics remains to be seen.

The Weak State Consensus

The notion that "the best state is a weak state" is intimately related to the consensus about neo-liberal economics. As we have just noted, the latter holds as a foundational principle that states should regulate as little as possible and that welfare states should be retrenched. Moreover, favouring market-based rather than state-managed economic strategies implies that state action will be limited. Despite the overlap in the two notions, it is useful to keep them distinct, both for analytic reasons and because there is an important non-economic dimension to a position in favour of a weak state.

The discussion is most frequently framed in terms of the relationship between civil society and the state. Liberalism's definition of civil society as everything which is not public, and therefore incorporating markets, families, and all sorts of cultural and social exchanges, has been widely appropriated. This means, then, that the state is a space or a set of institutions separate from civil society. It is by no means a reflection, a sort of condensed version of the power relations traversing civil society, as Marxists might have it. Nor is it an institutional form that can compensate for a weak or damaged civil society. Rather, in this agreed-upon vision, the state is the **competitor** of civil society, inherently oppressive even in its liberal democratic forms. Liberalism's proposition is that any strong state will undermine civil society. Therefore, the logical conclusion is that if a civil society is weak it is because the state is too strong. Clearly then, if neo-liberalism is premised on a preference for strengthening market signals and mechanisms in decision-making, it is crucial to weaken the state so as to allow this civil society to flourish. Such economic ideologues, localized at first in G-7 countries, have succeeded in transforming their local preferences into a global preference, via international institutions which promote retrenchment of the public sector and market flexibility.

But enthusiasm for a limited state, or more exactly for supposedly freeing up space for civil society, motivates more people than classical liberal free-marketers of the G-7 states. For example, the experience of "real existing socialism" also left many counter-hegemonic social forces in Eastern Europe and parts of Africa with a deep suspicion of state authority and a belief that a strong civil society is the only defense against the all-powerful states they have known. Their particular and local conditions have also put the state on trial, with their claims that as a hindrance to civil society, it must be severely limited (Offe 1985).

The consensus about a limited state has produced an interesting twist on classical liberal theory. For classical liberalism, beginning in the 18th century and throughout the next two that extended the Westphalian state system, state sovereignty was a crucial underpinning of its power. As Max Weber taught us, the very definition of the state was its capacity to exercise sovereign power over a given territory. Thus, accession to statehood, including the movement out of colonialism or other statuses linked to imperialism, required the capacity to exercise sovereignty. Expressions of sovereignty involved, in the Weberian formulations, the exercise of naked force to be sure, but they also involved the capacity to coerce through regulation. The consensus of the limited state, particularly as it is linked to neo-liberal economics, frequently abandons this second dimension of state sovereignty, particularly in peripheral and semi-peripheral states. The capacity, indeed the right, of the state to regulate is challenged by many in the name of the rights of other institutions, such as transnational corporations or transnational social movements. This restriction on state sovereignty, whether coming from capital or progressive forces, has consequences quite as important as the other types of limitations on state action. Such hollowing-out of state sovereignty has provoked counter-hegemonic mobilization in many parts of the world. Nonetheless, suspicion of a strong state has also led some transnational counter-hegemonic movements, with environmentalists and indigenous peoples in the lead, to celebrate their capacity to breach borders and impose their demands in states far distant from their area of primary mobilization. It is for all these reasons, then, that one can say that the concept of sovereignty has been significantly narrowed by the extension across space of enthusiasm for a limited state and a strong civil society.

Liberal-democratic Consensus

A consensus that liberal democracy is the only legitimate state form and that, within that form, only procedural democracy is possible arose from a long series of transitions from authoritarian rule (Przeworski *et al.* 1995). If the consensus was rendered unshakable by the fall of the Berlin Wall in 1989 and the collapse of the Soviet Union, it had been laid elsewhere. Beginning in 1970s, Southern Europe (Spain, Portugal, Greece) shook off aging dictatorships while in the 1980s, it was Latin America's (Argentina, Chile, Brazil, Uruguay, Bolivia) turn. By the first years of the 1990s, not only Central and Eastern Europe and the ex-USSR were establishing liberal democratic institutions, so too were several African countries (including very visibly South Africa), the Philippines, Nicaragua and Haiti.

Here, too, there is an overlap with the previous presented dimensions. Successive adjustments to liberal democratic theory allowed its possessive individualism to be extended from a description of utilitarian individuals engaged in competitive exchange in markets to a similar exchange in elections (Macpherson 1962). In addition, the space bounding this competition was the national state, whose self-creation was intimately linked to the institutionalization of mechanisms extending the right to consent to more and more categories of the population (Tilly 1990). Thus, in describing the dimensions of consensus about neo-liberal economics and a limited state, one arrives rather quickly at a consideration of the liberal democratic forms proposed as appropriate for hegemonic globalization.

Again we observe the rise of a globalized localism, the elevation of a particular local form – European and North American liberal democracy – to the status of model for all countries and contexts. According to this model, a fully realized set of liberal-democratic institutions should have the following features: elected government, in which all adult citizens are eligible to stand for election; free and fair elections in which each citizen's vote has equal weight; suffrage open to all citizens without respect to distinctions of race, religion, class, sex, and so on; freedom of conscience, information and expression on all public matters broadly defined; and the right to oppose, including the right to autonomous association in social movements, interest groups and political parties (Held 1993: 21).[3]

Judged against this ideal-type, it is evident that most liberal democracies have not achieved these standards. In particular, socially correlated limits exist to participation, whether as candidates, in independent associations, or as voters. Therefore, Western Europe and North American states have tended to confine their measure of their own democratic credentials to regular elections, transfer of power from the defeated to the elected candidates and parties, and formal equality rights for participation and eligibility. This local model is now used to judge the achievements of the new democracies, as hosts of foreigners flown in from across the globe to observe elections – in Mexico, Nicaragua, Hong Kong, Bosnia-Herzgovina, Mozambique, etc. – can testify. Alternative models using standards of effective access, or substantive rights rather than formal rights, or measuring the organizational capacity or actual participation of disadvantaged groups, have simply been rendered irrelevant or utopian. And considered even less pertinent are alternatives seeking economic and social democracy, as in locales where social democratic and socialist political forces have some presence. They are simply dismissed as local peculiarities, for example as a Nordic particularity that could not be replicated elsewhere.

The Rule of Law and Judicial Consensus

This shrinking of the standards of liberal democracy to their most procedural and narrowly defined features signals the presence of the fourth dimension of globalization about which there is a hegemonic consensus. This is the elevation of formal, state law and judicial adjudication to the status of sole criterion for the evaluation of political action and state intervention. The liberal-democratic and rule of law dimensions reinforce each other. For example, judges oversee electoral processes to ensure that formal legal norms and formalities are fulfilled; they can do no more than this. But the consensus about the weak state and neo-liberal economics is also implicated. The provision of a legal framework and responsibility for its enforcement has become the *raison d'être* for the state. Such an enforceable framework depends on the state providing a judicial system which can maintain the rule of law. A well-functioning judiciary in which judges apply the law in a fair, even, and predictable manner without undue delays or unaffordable costs is part and parcel of the rule of law (Shihata 1995: 14).

But why is the rule of law so necessary? The implications of its absence have finally become evident to those international organizations most involved in transmitting and institutionalizing the principles of this dimension as well as the others. Indeed, they have recently suggested that the whole edifice might depend on this fourth pillar. As World Bank officials confess (and "confess" seems the correct word; they seem to be atoning for past sins), it has taken failures of government in Africa, the collapse of dictatorships in Latin America and profound transformations in Central and Eastern Europe to manifest that, without a sound legal framework, without an independent and honest judiciary, economic and social development risk collapse (Rowat *et al.* 1995: 2).

From the perspective of hegemonic globalization, the alternative to the rule of law is chaos. Only if the rule of law is widely accepted and effectively enforced can actors with global pretensions have any confidence that certainty and predictability will be guaranteed, transactions costs lowered, property rights clarified and protected, contractual obligations enforced, and regulations applied. From this perspective, the judiciary becomes responsible for delivering equitable, expeditious and transparent judicial services to citizens, the state, and corporations both domestic and foreign.

Case Studies of Embedding and Resisting

The previous section has stressed the existence of consensus around four dimensions of globalization. It also suggested that in each case a local form was elevated to the status of the global. These forms can rarely, if ever, apply as such, as a kind of "one size fits the global wardrobe." In order to diffuse efficiently, processes must be made local. In each case, the general must be given particular form, specific content. There is no single way to institute neo-liberal economics, to limit the state, to organize liberal democracy or even to grant primacy to the rule of law and to judicial action. If globalization means extension across space, it does not mean that this stretching is like that of an inanimate object such as an elastic band. The proper comparison is to a vine, whose wide-reaching branches must be anchored in order to survive. Without tendrils which securely attach it to the varied terrain it traverses, its future is hardly assured.

Therefore, this section turns to the specifics. To do this, as we have already suggested in our definition of globalization, is to uncover the ways in which the social relations of globalization, traversed by unequal power relations, are localized. Such a theoretical stance implies a particular approach to the empirical world. It requires detailed examination of the complex patterns of implantation of the global in local spaces. It requires case studies.

Understandably enough, the variety of the particular mixes of local embeddedness and translocal correspondences or complicities is immense, the more so if the locales involve, as they do here, places as different as Canada, Brazil, South Africa, France, India, Sweden, Colombia, the USA, Turkey and Hawaii. Within such variety we can nonetheless identify some common themes and struggles, corresponding to one or more of the dimensions of globalization.

The impact of the neo-liberal economic consensus on national and local conditions looms large in this volume and it is the object of detailed analysis of several chapters in Part I. The first two chapters focus on Canada, providing case studies of two general processes. Harry Arthurs examines the changing strategies of a core institution of economic globalization, the transnational corporation, and the growing concentration of corporate power made possible by telecommunications and information technology. The concentration of producer services in global cities engenders a hollowing out of other communities through the elimination of local boards of directors, declining demand for producer services, reduced autonomy of the subsidiaries and the consequent insensitivity to local conditions in general and to local managerial vernaculars in particular. The globalization of New York or Los Angeles is engendering the localization of Toronto.

This story has two sides. The same global strategy that produces the concentration of producer services may also produce the dispersal of consumer services. Ruth Buchanan raises this aspect in her analysis of the flourishing call-centres in the province of New Brunswick. This sector of services encompasses both inbound telephone services via 1-800 numbers provided by a range of firms from courier companies to airlines, hospitality industries and financial institutions. There are also outbound telephone services, such telemarketing, survey research, and fund raising. The contrast – or rather complementarity – with Arthurs' chapter is striking. While global strategies of transnational corporations may depend little on local managerial culture, they depend greatly on local conditions such as workers' linguistic skills, labour markets and regulations.

Such adaptations of local conditions to shifting patterns of trade and production are hardly new, of course. For centuries, the arrival of those capable of claiming hegemony for their visions of social and political as well as economic forms have reshaped local landscapes. Of particular importance, as we argued above, is the link between such patterns of trade and the installation of the "rule of law." Sally Merry recounts a transnational legal battle in Hawaii in the early 19th century between British sailors and North American missionaries over access to the sexual services of Hawaiian women. In a nutshell, the case illustrates how wandering institutions operate by complex combinations of global and local inputs. Although the conflict was among foreigners and the debate was framed in the terms of global politics and laws, the resolution of the conflict could happen only once local authorities agreed to act.

The next section presents four chapters that illustrate resistances and opportunities for the subaltern that may arise within globalization's intense and diversified interactions and institutions as they adapt to spaces that have their own histories, needs, and practices. Maria Celia Paoli's chapter highlights such processes by examining the making and unmaking of workers' social and economic rights in Brazil. Playing against a history of authoritarian labour policies and benefiting from the democratic energies released in the aftermath of the dictatorship, parts of the labour movement could promote institutional innovations geared to making the demands of global economy compatible with industrial democracy. In doing so they strengthened the articulation between labour activism and active citizenship. Such institutional innovations and resistance to the exclusionary features of neo-liberal globalization did not succeed. The state withdrew the support it had previously granted them. By yielding to ideological visions of the advantages of a weak state, Brazilian governments inaugurated a new form of state authoritarianism, using its own autonomy from civil society to act freely as an agent of neo-liberal economic globalization.

Gay Seidman deals with South Africa's democratic transition and the contribution of feminism. She shows how the national political process and the democratic aspirations it contained were redefined and amplified to include some degree of gender equality. One reason that women could gain such visibility in the South African transition was that they had ties to a transnational feminist movement. Seidman's analysis also shows how difficult and complex it is at times to distinguish between hegemonic and counter-hegemonic globalizations. Feminism is sometimes now viewed as a form of western cultural imperialism. Indeed, the ANC-leadership tended to see it that way for a time. On the other hand, mobilized resistance to gender discrimination by South African women gained resources as well as prominence by being inscribed in a larger movement which allowed them to contribute oppositional and gendered collective identities to the construction of South African liberal democracy.

Indeed, the appropriation of global interactions through the creation of oppositional collective identities to be activated in local and national counter-hegemonic struggles epitomizes the new profile of resistance in an epoch of multiple and contradicting globalizations. But resistance can equally be anchored in the individual strategies of people caught up in global forces. This is clearly shown in Lucie White's analysis of the ways in which immigrant women in Los Angeles have been able to use Project Head Start to develop new practices of citizenship. To these women, as to many ordinary people, globalization is an all-too-close and real experience. Their journey North composes a harsh picture of lives caught up in global forces that both rely on women's labour and hunt them down. The innovative appropriation of a welfare program can give an insurgent meaning to victimization by a hegemonic state that both opens and closes its borders according to the needs of hegemonic economic globalization.

Border crossings also dominate Barbara Yngvesson's chapter. If Lucie White focuses on the lives of women caught up in globalization, in Yngvesson's chapter children's lives are the central concern. Adoptable children are caught up in a global market of inter-country adoption. Focusing on Sweden as an adopter country, and India and Colombia as countries from which children come, this chapter illustrates how unequal exchanges in global interactions extend, in complex constellations of meaning, from the economic to the symbolic and emotional realms. The diffusion of the sentimentalized child is a form of cultural globalization underlying inter-country adoption that coexists with a symbolic transformation of the child as a commodity into the child as a national resource and as a bearer of rights. Such institutional transformations have enabled adoptees to reconstruct their identities, combining birth and adoption identities, thereby interjecting cosmopolitan, counter-hegemonic voices not originally contemplated in the global adoption script. The chapter also shows how contingent narratives of identity enable adoptees to design counter-hegemonic strategies that may even destabilize the hegemonic globalization of inter-country adoption.

The final section of the book addresses the changes in democratic and legal practices associated with globalization. The intersection of the politics of identity with state policies, which in the previous section took place at the micro-level of immigrants and adoptees, can also be analyzed at the macro-level. Fuat Keyman provides an analysis of Turkey's shift in the 20th century between alternative politics of identity. Here again, the state is both a local broker of global flows and an active agent of their localization. Subjected to a variety of global pressures, the state in each period provides the institutional and political context in which different politics of national identity are embedded. Until recently, state action was viewed as key to development and western-style secularist modernization provided the model for Turkey's "will to civilization." This was re-made locally in a specific political form, Kemalism. In the last two decades, however, both the neo-liberal economic consensus and the weak state consensus dismiss the state from this central position in modernization. A political void exists, which, in the specific Turkish conditions, has been filled by an alternative politics of national identity, the rise of Islam and its language of difference.

By providing a comparison of two cases, Jane Jenson's chapter exposes in a side-by-side fashion the differential effects of globalizations for post-war citizenship regimes. Both the Canadian and French women's movements linked their claims-making from the 1960s through the 1980s to expanding the social rights of citizenship. However, as the progressive alliance against North American free trade in which the Canadian movement had inscribed its action went down to defeat, so too did many of its projects for social citizenship. In France, in contrast, a wing of the women's movement caught the wave of neo-liberal citizenship, stressing liberal democratic forms and rule of law, by elaborating claims in more limited forms. Their demand was for gender parity in electoral institutions. The cost of their victory was a pared-down agenda of resistance and full acceptance of the narrow procedural definition of democracy.

The first three dimensions of consensus provide the foundation for the fourth, the rule of law and judicial consensus. The last chapter focuses on this, showing that the globalization of the rule of law, while being an old feature of western dominance, has recently assumed new prominence as global capitalism subjects more and more social interactions to its logic. Boaventura Santos analyses the most recent manifestations of the globalization of the rule of law. In particular, he asks how the judicial system – which has in most countries been up until now an obscure, weak and often corrupt institution – has been called upon in the last two decades to take a prominent role in the expansion of both global capitalism and liberal democracy. The extent to which subordinate social groups can appropriate this form of hegemonic globalization for counter-hegemonic purposes remains an open question.

Taken together, the three sections of this book all provide, by means of their case studies, concrete evidence about wandering institutions. These institutions traverse a web of globalizations and localization, supporting either hegemonic or counter-hegemonic claims and sometimes both. As they travel they alter the context, the constraints and the opportunities within which individuals and social groups make sense of the world, or rather of the worlds, in which they live. This, ultimately, is the heart of globalizations.

Notes

1. On the concept of globalized localisms and localized globalisms conceived of as modes of production of globalization see Santos (1995: 252-268).
2. This definition is drawn from Santos (1997: 3).
3. An alternative set of characteristics can be found in Dahl (1989: 221) and in O'Donnell (1996: 35).

References

Boyer, Robert, Drache, Daniel (eds.) 1996, *States Against Markets: The Limits of Globalization*, New York: Routledge.
Castells, Manuel 1996, *The Rise of the Network Society*, Cambridge: Blackwell.
Dahl, Robert 1989, *Democracy and its Critics*, New Haven: Yale University Press.
Featherstone, Mike, Lash, Scott, and Robertson, Roland (eds.) 1997, *Global Modernities*, London: Sage.

Ferguson, Thomas, Rogers, Joel 1986, *Right Turn: The Decline of the Democrats and the Future of American Politics*, New York: Hill and Wang.

Ferro, Cristina 1995, 'The Will to Civilization and its Encounter with *Laisser-faire,*' *Alternatives* 27: 89-103.

Fukuyama, Francis 1992, *The End of History and the Last Man*, New York: Free Press.

Giddens, Anthony 1990, *The Consequences of Modernity*, Stanford: Stanford University Press.

Held, David 1993, 'Democracy: From City-states to a Cosmopolitan Order,' in David Held (ed.) *Prospects for Democracy*, Stanford University Press, pp. 13-52.

Hirst, Paul Q. and Thompson, Graham 1996, *Globalization in Question: The International Economy and the Possibilities of Governance*, Cambridge: Polity Press.

Huntington, Samuel 1993, 'The Clash of Civilizations?,' *Foreign Affairs* LXXII: 3-12.

Jenson, Jane and Ross, George 1985, 'Pluralism and the Decline of Left Hegemony: The French Left in Power,' *Politics and Society* 14: 147-184.

Leys, Colin 1986, *Politics in Britain: An Introduction*, London: Verso, 2nd ed.

Macpherson, C. B. 1962, *The Political Theory of Possessive Individualism: Hobbes to Locke*, Oxford: Oxford University Press.

O'Donnell, Guillermo 1998, 'Horizontal Accountability in New Democracies,' *Journal of Democracy*, 9(3), 112-126.

Offe, Claus 1985, *Disorganized Capitalism: Contemporary Transformations of Work and Politics*, Cambridge: MIT Press (edited by J. Keane).

Przeworski, Adam 1985, *Capitalism and Social Democracy*, Cambridge/New York: Cambridge University Press.

Przeworski, Adam 1995, *Sustainable Democracy*, Cambridge: Cambridge University Press.

Robertson, Roland 1992, *Globalization*, London: Sage.

Rowat, Malcom 1995, "Judicial Reform in Latin America and the Caribbean: Operational Implications for the Bank" in Rowat *et al*, 16-18.

Rowat, Malcom, Malik, Walled and Dakolias Maria (eds.) 1995, *Judicial Reform in Latin America and the Caribbean*, Washington: The World Bank.

Santos, Boaventura de Sousa 1995, *Towards a New Common Sense: Law, Science and Politics in the Paradigmatic Transition*, New York: Routledge.

Shihata, Ibrahim F.J. 1995, "Legal Framework for Development: The World Bank's Role in Legal and Judicial Reform," in Rowat *et al.* (eds.), 13-15.

Tilly, Charles 1990, *Coercion, Capital and European States, AD 990-1990*, Cambridge: Blackwell.

PART I
GOING GLOBAL:
BUSINESS AND TRADE

1 The Hollowing Out of Corporate Canada?

HARRY W. ARTHURS[1]

The business corporation – seldom used by 19th century business – became the indispensable and characteristic institution of capitalism during the 20th century. In the specific context of globalization, transnational corporations hold sway as objects of admiration and fear, as repositories of vast power and wealth,[2] and especially as dominant actors in the construction and operation of markets. These corporations claim credit – and are assigned blame – for world-wide flows of trade, investment, technology, products and ideas and for consequential changes in society, culture, politics and the natural environment. Without the transnational corporation, globalization is almost unthinkable.[3]

The impact of globalization on specific places and populations is very much tied to the particular aspect of corporate activity with which they are associated (Storper 1993). Traditional *entrepôts* such as Singapore, the degraded *maquiladora* zones of Mexico, and born-again Welsh manufacturing towns are very different from each other and from the high-skill, high-trust production centres of Emilia-Romagna. Thus, transnational corporations can be viewed as institutions (Robé 1997; Muchlinski 1997) whose governance structures, deliberative processes, business practices and market decisions not only produce the aggregate effects which we call the global economy, but as well the "localized globalisms" (Santos 1995) experienced by particular communities and their populations.

At the same time, transnational corporations are neither immune from these aggregate effects nor immutable in the face of them. New technologies of production, distribution and communication, liberalized trade regimes and deregulation are changing not only how corporations operate but how they are governed. Changes in governance structures, in turn, have particular consequences for "global cities" like London, New York or Tokyo, with their characteristic concentrations of corporate head offices and of the specialized service enterprises which support them (Sassen 1994). Moreover, the growing concentration of corporate power in these global cities has potential implications for other communities quite distant from them, which are experiencing a commensurate "hollowing out" of their corporate cadres. This chapter uses the experience of Canada to explore the possibility that by intensifying concentrations of economic power within and around transnational companies, globalization may directly and indirectly contribute to a "hollowing out" not only of business communities but of cities, regions and countries around the world.

The Changing Governance of Transnational Corporations

Lawyers and economists tend to perceive the corporation as simply "a structure through which production is made to occur," as a "nexus of contracts," as a rational economic actor or as a disembodied juridical person pursuing profit under the direction of a single intelligence (Flannigan 1995). By contrast, Galbraith argued decades ago that a corporation is "a large and complex organization [in which] individuals align themselves with its goals in response to diverse motives" (Galbraith 1967:149). His definition enables us to see the corporation as a site of multiple intelligences and competing "rationalities," of ongoing contestation and tenuous cooperation between holders of debt and equity, between shareholders and other "stakeholders" such as workers, between management and directors, and amongst members of its "technostructure" with differing degrees of influence on the central direction of the company and differing mandates and technical skills (Galbraith 1967). At some level, all these groups and individuals share a commitment to the corporation's financial success, but they compete for power and influence within corporate structures, and favour corporate strategies which incidentally enhance their own financial prospects, careers or human capital. This insight also surfaces in studies of organizational change (Mastenbroek 1993), industrial innovation (Wiseman and Gomez-Mejia 1998), responsibility for corporate wrong-doing (Lee and Sanders 1996), labour relations (Burawoy 1979; O Connor 1997) and the effects of national culture on transnational management (Jackson 1993; Kustin and Jones 1995).

The ensuing variability and volatility in decision-making poses a special problem for large, transnational corporations. Such corporations usually comprise a congeries of units, each with its own history, mandate and managers. Some of these units may have been designed to deflect regulatory, anti-trust or tax laws; others may have emerged from financial manoeuvres such as leveraged buy-outs; and still others may have been defined in terms of product, function or geography. Some may be organized as departments or divisions within the corporation's "core" organization; others – for various reasons: to facilitate specialization and flexibilization, to enhance accountability and competitiveness, to access particular supplies or penetrate specific markets – may function as subsidiaries. And all of these may be linked in turn to a network of suppliers and distributors, corporate allies, franchisees and licensees, partners and co-venturers, some genuinely autonomous enterprises, others merely the *alter ego* of the firm itself.

This dispersal and complexification of corporate functions and structures obviously creates a problem of integration and coordination. In a superficial sense, the problem has been addressed by the development of advanced communications technologies which facilitate the movement of information from the corporate periphery to the centre, and of detailed direction from the centre to the periphery. However, technology does not invent or deploy itself. It is adopted because it performs some necessary or desired function; and once adopted, it is likely to bring about significant changes in management strategies and structures.

Thus, the ultimate resolution of the problem of coordination and integration is, indeed, found in the realm of corporate governance. Conventional wisdom once favoured the "control" model: the board and senior executives of the parent company were perceived as the directing intelligence – the technologically-enhanced "brain" of the extended corporate family – making use of defined mandates, hierarchical reporting relationships and performance measures to direct, coordinate and integrate the activities of all core and subsidiary units, as well as those of external organizations such as suppliers, vendors and partners.

By contrast, more recent management theories (Hoffman 1994) argue that technology makes possible – and globalization makes necessary – leaner, less hierarchical, more "hetrarchical" and reflexive organizations in which considerable authority is devolved to units and partners. Adherence of the components to the organization's overall goals – they contend – is to be achieved by "normative means [transmitted] through corporate culture" (Sölvell and Zander 1995: 26) rather than by explicit commands, as in the "control" model. This more flexible model of management envisages a more "strategic" relationship in which corporate headquarters, widely-dispersed functional service units, subsidiaries, and outside firms are all linked through strategies of "complex integration" (UNCTAD 1994: 139-140).

However, it is not at all clear whether, and to what extent, these new management theories have taken hold. Undoubtedly, flexibilization and globalization did generate a new logic of intra-firm governance. Down to the 1970s and 1980s, most subsidiaries of transnationals – Ford (United Kingdom) or GE (Canada) – were "local implementers" or "miniature replicas" of the transnational itself (Birkinshaw and Morrison 1995). They produced a variety of goods and services, raised capital from local investors, reported to their own boards of directors, supported a significant management cadre responsible for functions ranging from human resources to production to marketing, and often developed their own networks of local subsidiaries and contractors. True, we must be careful not to apply too much gilt to this particular lily: for good reasons "branch plants" acquired a pejorative connotation in host countries such as Canada. "Miniature replica" subsidiaries seldom undertook their own research and development (R&D), produced a full range of product lines, or enjoyed complete financial autonomy. Their presidents and senior officers – individuals of some importance in the host country – were not necessarily influential within the parent firm; their boards – mostly appointees of the parent transnational, the subsidiary's dominant shareholder – usually had to acquiesce in decisions emanating from the parent board or its proconsul, the president of the subsidiary. Nonetheless, for all their limitations, semi-autonomous "miniature replica" subsidiaries were a powerful presence in the local corporate community and in the host country more generally.

More recently, however, the attraction of "miniature replica" subsidiaries has diminished and their numbers have dwindled. Parent transnationals have rationalized and restructured their operations in order to achieve efficiency gains through a new division of labour, by which subsidiaries each produce a narrow range of products in large numbers for world or regional markets (Morrison, Ricks, and Roth 1991), rather than many products in small numbers for local consumption. In many cases, indeed, subsidiaries were restructured, so that they could function as "specialized contributors" of particular components destined to be incorporated into products made or assembled elsewhere.

By creating narrowly-mandated and "specialized contributor" subsidiaries, transnationals sought greater coherence and more complex integration of local and transnational managerial functions. It could hardly be otherwise. The international division of labour implied its ultimate re-integration. The activities of "specialized contributors" to an integrated product line ultimately had to be closely coordinated with those of the other contributors. Subsidiaries with world or regional product mandates had to live within them, geographically and functionally, so that they would not impinge on the mandates of other units. All parts of a transnational company had to adhere to financial targets and maintain quality standards, in order to avoid threatening the stability and reputation of the rest. For all of these reasons, transnational corporations had to seek greater coherence amongst, and integration of, their constituent units.

The new logic of globalization also required a change in the governance of what were formerly "miniature replica" subsidiaries. These subsidiaries were until fairly recently organized as publicly-held "national" companies whose relative autonomy was emphasized, symbolically and functionally, by the presence of a significant body of local shareholders, local boards of directors, and CEOs with a considerable degree of authority. But as autonomy has increasingly come to be seen as counter-productive, many of these companies have been wound-up and either closed down altogether or reconstituted as private companies wholly-owned by the foreign parent or one of its proxies. And even where economic logic or political expediency has required that the previous formal structure of a particular subsidiary should be preserved, it is likely to operate with reduced autonomy, a smaller, less powerful executive cadre, and a more limited repertoire of managerial and technical functions.

A commensurate change in the managerial culture of transnational corporations seems likely to ensue. In the new dispensation, local managers of subsidiaries must learn to become more responsive to the corporation's global aspirations, strategies and interests, and less so to those of their particular unit – even if it means putting their own personal interests at risk. This may entail, for example, disclosing to the parent company their special knowledge of local conditions (Holm, Johanson, and Thilenius 1995) – the source of their indispensability as managers – or performing such self-effacing assignments as downsizing or closing their own operations. One might expect that in return the central direction of transnationals would respond more sensitively to local interests, sensibilities and ways of doing business. But the contrary is often true. With few exceptions,[4] transnational companies remain closely identified with their country of origin. Their global boards of directors continue to be almost entirely composed of appointees from the home country,[5] and very much attuned to its interests (UNCTAD 1994:146), and management styles from the home country to a surprising degree continue to shape those of foreign subsidiaries (Kustin and Jones 1995).

To recapitulate, changes in manufacturing technology and flexibilization strategies have indeed made possible the rapid adjustment of output to changing markets and new manufacturing techniques, and have facilitated cost-effective spatial and functional divisions of labour, economies of scale and the pursuit of comparative advantage; but they have also narrowed the range of activities conducted in any particular location, and subordinated each to the discipline of a collective bottom line. Changes in communications and information technology may have made possible the wider dispersal of corporate activities; but they have also extended the reach of head office control. Changes in management theory may have revealed the logic of leaner, less hierarchical, more reflexive organizations; but management practice has, in many respects, become more centralized. And the rhetoric of networks, co-ventures, alliances and partnerships has conjured up the possible dawn of a new era of corporate comity and interdependence; but the reality is that flexibilization, enshrined in onerous relational contracts, has made smaller enterprises intensely vulnerable to the variable requirements of larger ones (Macneil 1980: 72 ff; UNCTAD 1994: 138 ff; Schanze 1991; Storper 1992). In short, transnational corporations seem less to have adopted new and open management cultures or more supple, disseminated institutions of governance than to have reinforced the centripetal forces already at work within the old, hierarchical arrangements.

Why does this matter? Perhaps – as the conventional wisdom contends – globalization and flexibilization will enhance the profitability of transnationals, and the prosperity of at least some host communities, managers, workers and suppliers; perhaps some of that profit will drift out to the periphery of the corporation rather than accumulating at the centre. But the restructuring of corporate governance, the increase of power at the centre, is not a neutral fact. The enterprise as a whole may profit; some of its subsidiaries may prosper in the short- to mid-term; but the parent corporation's directors and executives have assumed tighter control of its subsidiaries with the specific objective of generating "new" corporate behaviours and "improving" corporate results. They are, at least to some extent, people working within different frames of reference, national and local contexts, corporate-cultural environments, and reward structures. Their notion of what is "new" and "improved" will almost certainly differ from that of the dismissed directors and disempowered managements of restructured subsidiaries. And the effects are likely to be experienced by the host communities and countries whose fortunes wax and wane with the arrival or departure of transnational corporate activity, jobs and taxes.

The Local Consequences of Changes in Corporate Governance: the Impact on Producer Services

Of all the possible effects, none are more explicitly related to the restructuring of corporate governance than those involving so-called "producer services." As Sassen (1995: 778) has argued, "the more globalized the economy becomes the higher the agglomeration of central functions." A limited number of cities, she says, "concentrate the infrastructure and the servicing that produce a capability for global control. The latter is essential if geographic dispersal of economic activity . . . is to take place under continued concentration of ownership and profit appropriation" (1995: 778-79). Corporate head offices thus tend to function as economic nuclei, around which cluster providers of advanced and specialized producer services – consultants, lawyers, accountants, software houses, designers, advertising agencies – whose physical proximity to head office facilitates efficient interaction (Sassen 1994; Daniels and Moulaert 1991; Daniels 1993; Medcalf 1996).

Moreover, these producer service providers and their corporate clients are not merely key actors in the global economy; they comprise an affluent and dynamic segment of the local economy, a rich market for local enterprises, reaching right down the "food chain" to low-paid domestics and restaurant workers (Sassen 1994). Consequently, the arrival or departure, expansion or contraction, of global and regional head offices – the specific and tangible consequences of reorganizing corporate governance – implicates a "space economy" which differs in important ways from that associated with, say, manufacturing or distribution operations (Sassen 1995).

Localized Globalisms: The Canadian Case

If this three-fold process of consolidation is occurring – consolidation of corporate control, of head office functions, of producer services – one might expect that its consequences would affect Canada in particularly dramatic fashion. Much of Canada's wealth is owned by foreign – especially American – investors,[6] and many of its largest corporations[7] are actually subsidiaries of transnational corporations based abroad, principally in the United States.[8] Moreover, Canada's economy is heavily dependent on international trade,[9] a very high proportion of which is with the United States[10] and takes the form of intra-firm transactions.[11] And finally, integration of the two countries is proceeding apace at many levels (Arthurs 1998), facilitated by the North American Free Trade Agreement (NAFTA) and other regimes which have liberalized the rules for transnational trade and investment.

This process of integration provides the context within which corporate consolidation is occurring (Grinspun and Cameron 1993). It is a context fraught with risks. On the one hand, relatively few large transnational companies are Canadian-owned.[12] It is therefore unlikely that they represent the means whereby Canada will regain on the home-country swings what it loses on the host-country roundabouts. On the other, the Canadian federation – one of the most decentralized in the world – seems unwilling or unable to muster the will or mobilize the means to reduce its exposure to the consequences of business decisions initiated by foreign companies. Consequently, transnationals are, and likely will be for the foreseeable future, a dominating presence in the economy. Because they and their subsidiaries are employers, taxpayers, purchasers of goods and services, shapers of market behaviour and popular culture, political actors, and contributors to charities and civic culture, their three-fold consolidation is almost certain to have profound social, economic and political effects within Canada.

The Restructuring of Canadian Subsidiaries of Transnational Corporations

Considerable, but incomplete and somewhat anecdotal, evidence suggests that two related trends have indeed developed. First, changes in the governance of foreign-based (and especially American-based) transnationals have led to a corresponding decline in the autonomy, range of functions and actual numbers of their subsidiaries. Second, as predicted, these corporate changes may be affecting the market for producer services in cities where regional head offices tend to be located, such as Toronto, Montreal, Calgary and Vancouver (Sassen 1994: 82-85; Hutton and Ley 1987; Michalak and Fairbairn 1993; Coffey and Sheamur 1996). Before examining this evidence, however, it is important to understand the legal context within which subsidiaries operate.

(a) The legal context for Canadian subsidiaries of foreign-based transnationals Canadian law imposes few constraints on the corporate structures through which foreign-based transnationals do business.   For example, in Ontario – the country's commercial heartland – a company incorporated abroad may obtain a license as an "extra-provincial" company with only minimal formalities.[13] Even this small inconvenience can be avoided if the foreign company chooses to operate from its base abroad – for example, American border cities – and merely export goods to Canadian customers.[14] Nor do adverse tax consequences of any significance attach to firms doing business in Canada without incorporating there.[15] Only in a few policy-sensitive sectors – financial institutions, insurance, transportation and communications – are there specific requirements for a Canadian corporate identity, and for predominant local shareholding,[16] and these requirements

may soon be outlawed by some future version of the proposed Multilateral Agreement on Investment.[17]

Nonetheless, foreign transnationals doing business, producing goods or offering services in Canada have usually incorporated subsidiaries for that purpose. There were reasons to do so in earlier times: tariffs and other government policies gave advantages to industries which could identify themselves as "Canadian;"[18] and practical difficulties of transportation and communications argued for the creation of local management structures empowered to conduct business without frequent reference to a foreign head office. Then, as these original reasons for incorporating became less important, a new set of factors came into play. Subsidiaries might have better knowledge of local market conditions, media relations and labour practices. They might be better able to deal with governments and regulatory agencies, and to identify suppliers and attract customers. They might even attract a cohort of local investors not readily available to foreign transnationals, or gain access to capital or subsidies provided by financial institutions and governments to Canadian companies. And finally, in some cases at least, establishing a subsidiary might facilitate access by the parent transnational to other foreign markets (Anderson 1987).

Of course, like domestic firms, transnationals which opted to incorporate a subsidiary could choose amongst several structures: a wholly-owned private company, a public company in which the foreign parent was the dominant shareholder, a widely-held public company in which the parent's holdings were relatively dilute, or a joint venture or partnership with another firm. In recent years, however, trade liberalization, globalization and regional economic integration have redrawn the map of corporate responsibility and reporting. Many manufacturing subsidiaries – which formerly served the Canadian market as "miniature replicas" of their parent firms – now operate under world or regional mandates (Litvak 1990; 1993). Using improved communications technology, head offices now can (and do) exercise close control over Canadian finance, sales or human resources functions. The growth of electronically-accessible global capital markets has diminished the need for stocks to be listed on Canadian exchanges. And deregulation and tax reduction – proceeding apace everywhere (Arthurs 1996b) – have made local political sensitivity and influence less crucial to corporate decision-making. For all of these reasons, many foreign-based transnationals operating in Canada have opted to subordinate, simplify, even eliminate, the governance structures of their subsidiaries.

Formal corporate structures are often altered: many transnationals acquire 100 percent ownership of their publicly-held subsidiaries; public companies are converted into wholly-owned private companies – "taken private" in the parlance of the trade; the numbers of directors on subsidiary boards are reduced; and outside directors are replaced with insiders who are themselves officers or directors of parent firms. And, it appears, in addition to, or in lieu of, formal restructuring, parent firms informally tighten control over their subsidiaries by redefining their mandates, reducing the authority, status, and number of their executives or transferring key subsidiaries to head office. Each of these strategies will be explored below.

(b) The declining local character of foreign-owned subsidiaries: a preliminary study   Using widely-accepted lists of leading Canadian corporations,[19] as well as returns under the *Corporations and Labour Unions Returns Act* (CALURA),[20] I have undertaken a study of the largest 115 subsidiaries of foreign-based transnationals in 1985 and 1995. During this decade, the incidence of transnationals within the top echelon of companies declined somewhat. In 1985, the 115th-ranked subsidiary of a foreign-based transnational was 265th on the list of leading companies; in 1995, it was 299th. However, this does not indicate that foreign transnationals in the aggregate were any less dominant in the local economy, in terms of their income or the value of their investment (Statistics Canada 1997); indeed, it may simply indicate that, since the advent of the FTA/NAFTA, some transnationals have begun to serve Canadian markets by simply shipping goods across the border rather than by producing and distributing them through a Canadian subsidiary.

However, the character of subsidiaries of foreign transnationals changed considerably in the ten years after 1985. In 1985, 47.8 percent (55) of the top 115 foreign-owned subsidiaries were specifically identified as privately-held. In addition, a further 20.8 percent (24) whose public or private status was not specified were listed as being owned 100 percent abroad, presumably by a parent transnational firm. Thus, in total, 68.6 percent (79) of these companies had no Canadian shareholders. By 1995, 94 of the top 115 subsidiaries were specifically identified as privately held, while a further three, described as public companies, were owned 100 percent abroad, again presumably by a foreign transnational; in all, 84 percent (97) had no Canadian shareholders.

This impression of the increasing privatization of leading firms, and of their diminishing local ownership, is confirmed by tracing the metamorphosis of the top 115 firms from 1985 through to 1995. Of the 115 top foreign-owned subsidiaries in 1985, 45.2 percent (52) did not appear on the 1995 list of leading firms. Of these, 24.3 percent (28) were still operating, but were producing revenues too low to merit inclusion on the list. No information was available on two firms. The remaining 19.2 percent (22) disappeared from the list because they had experienced some sort of corporate transformation, as had a further 8.6 percent (10) which appeared on both the 1985 and 1995 lists. In all, 27.8 percent (32) of the 115 foreign-owned subsidiaries on the 1985 list went through a corporate transformation: 16 were converted from public to private companies, six were dissolved, 11 were amalgamated with privately held companies, and one was amalgamated with a public company.[21]

Nor was a change in corporate form the only indicator of increasing control by foreign transnationals of their subsidiaries. A change in the composition of the boards of directors of subsidiaries also occurred. Overall, companies which had been reorganized during this decade – for the most part, by being taken private – reduced the size of their boards by roughly half, from an average of 10.3 directors per company in 1985 to only 5.17 in 1995. The number of outside directors on their boards fell even more dramatically.[22] All of these companies had outside directors in 1985. By 1995, 55 percent (15) of those surviving had completely eliminated outside directors, and 28 percent (8) companies which had retained outside directors had reduced their complement from an average of 4.9 in 1985 to an average of 2.8 in 1995. On average, each company still-surviving from 1985, but reorganized and/or privatized, appointed only one external director in 1995.[23]

One must be cautious in drawing conclusions from these figures. However, comparison between major subsidiaries which were restructured and those which were not underlines the point. On average all major subsidiaries had boards comprising 8.57 directors in 1985; by 1995 that average had fallen to 6.68; on average they had 3.25 external directors in 1985, but only 2.35 in 1995. But as noted above, those which had been reorganized had even fewer directors, and considerably fewer external directors, than those which had not.

Because these companies were foreign-based transnationals, an attempt was made to identify the residence of board chairs, directors and CEOs in order to determine whether more direct personal control was being asserted over subsidiaries by the senior officials of their parent firm. Despite some gaps in the data, and recalling the overall reduction in both the size of boards and the presence of external directors, we can nonetheless draw some conclusions. From 1985 to 1995, while most directors were still Canadian residents, there was a discernible increase in the percentage of non-resident external directors – from 9.36 percent in 1985 to 16.6 percent in 1995; however, there was hardly any change in the percentage of non-resident internal directors – 36.8 percent in 1985 as opposed to 37.8 percent in 1995.

Likewise, there was a significant increase in the percentage of board chairs resident abroad – from 36 percent in 1985 to 44.6 percent in 1995, although only a handful of these were from outside the company. Finally, while 92.5 percent of subsidiaries had a resident CEO in 1985, that number had declined to 86.6 percent in 1995.

In sum, the data suggest that during the decade 1985-1995, a modest trend developed to appoint more non-resident directors, chairs and CEOs. It would be fair to assume that, to this extent at least, parent transnationals increased their control over subsidiaries. However, this development was overshadowed by the more striking trend toward smaller boards generally, the reduced presence of external directors, and especially the virtual disappearance of external directors from the boards of companies which had been taken private or otherwise restructured. To the extent that external directors once represented a potential source of power and influence in corporate decision-making, their ability to shape the destinies of subsidiaries of foreign-owned transnationals appears to have diminished considerably.[24] This last is subject to an important *caveat*: an extensive literature testifies to the difficulty generally encountered by directors (and shareholders) in seeking to control management (Berle and Means, 1968; Ziegel *et al.* 1994, c.5). Finally, the elimination of Canadian shareholders and directors from subsidiaries which have been taken private may well engender several adverse consequences on a broader scale: reduced portfolio choices and profits for Canadian investors, reduced exposure to advanced management techniques for local managers and directors and arguably, in the absence of local scrutiny, inflated dividends, management fees and other exactions paid by wholly-owned subsidiaries to their foreign parents (Sadeque 1991).

These developments reignited a debate over 1975 federal legislation requiring that the majority of a corporation's board and of each board committee be resident in the country.[25] The issue is, of course, whether the residence (or, for that matter, the nationality) of a subsidiary's directors or senior executives affects its behaviour *vis-à-vis* its employees, customers, suppliers, the communities in which it operates or its parent firm. A parliamentary committee expressed "agreement with the view that a company operating in Canada should have a Board that will provide a Canadian perspective on issues that are discussed in Board deliberations" and recommended retaining the residency requirement for the Board itself, although not for its committees (Senate of Canada 1996). However, several academic commentators contend that there is little correlation between the nationality or residence of directors and CEOs and their performance. Indeed, Daniels and Halpern have urged that "the absence of artificial entry barriers" to corporate office holders in Canada should be viewed in a positive light "especially when differences in the home and host country environments are relatively insignificant." Subsidiaries, in their view, have no need of a senior echelon of resident managers or directors; their corporate structures could be streamlined; and their conversion from public to private companies would enable them to make efficiency gains through the de-layering of management structures, and reduced filing, accounting and legal fees. So considerable are these potential savings, they argued finally, that protection for Canadian minority shareholders against the consequences of privatizing such subsidiaries should be limited, lest this "retard the timely rationalization of dysfunctional organizational structures" (Daniels and Halpern 1996). On the other hand, some academic commentators are less sanguine about entrusting the country's future to the unmediated self-interest of foreign-based firms (Courchene 1996: 208) and favour public policies which might resuscitate corporate Canada (Gillies 1992) – if indeed it is possible to do so in the face of opposition or non-cooperation from global investors and transnational corporations.

(c) Informal shifts in the structure of power within foreign transnationals As suggested above, transnationals appear to be reducing the autonomy of their subsidiaries, even without altering their formal structures, although this is difficult to document. A narrower mandate for the subsidiary, reduced power and responsibility devolved to its executives, less scope for locally-generated business initiatives, or the centralization of key functions such as R & D, may in fact be signs of diminished autonomy for the subsidiary, but will seldom be announced as such. Nor is it easy to detect or interpret more subtle indicators such as the seniority or personal reputation of the CEO appointed to run a subsidiary, the likelihood that that individual will be promoted to higher office in the parent firm, the reporting lines and required levels of approval which link the subsidiary's senior executives to their counterparts in the transnational. It is even difficult – without detailed case studies – to determine whether, in a specific case, the "hollowing out" of a subsidiary results from the parent firm's desire to consolidate and rationalize its global operations, or its wish to reduce its governance costs by "delayering" management.

However, acknowledging all these difficulties of evidence and evaluation, informed observers do detect a fundamental shift in the formal and informal governance structures of subsidiaries. For example, a 1994 survey of CEOs of Canadian foreign-owned subsidiaries reports that a significant number (over 40 percent) – especially those in the high tech manufacturing sector, in larger firms and in firms with US-based parents – perceived that during the past five years, their autonomy had been diminished, and that they had been subjected to closer oversight by the relevant operating division of their parent firm. These changes were often accompanied by a redefinition of the company's mandate, from purely Canadian to continental or global markets (Rhéaume and Warda 1995).

Academic research and anecdotal evidence reinforce the survey results. For example, case studies of efforts by subsidiaries to expand their mandates reveal, on the one hand, that aggressive pursuit of extended mandates by Canadian executives might sometimes succeed, but also that they would often be frustrated by head-office directives and the competing claims of other units, particularly those located in the United States (Birkinshaw 1995a). Newspapers have reported the resignation of the external Canadian directors and the CEO of a Canadian subsidiary in protest against the reduction of the subsidiary's autonomy by the parent firm (Schreiner 1995), the less frequent appointment of "locals" to senior executive positions in Canadian subsidiaries, with parent transnationals "preferring to call the shots from US headquarters" (Milner 1994) and other manifestations of "the absolute faith of the US parent in its central position within the global constellation" leading to "a fundamental lack of concern about the differences between the United States and Canada" (O'Neil 1996).

(d) The effects of diminished subsidiary autonomy on corporate behaviour and public policy Do these changes in the formal and informal governance of subsidiaries actually alter their behaviour? If so, are the changes positive or negative? And if negative, what public policies might provide an effective response?

On the one hand, it would be unwise to overestimate the potential autonomy of any subsidiary, whatever its formal relationship to its parent transnational, whatever its management culture. The parent company is almost always the dominant, if not the sole, shareholder in the subsidiary, and its nominees – increasingly "inside" directors – are almost always able to control board decisions. In the event that outside directors exhibit unseemly independence, the parent firm can replace them, take the subsidiary private or wind it up altogether. Senior executives of the subsidiary are usually appointed by the parent company, directly accountable to its officers and dependent upon them for career advancement. And operations of the subsidiary are often directly controlled by the transnational parent through contractual arrangements covering intellectual property, the supply of key parts and machines, product mandates, finances and other matters. In short, the subsidiary will almost always act in response to the directions of the parent firm.

But the issue, in reality, is not whether the subsidiary can act in contravention of its mandate, or against the wishes of its parent, but rather how the subsidiary can win the approval of its parent for its initiatives, how it can influence the parent's decisions to invest or disinvest, how it can become a more significant actor within the overall transnational organization, and especially how it can secure a wider margin of discretion to make decisions locally instead of referring them to head office. This latter point is especially important, as it speaks to the high volume, low visibility executive judgments which shape the character and profitability of the subsidiary – local sourcing of goods and services, sales strategies which take account of local market conditions, industrial relations policies which reflect local law and practice (Kumar and Holmes 1997). Such interstitial judgments, indeed, are particularly likely to reflect a tendency by local executives to internalize the values, customs and style of the host country (Drache 1994; Milkman 1991), a well-known phenomenon amongst diplomats who, for this very reason, are regularly reassigned from country to country and from foreign to domestic postings.

It is not that an ardent host-country nationalism will necessarily corrode strong corporate loyalties or subvert corporate plans. On the contrary, utilization of local methods, vocabularies and contacts may be the best way, in specific contexts, to achieve the transnational's goals. However, even when recast in these more modest and potentially positive terms, the capacity of subsidiaries to influence decisions of the parent transnational must surely be declining. In this current phase of globalization, the "leverage" of their directors and senior officials – their Canada-specific knowledge and influence – is a wasting asset. To the extent that global capital markets have diminished the importance of access to local financing, external directors are no longer needed to reinforce the company's credibility with local banks and pension funds. To the extent that NAFTA, the GATT and ultimately the MAI have erased tariffs and diminished other disadvantages for foreign firms, the need for local directors to influence government policies diminishes. To the extent that improved communications technology allows the parent to monitor more closely the performance of its subsidiaries, the oversight functions of the subsidiary board are arguably made redundant. To the extent that marketing is now undertaken by means of transborder advertising prepared by American advertising agencies and disseminated by American television and magazines, Canadian managers need no longer concern themselves with such matters. These facts may explain why as transnational corporations alter their governance structures, to reinforce centralized control and diminish the autonomy of their subsidiaries, "Corporate Canada" – the community of directors and senior executives of Canadian domestic corporations and foreign-owned subsidiaries – is being "hollowed out."

Conclusion: Does the "Hollowing out of Corporate Canada" Adversely Affect Anyone Other than Members of a Highly Privileged Business Elite?

If we accept the rigorous logic of trade liberalization and continental integration, Canadians should generally benefit from the country's unique form of "localized globalism," which makes it so easy for transnationals in effect to treat their disempowered subsidiaries, in Canada and elsewhere, as an integral part of their "home country" operations. These subsidiaries can operate with minimal corporate structures, minimal requirements to adapt to local laws and labour markets, and minimal inconvenience in terms of socio-cultural and physical distance. They can often secure *de facto* subsidies – for example health care, training and improved infrastructure – which lower the costs of production. They can restructure their Canadian operations to achieve continental economies of scale with relatively little risk of political or regulatory reprisals, especially now that their subsidiaries enjoy privileged access to the American market under NAFTA. If these advantages lead transnationals to increase investment in their Canadian subsidiaries, if those subsidiaries acquire more extensive facilities, a greater share of global production, new technologies, and improved job opportunities, the economic benefits can be expected to trickle down to employees, suppliers and local communities.

However, such potentially positive results – which are by no means guaranteed, and which did not materialize during the first half of the 1990s (Merrett 1996) – must be balanced against possible negative consequences, many of which flow from the "hollowing out of corporate Canada." Less autonomy and less leverage for the executives of subsidiaries within the transnational corporate structure may lead to fewer Canadian-based initiatives and greater exposure to adverse investment decisions and job losses decreed at head offices. Less tolerance for a distinctive local managerial vernacular may lead to the erosion of Canadian commercial practice and industrial relations conventions. And fewer specialized functions being performed in fewer and less powerful subsidiary head offices may lead to a declining market for producer services in Canada's major cities. Indeed, some studies are beginning to suggest that we may see a decline in demand for producer services (Daniels and Moulaert 1991; Harrington 1989; Francois 1990; Nicolaïdis 1993) such as legal services (Arthurs 1996b) and industrial R & D (Birkinshaw 1995a). If this trend develops, consequential effects are likely to include declining urban economies, a falling-off of much-needed private support for higher education and the arts (Murray 1991), exacerbated industrial conflict, (Arthurs 1996a; Lucio and Weston 1994) and the ramifying consequences of all of these upon the quality of community life. For instructive examples, we need look no further than the decline of economic, social and cultural activities in American cities such as Buffalo, St. Louis and Pittsburgh – all of which have suffered the departure of head offices and of activities symbiotically related to them.

The essence of the problem is that transnational companies and their subsidiaries constitute a considerable presence in Canada – a social, political and cultural presence as well as an economic presence. They are major consumers of producer services, powerful participants in policy networks and public debates, benefactors or sponsors of artistic, educational, sporting and humanitarian organizations and events, shapers of land markets, urban skylines and popular culture and, through the example they set in their employment practices, influential in defining local attitudes concerning gender, race and class. Moreover, their executives and employees – in their personal capacities – are often an important clientele in metropolitan markets for specialized goods such as upscale clothing, food and housing. Consequently, consolidation within transnational corporations, which weakens the form, function, character and leadership of their subsidiaries, is likely to have important effects on the life of all communities in which they are a significant presence.

Canada is obviously not the only country which might be affected by changes in the operational and governance structures of transnational corporations. But Canada is more vulnerable than most because of its geo-political location, its dependency on exports, its willing accession to junior partnership in an integrated continental economic system, its ongoing constitutional and political crises and its failure to develop a significant number of home-grown transnationals. True, these vulnerabilities can, to an extent, be seen as merely the obverse of all the favourable factors which make Canada an attractive destination for American and other foreign investors; and it is possible that with hindsight we will be seen to have gained more than we have lost as the result of our unique encounter with globalization. However, for the present, each time a transnational corporation rejigs its organization chart, each time the role and structure of its subsidiaries is redefined, not just an enfeebled and vulnerable Corporate Canada but all Canadians are put at risk.

Canada's experience of globalization is unique: the experience of all countries is unique. But it is an experience from which, perhaps, other countries can learn. It invites scholars and policy makers to move beyond generalizations about the aggregate effects of the global economy to more nuanced and empirically-grounded accounts of what globalization portends for particular states, communities and economic sectors. It serves as a reminder that globalization is no respecter of persons, that it can adversely affect privileged local elites – often its principal enthusiasts – no less than the poor and powerless. And finally, Canada's experience suggests that globalization may succeed in insulating the central institutions, agencies and processes of corporate governance not just from national laws and policies, not just from the implicit responsibilities of membership in civic society, but even from the socializing influences which help management to operate effectively within specific circumstances, communities and cultures. Can globalization survive such success?

Notes

1. I would like to express my appreciation to the Canadian Institute for Advanced Research and the Social Sciences and Humanities Research Council of Canada for their financial support; to Aine O'Flynn, Troy Ungerman, Kelly Gallagher-Mackay and Raziel Zisman for their research assistance; and to the editors, as well as Stan Beck, Mary Condon, Ron Daniels, Wendy Dobson, James Gillies, Ed Waitzer and many others for their insightful comments.
2. During the early 1990s, 37,000 parent firms – 90 percent originating in the developed countries – controlled over 200,000 foreign subsidiaries or affiliates. The largest 100 of these firms – excluding banking and financial institutions – owned total assets of about US$3.4 trillion, of which about US$1.3 trillion was held abroad, comprising one-third of the foreign direct investment originating in their home countries (UNCTAD 1994). According to another estimate, using different parameters, 83 transnationals are responsible for 70 percent of all foreign direct investment (Gillies and Morra 1996).
3. Likewise, one might argue that without globalization, the corporation itself would have been unthinkable: many of the earliest European corporations were established specifically to conduct trading ventures in Asia, the Americas and Africa. However, an early and still persisting alternative form of globalization was undertaken by ethnically-homogeneous trading networks of Jewish, Chinese, Lebanese and East Indian traders (Landa 1994).
4. The Royal Dutch/Shell Group of Companies was created in 1907 when a British and a Dutch firm merged whilst retaining their separate identities. In 1930, Lever Brothers and Margarine Unie created the Unilever Group comprising a British entity, Unilever PLC,

and a Dutch one, Unilever N.V. More recently, in 1988, ASEA of Sweden and BBC Brown Boveri Ltd. of Switzerland formed ABB Asea Brown Boveri Ltd.

5. A survey of 83 transnational firms responsible for 70 percent of the world's foreign direct investment, concludes that "only a few . . . have foreign representatives on their boards [which] are predominantly made up of citizens of the home country of the company" (Gillies and Morra 1996: 33).

6. American-owned companies control 11.4 percent of the assets of Canadian companies, but a strategic 20 percent share of the operating revenues; other foreign transnationals own 10 percent of the corporate assets and account for 10 percent of the operating revenues of Canadian companies (Statistics Canada 1997).

7. Transnationals comprised 5 of Canada's top 10 companies (by revenue) in 1985, and 37 of its top 100 companies (Canadian Business 1986). In 1995, the numbers were almost identical: 5 of the top 10 companies, and 35 of the top 100 (Composite of annual surveys from *The Globe and Mail's* Report on Business Magazine, "The Top 1000;" The *Financial Post*, "The Financial Post 500;" and *Canadian Business*, "The Performance 500").

8. As of 1991, the United States accounted for 63.3 percent of Canada's foreign direct investment. All the EU countries collectively accounted for 23.4 percent and Japan for 4.1 percent (Niosi 1994). Foreign-controlled firms earned more revenue per dollar of assets (and paid a higher ratio of taxes to profits) than Canadian firms (Statistics Canada 1997).

9. Exports account for 40-45 percent of the Canadian GDP (Historical Statistical Supplement 1995/96), a greater proportion than in any other G-7 country except Germany (Blank 1993).

10. Over 80 percent of Canada's merchandise exports go to the United States (Weintraub 1994).

11. Transactions involving Canada's American-owned subsidiaries and their parent firms are estimated to account for over 60 percent of Canada's total exports to the United States (Krajewski 1992). Weintraub suggests that fully 70 percent of Canada's merchandise exports to the United States are not at arm's length: about 40 percent are intra-firm transfers, and another 30 percent result from licensing and inter-firm understandings (Weintraub 1994).

12. UNCTAD ranks three Canadian-based transnationals as 34th, 65th and 74th amongst the largest 100 such companies, only one of which is listed as "high growth." The other two are listed as "no growth" and "decline." In all, the survey identifies 1,396 Canadian-based transnationals amongst a world total of 37,530. Some of these may themselves be subsidiaries of foreign-based transnationals (UNCTAD 1994: c. 1).

13. *Extra-Provincial Corporations Act*, R.S.O. 1990, c. E.27. See generally Van Duzer (1997: 135-38).

14. The obligation to obtain an extra-provincial license arises when a corporation begins to carry on business in a province. For example, in *Success International Inc.* v. *Environmental Export International of Canada Inc.* (1995), 23 O.R. (3d) 137 (Gen. Div.) the plaintiff, an "extra-provincial corporation" which had carried on business in Ontario but had failed to comply with licensing requirements, was found not to be entitled to seek access to the courts to enforce an arbitrator's award. In Ontario, taking orders or buying or selling goods or services through travelling representatives, advertisements or the mail is not deemed as carrying on a business (Van Duzer 1997: 138).

15. A pending amendment to s. 219 of the *Income Tax Act*, RSC 1985 (5th Supp.) c. 5., appears to place "branch operations" of non-resident companies in the same position for tax purposes as subsidiaries which are incorporated in Canada.
16. See e.g. *Telecommunications Act*, S.C. 1993, c. 38. and *Bank Act*, S.C. 1991, c. 46.
17. A draft version of the MAI, whose discussion was abandoned by the OECD in 1998, contemplated that in principle country-specific exceptions or reservations could be negotiated among the Parties to the Agreement, so that a country could maintain laws and regulations which did not conform to MAI disciplines (OECD 1997). The reality is that these exceptions or reservations would not likely survive the negotiating process or if they did, they would have to be abandoned due to the competitive pressures generated by the implementation of the MAI. The Seattle Round of WTO negotiations addresses many of the issues raised previously in OECD discussions of the MAI.
18. Under the National Policy of Sir John A. Macdonald, tariffs, subsidies and other positive and negative measures were used to encourage the development of Canadian manufacturing, transportation, resource and commercial enterprises. This policy was followed, with some deviations, until the movement toward trade liberalization following World War II and even, to some extent, until the advent of free trade with the United States in 1988 (Supply and Services Canada 1985).
19. See note 7, *supra.*
20. R.S.C. 1985, c. 43. The legislation requires all foreign-based corporations and labour unions in Canada to file annual returns revealing (in the case of corporations) their dominant shareholders and the names and addresses of their directors and senior executives. While most corporations appear to comply with the legislation, the information supplied is clearly incomplete and subject to the normal frailties of self-reporting.
21. Total exceeds 32. Two companies were first taken private and then dissolved.
22. "Outside directors" are those who do not hold a management position in the company, its parent or affiliates.
23. Six companies had been dissolved by 1995, and no information was available for the remainder.
24. American-based transnationals have historically tended to use subsidiary boards less extensively than other transnationals (Kriger and Rich 1987).
25. *Canada Business Corporations Act*, R.S.C. 1985, c. 44, ss. 114(3) and 115(2).

References

Anderson, Anne 1987, *The Autopact: Past Achievements and Current Concerns*, Toronto: Legislative Research Center, Current Issue Paper #71.

Arthurs, Harry W. 1996a, 'Labour Law without the State?,' *University of Toronto Law Journal*, 46:1.

--------- 1996b, 'Lawyering in Canada in the 21st Century,' *Windsor Yearbook of Access to Justice* 15: 202.

--------- 1997, 'Mechanical Arts and Merchandise: Canadian Public Administration in the New Economy,' *McGill Law Journal* 41: 29.

--------- 1998, 'Globalization of the Mind: Canadian Elites and the Restructuring of Legal Fields,' *Canadian Journal of Law and Society* 12: 219.

Berle, Adolf. A and Means, Gardiner C. 1968, *The Modern Corporation and Private Property*, New York: Harcourt, Brace & World (rev. ed.).

Birkinshaw, Julian 1995a, *Business Development Initiatives of Multinational Subsidiaries in Canada*, Ottawa: Industry Canada, Occasional Paper No. 2.

--------- 1995b, 'Taking the Initiative,' *Business Quarterly* 59: 97.

Birkinshaw, Julian and Morrison, Allen J. 1995, 'Configurations of Strategy and Structure in Subsidiaries of Multinational Corporations,' *Journal of International Business Studies* 4: 729.

Blank, Stephen 1993, *The Emerging Architecture of North America*, Miami: North-South Center, University of Miami, Paper No. 1.

Buchanan, James M. 1984, 'Politics without Romance: A Sketch of Positive Public Choice Theory and its Normative Implications,' in Buchanan and Tollison (eds.), *The Theory of Public Choice II*, Ann Arbour: University of Michigan Press.

Burawoy, Michael 1979, *Manufacturing Consent: Changes in the Labor Process Under Monopoly Capitalism*, Chicago: University of Chicago Press.

Coffey W. and Sheamur R. 1996, *Employment Growth and Change in the Canadian Urban System, 1971-94*, Ottawa: Canadian Policy Research Networks/Renouf Publishing Co.

Courchene, Thomas J. 1996, 'Corporate Governance as Ideology', *Canadian Business Law Journal* 26: 202.

Daniels, Peter W. 1993, *Service Industries in the World Economy*, Oxford/Cambridge: Blackwell.

Daniels Peter W. and Moulaert, Frank (eds.) 1991, *The Changing Geography of Advanced Producer Services*, London and New York: Belhaven Press.

Daniels, Ronald J. and Halpern, Paul 1995, 'Too close for comfort: the role of the closely held public corporation in the Canadian economy and the implications for public policy,' *Canadian Business Law Journal* 26: 11.

Drache, Daniel 1994, 'Lean Production in Japanese Auto Transplants in Canada,' *Canadian Business Economics* 45.

Flannigan, Robert 1995, 'The Economic Structure of the Firm,' *Osgoode Hall Law Journal* 33: 105.

Francois, Joseph F. 1990, 'Trade in Producer Services and Returns due to Specialization under Monopolistic Competition,' *Canadian Journal of Economics* 23: 109.

Galbraith, John K. 1967, *The New Industrial State*, Boston: Houghton Mifflin Co.

Gillies, James M. 1992, *Boardroom Renaissance: Power, Morality, and Performance in the Modern Corporation*, Whitby: McGraw-Hill Ryerson.

Gillies, James M. and Morra, D. 1996, 'Stakeholders and Shareholders in a Global World,' *Policy Options* 17: 32.

Grinspun, Ricardo and Cameron, Maxwell A. 1993, *The Political Economy of North American Free Trade*, New York: St. Martin's Press.

Harrington, James W. 1989, 'Implications of the Canada-United States Free Trade Agreement for Regional Provision of Producer Services,' *Economic Geography* 65: 314.

Historical Statistical Supplement 1995/96, *Canadian Economic Observer*.

Hoffman, Richard C. 1994, 'Generic Strategies for Subsidiaries of Multinational Corporations,' *Journal of Management Studies* 6: 69.

Holm, Ulf, Johanson, Jan and Thilenius, Peter 1995, 'Headquarters' Knowledge of Subsidiary Network Contexts in the Multinational Corporation,' *International Studies in Management and Organization* 25: 97.

Hutton, Thomas and Ley, David 1987, 'Location, Linkages and Labour: The Downtown Complex of Corporate Offices in a Medium Size City, Vancouver, British Columbia,' *Economic Geography* 63: 126.

Jackson, Terence 1993, *Organizational Behaviour in International Management*, Oxford: Butterworth-Heinneman.

Krajewski, Stephen 1992, *Intrafirm Trade and the New North American Business Dynamic*, Ottawa: Conference Board of Canada.

Kumar, Pradeep and Holmes, John 1997, 'Canada: Continuity and Change' in Kochan, Lansbury and MacDuffie (eds.), *After Lean Production: Evolving Employment Practices in the World Auto Industry*, Ithaca and London: ILR Press.

Kustin, Richard and Jones, Robert 1995, 'The Influence of Corporate Headquarters on Leadership Styles in Japanese and US Subsidiary Companies,' *Leadership and Organization Development Journal*, 16: 11.

Landa, Janet T. 1994, *Trust, Ethnicity and Identity: Beyond the New Institutional Economics of Ethnic Trading Networks, Contract Law, and Gift-exchange*, Anne Arbor: University of Michigan Press.

Lee, Hamilton V. and Sanders, Joseph 1996, 'Corporate Crime Through Citizens Eyes: Stratification and Responsibility in the United States, Russia and Japan,' *Law and Society Review*, 30: 513.

Lucio, Miguel Martinez and Weston, Syd 1994, 'New Management Practices in a Multinational Corporation: The Restructuring of Workers' Representation and Rights?,' *Industrial Relations Journal* 25: 110.

Mastenbroek, Willem F.G. 1993, *Conflict Management and Organizational Development*, Chichester: John Wiley and Sons.

Medcalf, L. 1996, 'Is Canadian Marketing on the Line,' *Marketing Magazine*, July 1, p.1.

Merrett, Christopher. D. 1996, *Free Trade: Neither Free Nor About Trade*, Montreal: Black Rose Books.

Milner, Brian 1994, 'Free Trade Wave Rocks the Canadian Boat,' *International Business*, August, p. 79.

Milkman, Ruth 1991, *Japan's California Factories: Labor Relations and Economic Globalization*, Los Angeles: Institute of Industrial Relations, University of California.

Morrison, Allen J., Ricks, David A. and Roth, Kendall 1991, 'Globalization versus regionalization: Which way for the multinational?,' *Organizational Dynamics* 19: 17.

Muchlinski, Peter T. 1997, 'Global Bukowina Examined: Viewing the Multinational Enterprise as a Transnational Law-making Community,' in G. Teubner (ed.), *GlobalLaw Without the State - Studies in Modern Law and Policy*, Aldershot/Brookfield: Dartmouth Publishing.

Murray, Victor V. 1991, *Improving Corporate Donations: New Strategies for Grantmakers and Grantseekers*, San Francisco: Jossey-Bass.

Nicolaïdis, Kalypso 1993, 'Mutual Recognition, Regulatory Competition and the Globalization of Professional Services,' in Aharoni (ed.), *Coalitions and Competition: The Globalization of Professional Business Services*, London and New York: Routledge.

Niosi, Jorge 1994, 'Foreign Direct Investment in Canada,' in Eden (ed.), *Multinationals in North America*, Calgary: University of Calgary Press.

O'Connor, Marleen A. 1997, 'Global Capitalism and the Evolution of American Corporate Governance Institutions,' in Macmillan Patfield (ed.), *Perspectives on Company Law: 2*, London and Boston: Kluwer Law International.

OECD 1997, *MAI, The Multilateral Agreement on Investment*, Paris: OECD Policy Brief No.2. <http://www.oecd.org/publications/Pol_brief/9702_pol.htm#6> (30 Jan. 1998).

O'Neil, M. 1996, 'Inching Toward Hegemony,' *Canadian Computer Reseller* (March 6) 14.

Rhéaume, Gilles and Warda, Jacek 1995, *The Role of Foreign-Owned Subsidiaries in Canada*, Ottawa: Conference Board of Canada.

Robé, Jean-Philippe 1997, 'Multinational Enterprises: The Constitution of a Pluralistic Legal Order,' in G. Teubner (ed.), *Global Law Without the State - Studies in Modern Law and Policy*, Aldershot/Brookfield: Dartmouth Publishing.

Sadeque, Zulfi 1990, *Canadian Minority Equity Participation in Foreign Controlled Subsidiaries*, Ottawa: Investment Canada, Working Paper No. 1990-I.

Santos, Boaventura de Sousa 1995, *Towards a New Common Sense: Law, Science and Politics in the Paradigmatic Transition*, New York: Routledge.

Sassen, Saskia 1995, 'When the State Encounters a New Space Economy: The Case of Information Industries,' *American University Journal of International Law and Policy* 10: 769.

Senate of Canada 1996, *Corporate Governance: Report of the Standing Senate Committee on Banking, Trade and Commerce*, Ottawa: Senate of Canada.

Sölvell, Örjan and Zander, Ivo 1995, 'Organization of the Dynamic Multinational Enterprise,' *International Studies of Management and Organization* 25: 17.

Statistics Canada 1997, *Foreign Control in the Canadian Economy, CALURA: Pt. 1, Corporations 1995*, Ottawa: Statistics Canada.

Storper, Michael 1992, 'The Limits to Globalization: Technology Districts and International Trade,' *Economic Geography* 68: 60.

Supply and Services Canada 1985, *The Royal Commission on the Economic Union and Development Prospects of Canada (The MacDonald Commission)*, Ottawa: Supply and Services Canada.

UNCTAD 1994, *World Investment Report 1994: Transnational Corporations, Employment and the Workplace*, New York/Geneva: United Nations.

Van Duzer, John A. 1997, *The Law of Partnerships and Corporations*, Concord: Irwin Law.

Weintraub, Sidney 1994, 'Current State of US-Canada Economic Relations,' *American Review of Canadian Studies* 24: 473.

Weisman, Robert M. and Gomez-Mejia, Luis R., 'A Behavioural Agency Model of Managerial Risk-Taking,' *Academy of Management Review* 23: 133.

Ziegel, Jacob S. *et al.* 1994, *Cases and Materials on Partnerships and Canadian Business Corporations*, Scarborough: Carswell. 3rd Ed.

2 1-800 New Brunswick: Economic Development Strategies, Firm Restructuring and the Local Production of "Global" Services

RUTH BUCHANAN

In New Brunswick, a small, underdeveloped and relatively isolated province on the Atlantic Coast of Canada, the tides of global economic transformation can be seen from a distance. At least, this is what I believed when, as a young academic interested in globalization, I relocated to Fredericton in 1993. I assumed this because globalization scholars at the time tended to be located in and focus their attention on major urban centres. Their arguments suggested that if the virtual networks that made up the global economy could be described as located in any place, it had to be a global city. The nearest one could actually get to globalization from Fredericton, I imagined, would be Boston, or better, New York. Although those cities were not far away geographically, within the hierarchy of the global economic order, it seemed as if they couldn't get any farther.

However, I soon came to understand what this chapter intends to illustrate: that processes of globalization are also taking place in New Brunswick, albeit in forms quite distinct from that of the global centre. I wasn't in the province very long before I noticed a number of recognizable themes emerging in local economic news: the implications of new telecommunications technologies, restructuring and reorganizations by firms, and the shifting roles of local, provincial and federal governments. In particular, between 1991 and 1996, a convergence of strategies being pursued by government, firms, and workers created an attractive environment within the province for the location of call centre operations.[1] Call centres are centralized offices where large numbers of employees perform most of their work over the telephone. The call centre industry encompasses both inbound telephone services via 1-800 numbers provided by a wide range of firms (from courier companies to airlines, hospitality industries and financial institutions) as well as outbound telephone services like telemarketing, survey research and fundraising. Firms reorganizing to reduce costs are increasingly turning to the creation of call centres through which a diverse range of functions can be centralized, at some distance from both customers and head office, for more cost-efficient delivery. New Brunswick early on realized that it could market itself as a cheap, productive location for these types of operations. Between 1991 and 1997, the teleservices sector accounted for a significant proportion of job creation in the province, providing approximately 6,000 new jobs in a province of less than three quarters of a million people. The provincial government played an essential role in both initiating and encouraging the sector's growth, actively soliciting firms and offering incentives to those which chose to relocate. The implementation of the call centre development strategy happened to correspond with a second wave of consolidation and restructuring of call centre operations by many firms, which contributed to the province's success in attracting nearly 40 such centres by 1997.

As I began to realize that the intersecting dynamics at work in New Brunswick were also linked to what I had understood as globalization, yet operated according to a distinct logic of their own out on the periphery, it was necessary to revisit my assumptions about current processes of economic transformation. Globalization is not a single process that radiates outward or downward from an integrated core; rather globalization(s) can be seen as an amalgamation of processes that draw on the particularities of local history and the agency of local workers and communities as much as larger forces of economic integration or transformation. Globalization(s) occur through a multiplicity of interactions and institutions that are necessarily localized, in spaces that have their own histories, needs and instrumentalities.[2] This chapter is an effort to illuminate the complex ways in which global processes are interpreted and transformed by institutions and actors operating within more circumscribed scales of influence; or put simply, how the global is (re)made in the local.

From this perspective, the New Brunswick call centre story can be understood as an important piece of the globalization puzzle, in which transformation and growth within the services sector are crucial. While at one time the economic role of services was seen as secondary to the role played by production in economic activity, services are now understood as central to current processes of spatial and institutional restructuring. In particular, attention has been paid to the increasing significance of intermediate activities such as the provision of legal, marketing, financial and management expertise to businesses (producer services). Both the rapid expansion of producer services and their consolidation as the economic core of major cities have been identified as key factors in the spatial and institutional reorderings currently underway (Sassen 1991; Castells 1996). Yet, the emergence of global cities is only one piece of a two-fold process. Intensified polarization of economic activity is producing both agglomeration and decentralization. While uneven development is not a new feature of capitalist forms of social organization, both the sheer intensity and the geographic and institutional forms characterizing current restructuring point toward a need to understand decentralization as much as agglomeration.

While much useful empirical work has been done recently on the growth of producer services in core areas, this focus fails to answer questions about how the new dynamics of uneven development may have also transformed the processes through which workers and communities on the periphery are positioned in relation to these emerging centres. Nor does it examine sufficiently the ways that firms participate in these changes, through both spatial restructuring and the internal reorganization of work processes. This chapter begins where this existing research leaves off.

Through the presentation of a case study of the New Brunswick call centre industry, it will be possible in this chapter to examine the intersection of forces which are producing current restructuring, and to highlight the interaction between three separate sets of actors: multinational firms, regional government, and the individuals who make up local labour markets. First, as I've already suggested, by selecting a case study far from global centres and in the context of the production of routine consumer marketing and services, this chapter will examine the interlinked spatial and organizational dimensions of restructuring by firms.

Second, it is important to observe that the new economy has ushered in not only this 'new geography of centrality and marginality' but also a new set of institutional relationships and instrumentalities through which this geography is produced, and these relationships restructured (Sassen 1996). One of the most important of these is the state, albeit often a regional state. Much initial research on the state in conditions of globalization lent itself most readily to propositions that states are losing their role in the regulation of economic activity, both domestic and transnational. Recently, another current aspect of research has emerged which has focussed on the region as an essential level of coordination of economic activity in the context of late 20th century capitalism (Storper 1997). One can find many examples of regional and local governments which have used regulatory and marketing initiatives to expand their role in economic development, often far away from global cities or national capitals (Sabel 1996). This study adds to the evidence that the state is not simply being "hollowed out," but that governments frequently play an important role in the current economic transformation through their interaction with restructuring firms. Hence, this chapter also examines the changing institutional role of the state, and the state as an instrument of restructuring, through the example of the provincial government of New Brunswick during the leadership of former Premier Frank McKenna.

Third, while the co-existence of these simultaneous tendencies of agglomeration and decentralization is structured by the relationship between two evolving institutional frameworks – the state and the firm – it is not determined by them. In order to fully explain the trajectory of restructuring in any particular locality, it is necessary to examine not only transformations in the organization of firms, and in the regulatory apparatus of the regional state, but also the responses of local actors in adapting to and/or resisting the changes brought about in their communities through these larger processes. In the New Brunswick example, the attitudes of workers and the public toward the jobs created by the call centres also played a significant role in the largely successful unfolding of the call centre strategy, a role which was well understood by both the firms and the provincial government. Initially, the availability of capable potential employees was a significant factor in bringing firms to the province, while low turn-over rates and high productivity of New Brunswickers employed as call centre workers helped to make many of the new centres successful by firm standards. However, low wages and difficult working conditions at some call centres created significant pressures for the employees, straining their coping skills, their sense of fairness and propriety and leading them to become more publicly demanding. Both the government and the firms took seriously the ongoing need for compliant labour from the start, and continued to work at constructing a public image of the call centres as providing valued and respectable work. It was the interaction between these localized struggles of workers, restructuring strategies of firms, and economic development efforts of government that collectively functioned to produce and reproduce the call centre industry in New Brunswick. This is the process, the global being made and remade in the local, that this chapter seeks to examine.

The Local Production of 1-800 Services: Restructuring Firms, Reorganizing Work

The spatial reorganization of firms that underpinned the rapid growth of the number of call centres in New Brunswick over the past six years is called "back officing" in industry circles. Certain lower skilled jobs such as telemarketing, teleservice, data entry, rate or credit checking are separated from the rest of a firm's operations and relocated to a suburban or offshore location where labour, rents and other costs are generally lower. By relocating to sites where suitable employees are cheap and plentiful, and there are few other employment options, the productivity returns for firms can be quite significant.[3] However, the gains produced by relocating production are usually limited; firms seeking further cost savings must eventually either increase the productivity of their workforce by other means, or relocate production further offshore in search of even cheaper labour (Appelbaum 1993). Recent studies of corporate reorganization and labour identify two approaches to increasing productivity in the context of the current volatile economy (Economic Council of Canada 1990; Duffy, Glenday and Pupo 1997). These correspond to two ideal types: the sweatshop and the flexible firm. Firms which choose the low road of the sweatshop depend on a steady supply of ready labour, investing as little as possible in their employees, who tend to burn out and turn over at a high rate. At the other end of the spectrum, firms seeking to "flexibilize" may invest heavily in their labour force, rely on internal labour markets and depend on being rewarded with greater loyalty, commitment and productivity from employees. For employees, this can either mean increasing demands for more work with negligible wage increases or further opportunities for training, skills utilization and autonomy within the labour process.

While these ideal types capture many important features of the structural dynamics of current restructuring, the dichotomy they present is not always neatly reflected in particular cases. This is because the current process of economic transformation, of which the New Brunswick story is one example, is also a product of ongoing conflicts and accommodations among locally situated social actors. Therefore, this chapter examines the differences among the ways that firms have approached the reorganization of their operations to incorporate telephone services provided from New Brunswick for their Canadian, or in some cases, North American customers, and explores some of the implications of these different routes on the relationships among the firm, its employees and customers. The choice of low or high road does not appear, in this context, as distinct or predetermined as theorists have presumed. Several firms have, while locating telephone service operations in a site where labour is relatively cheap and there are few strong local regulatory disincentives, avoided the classic "low road" approach. Rather, they may emphasize the quality of calls as well as – or even more than – quantity in evaluating worker productivity; they may invest more in training and compensating workers; they may use teams to motivate employees to work together, and they may encourage promotion within the firm.

The spatial restructuring, driven by the search for the ideal combination of cheap and productive labour, that brings firms to New Brunswick often takes place at the same time as, and is connected to, changes in the ways in which firms utilize information technologies and how they organize work. Call centres locating in the province share basic forms of organization, information technologies and geographically oriented restructuring strategies, although there are a few significant differences among them. The companies relocate only their telephone operations to the province, leaving higher paid employees in creative, managerial, and marketing functions in other locations. Physical separation from the rest of the operations can lead to increasing skills polarization and literal disappearance of the segregated workers from career paths within the firm (Belt, Richardson and Webster 1999; Shalla 1997). It also permits the implementation of significantly different expectations in terms of shift work, productivity quotas, salaries, and seniority from a firm's employment practices in other locations. Many of the firms locating centres in New Brunswick are consolidating operations formerly carried out in a number of sites into one "national" centre. Most of the centres in the province make or receive calls throughout Canada. Some provide support or backup to centres located in the United States as well.

The provision of services by telephone has been rapidly expanding over the past decade. With the establishment of sophisticated networked databases, firms that provide reservation services, for example, can provide detailed "local" information about a specific hotel such as how far it is from a corner store, a gym or a park.[4] That this information can be provided despite the despatialized nature of the linkage between the telephone service representative and the customer is an important aspect of quality service. In addition to the hospitality sector, airlines, banks, courier companies, and office equipment suppliers have all recently expanded or consolidated call centres in New Brunswick. The service centres make it possible for the firms to claim that they are improving access to their services by offering the 1-800 number through extended hours (in some cases 24 hour service). At the same time it reduces both labour costs and overhead through locating a large group of (usually) new employees under one roof. In some cases, it has the added advantage of enabling the reduction or elimination of unionized locations elsewhere. While some of the larger firms which have opened centres in New Brunswick have offered employees the opportunity to transfer to the new centre, most of the employees who currently work in the centres are New Brunswickers.

Most of the call centres require their employees to adhere to carefully worded scripts. While some of these scripts are necessary to comply with regulatory standards, as in the sale of insurance, much of the scripting is intended to bring employees into conformity with a company-dictated standard of good service. Just as the computer database inadequately replaces local knowledge, the scripts that many of the telephone workers are required to adhere to (for both inbound and outbound calls) are a poor substitute for the interpersonal engagement of the face-to-face encounter. Yet, if employees seek to deviate from the scripts to improve the effectiveness of the call, they can be disciplined. The highly monitored nature of the call centre environment, which one worker described as "Big Brotherish," makes deviation without detection difficult. However, there are often significant incentives to amend the scripts, particularly in a telephone sales environment where performance bonuses can make up a large proportion of employee income. Sometimes supervisory staff collude with this process. In one American owned telemarketing firm it was widely recognized that the scripts sent by the American head office were highly ineffective for selling to a Canadian public much less used to "hard-sell" techniques. Changes were made in the New Brunswick office for the use of the local callers. When head office called in from its location in the southern United States to remotely monitor calls at the New Brunswick office, local management warned employees so that they could return to the original scripts.[5]

Interviews with call centre employees reinforced the suggestion that productivity requirements and working conditions in New Brunswick compared unfavourably with those in other parts of the country. An employee with one firm that had another call centre in London, Ontario said, "People sort of know that the rules are quite different in London – they don't know in a big way, but they don't work overnight shifts. They, you know, I think they've got more clout in London."[6]

A similar observation was made by a local union representative who had transferred to a newly opened call centre from Ontario.[7] Based on information that he had gained from his many years of experience with the company, and from reviewing logs at other call centres after his election to the union position, he was convinced that the company was selectively trying to establish higher productivity quotas at the new New Brunswick location so that it would then be able to phase out centres in other locations by claiming that they were not performing as well.

In a mail-out survey I conducted in the summer of 1996, firms were asked to indicate a number of factors influencing their decision to select New Brunswick as a site for their consolidation or relocation. The one factor selected by almost all the firms was the telecommunications infrastructure in the province, which, through interviews, I came to understand as including both the technology offered by NB Tel and the support services it provided for call centre operations. The availability of a bilingual workforce and government incentives were next, followed by wage rates and the educational accomplishments of the workforce. Notably, the two factors which set New Brunswick apart from other sites in the view of these firms are both outcomes of the distinct local history of the province. While each of these histories can be elaborated upon in much more detail, I can only briefly indicate their particularities here.

In the 1970s, NB Tel made a series of decisions about infrastructure development which turned out to be crucial in giving them a head start on developments in the 1990s. The decisions were determined by two things: the lack of a single large urban centre in the province and the fact that one of the two multinational companies operating out of the province, owned by the McCain family, was located in the hamlet of Florenceville, in a relatively remote northwest area of the province. Instead of introducing more advanced services only in one or two large urban centres, as most other telephone companies were doing at the time, NB Tel had strong incentives to make its most advanced digital network ubiquitous throughout the province from the start. Thus, as more advanced uses of telephones became widespread through telematics, New Brunswick found itself already equipped with a fully digital network.[8]

Similarly, the labour force in New Brunswick has been shaped by a long history of economic disadvantage and high unemployment, recently buttressed by the decline of formerly key sectors such as the fisheries, mining and shipbuilding. A significant proportion of the income level of New Brunswickers had traditionally been made up through social programmes, funded by federal transfer payments. By the early 1990s, reform of both the nationally regulated unemployment scheme and the provincially governed welfare benefits had introduced strict new eligibility requirements and reduced benefits. At the outset, the call centre job creation strategy was envisioned by the provincial government as tied to its efforts to move welfare recipients off the roles and into paid employment.[9] This initiative quickly dropped from public view when it became clear that there was an abundance of educated New Brunswickers not on welfare in line for the new jobs. Many of them were young people, university or college students or recent graduates who might otherwise have had to leave the province to look for work. Most of this generation of workers did not look favourably upon unions[10] and didn't have pre-conditioned expectations about what a workplace would provide to them. In this way, they were ideal employees for companies coming to New Brunswick looking for higher productivity, a lot of flexibility (many of the centres have demanding shift schedules) and fewer demands from their workforce.

The firms that reorganized to place centralized calling operations in New Brunswick were at the same time reorganizing space within the workplaces themselves. Generally, the call centre environment tends to resemble Bentham's Panopticon.[11] Employees in call centres work in public isolation: in a large room filled with cubicles, grouped in islands or rows, each equipped with headsets and computers. One of the larger call centres I visited resembled a large aeroplane hanger with hundreds of diminutive cubicles arranged in clusters throughout the wide open space. Very little personalization of workspaces is permitted. While each individual is tethered to his or her own workspace by the headset, supervisors can monitor the calls of any worker at any time without their knowledge. In addition, for each employee, at the end of the day, a computer printout can be produced which provides an exact statistical breakdown of that caller's daily output.

Through the combination of random in-person monitoring and constant on-line monitoring, individual employees' performance is rendered highly visible to management, as well as to other employees (Clement 1992; Belt, Richardson and Webster 1999). Both inbound and outbound centres often use large visual displays to publicize performance levels and goals. In inbound centres, electronic displays may show the number of calls (or minutes per call) in the queue at any given time; outbound centres may display sales figures for various "teams." It is important that calls neither wait too long in the queue, nor that callers have to make repeat calls to solve one problem. However, what most call centres do not explicitly acknowledge is that these goals are in conflict, and as the section below on the role of call centre workers will examine, call centres are organized so that it falls to individual employees to develop strategies for successfully negotiating the contradiction between providing good service to each customer and meeting productivity quotas for dealing with high volumes of calls.

Many call centres have recently adopted what they call a "team" approach, although the impact of teams on the organization of work is often quite insignificant. In outbound centres, productivity is generally measured quantitatively on the basis of sales figures, or by a combination of percentage of successful sales and "talk time" (the length of each call). Teams are used either to keep track of employees selling particular campaigns, which are usually associated with particular incentive structures dictated by the client, or within a particularly large campaign, they may be used for in-house motivational purposes, with charts and displays showing the relative performance.

Within firms operating large in-house customer service bureaus the impact of the transition to a "team-oriented" workplace can be more substantial, yet as an employee interviewed at one very large firm observed, the implementation of a "team-oriented" approach can be done in a way that significantly increases workloads without reorganizing work. By reorganizing workers into teams, her company had saved cost by eliminating a higher paid level of supervisory positions, while transferring those responsibilities onto the interviewee, who was an already overworked and less-well-paid team leader. However, employees interviewed at other firms reported that they welcomed the additional responsibilities that came with membership in a "team" since they offered chances for collaboration, creativity or problem solving, were perceived as routes to career advancement or simply as a break from the monotony of the phones. The difference seemed to lie in whether the firm organized employee time in such a way that additional work responsibilities attached to team work were recognized and accounted for in the context of the employee's workday. Those firms most wedded to the Panopticon model of supervision appeared least able to make this shift. This often-touted "high road" to flexibility seems to require a much more decentralized workplace, with greater autonomy and less supervisory scrutiny of individual employees than is common among call centres.

"If You Have the Work, We Have the Force": Inventing a Local Economic Development Strategy[12]

Call centres are made possible by telematics, the combination of telecommunications and software technologies that can coordinate, through the predictive dialling of outbound or switching of inbound calls, the simultaneous connection of a telephone call and the display of account information to a service representative. Although this technology is not particularly new, its dissemination to places like New Brunswick has facilitated the corporate reorganizations that are bringing the call centres there as well. However, back-officing is a both a fickle and footloose type of investment. Most firms rent their premises and bring in computers and other equipment purchased elsewhere. The government of New Brunswick had to work to distinguish itself from the plethora of other possible generic locations for this type of work and establish the province as an attractive "site" for call centre operations.

There were a number of factors that made this an attractive initiative for the government of Premier Frank McKenna early in its mandate. Firstly, the McKenna government took initiatives to reform welfare and other social programmes along fiscally conservative lines in the early 1990s, for example by developing workfare programmes (in some cases mandatory) and strengthening enforcement against welfare fraud, to reduce disincentives to work. To make those initiatives politically palatable, however, it was necessary to also produce a serious job creation initiative. At the outset, call centres were discussed in the context of welfare reform, and a programme was conceived, and briefly implemented, which put welfare recipients to work on the phones.[13] This programme didn't last very long as it soon became clear that there were many more qualified people, not on welfare, who would line up for these jobs. Although government officials were always careful to point out that the call centres were only a small part of a more comprehensive job creation strategy for the province, at least in terms of numbers of jobs created, the call centre strategy eventually grew to become the cornerstone of the provincial government's job creation efforts.[14]

At first, the strategy was to establish that it was possible to compete with most other places in North America on purely economic logic. Wages and rents were low, payroll taxes non-existent and workers' compensation very affordable in the province compared to other locations. In addition, the way in which the New Brunswick Telephone Company was organized made it possible to lease the phones and switching technologies that firms required at relatively low rates (compared to the costs of purchasing this type of equipment elsewhere). While NB Tel is in the private sector, both government sources and those interviewed at NB Tel referred to the working relationship between the two entities as a "close" one. While the precise extent to which NB Tel, a private company, and the provincial government collaborated on the call centre strategy is not clear, it is significant that the original impetus for the strategy came from a government employee who had recently relocated from NB Tel.[15] While the government appeared to take the lead in initiating a firm's move to the province through marketing, providing cost/benefit analyses, and financial incentives, the service provided by NB Tel was identified by most firms as a major factor in the decision to relocate.

In addition to providing a favourable cost comparison to firms considering relocation, the province also offered forgivable loans to offset costs to firms associated with start-up and training of new employees. In the first five years of the programme, the province paid out more than 28 million dollars to call centres.[16] According to Premier McKenna, this amount was necessary in order to compete with similar offers from other jurisdictions.[17]

The amounts of the loans were public information, but the basis on which they were calculated was not.[18] A very general estimate based on the relationship between the size of the operation and the "loan" would place the amounts at approximately $10,000 per job. Most of the grants were contingent on the creation by a firm of a specified number of full-time equivalent positions over a period of three years. Failure to do this could result in a loan being called, although this had not occurred as of May, 1997. Firms were reluctant to comment on the role played by the loans in encouraging their relocation to New Brunswick rather than another province, although they appear to have had some influence. Finally, in terms of more formal, statutory changes, while the province did eliminate the provincial sales tax on 1-800 numbers, it appears to have passed no other legislation specifically to attract call centres.[19] While economic factors such as local labour and real estate costs, the technological services and support offered by NB Tel, and the payment of financial incentives go some way in explaining the relocation of a few firms to New Brunswick, they do not tell the whole story.

In order to adequately explain the rapid emergence of a market for call centres in New Brunswick, one needs to integrate an analysis of shifts and initiatives at the level of discourse with these economic realities. While few would argue that ideas and images circulating in the mainstream media have had both a powerful constraining and enabling influence on public perceptions about the economy, and on policy makers, the work of the imagination is not frequently singled out as a driving force in the transformation of either economic relations or regulatory institutions.[20] Yet, I would argue that the strategic marketing of New Brunswick as a site for call centre operations involved the constructive work of the imagination along two intersecting dimensions: first, in realizing New Brunswick's aspirations to become a desired location for call centres, and secondly, in constituting a willing, committed and docile labour force to work at those centres. In order to transform external perception of itself into an attractive site for this type of investment, the province commissioned studies, placed advertisements, sent representatives to telemarketing conferences, arranged private meetings between the Premier and corporate heads and offered significant sums to firms choosing to relocate. Throughout, it held out the existence of a large, willing, well educated, bilingual workforce as one of the key factors in attracting firms. The success of the strategy depended in large measure upon the truth of that claim.

At the same time as it was seeking out the call centres, the province also had to market at another level, promoting the centres to New Brunswickers as a good place to work. The call centres were tied to a wider set of policies intended to promote information technology and computer literacy within the province. People were promised that the call centres would be their "on-ramp to the information highway." They were touted by the Premier as "high-skill, high wage, pollution free jobs."[21] At least in part, through actively disseminating its vision of a potential teleservice and telemarketing industry both within the province and outside of it, the government was able to bring one into being, even though the reality may have failed to match the rhetoric in many cases.[22]

This two-level process – marketing a distinctive local labour force while actively engaged in constituting it – was most vividly illustrated by a particular teleservice industry event which I attended in Moncton, NB in 1996. I found myself seated in a ballroom overflowing with people first thing in the morning. The crowd was mixed, men and women, some in business dress, some casual, and they ranged widely in age. The event had been advertised as a teleservice industry job fair, one of the first of its kind in North America. What made it unique was the fact that no actual jobs were involved. None of the firms which attended the fair said that they were using it to fill immediate employment requirements.[23] The primary purpose of the job fair, put on by a group called the "Teleservice Labour Force Development Committee" which appeared to be tied to the Greater Moncton Economic Development Committee, was to generate a database of "potential call centre employees" for the local Chamber of Commerce.

Each of the several hundred people who attended one of the three "information sessions" during the day was asked to fill out a form listing his or her name, age, and qualifications, including language skills. The data were then entered on to a list which would primarily be used to assure companies considering locating in the province that there continued to be a large pool of eager, well educated and bilingual people in Moncton waiting for the chance to work at a call centre. The job fair followed a period in which the press had reported that the incredible Moncton success story had tapped out the local labour market, and that companies were choosing to locate in competing locations, including most obviously neighbouring Charlottetown, PEI, rather than take their chance on Moncton's dwindling labour force.

As the crowded ballroom and conversations with call centre managers in Moncton attested, the reports of the labour pool's demise was premature at best. Few, if any, of the call centres found it necessary to advertise for employees. Most received at least ten unsolicited applications for every position they needed to fill and continued to receive a regular flow of enquiries on an ongoing basis, whether or not they were hiring. Many preferred to conduct their hiring through local temporary services agencies, by employing a regular percentage of their staff (sometimes as much as 50 percent) through the agency, and hiring as permanent employees a select few after they had worked at the firm full-time for several months or even a year.

In the ballroom, there was a screening of a ten minute promotional video intended to market Moncton to potential call centre employers. It emphasized the high degree of education, training and specialization of the "new talent" located in the area, the low cost of doing business in the region, including reduced operating expenses and cost of living savings. The technological and service advantages offered by NB Tel were also praised. After the video, human resources managers from several of Moncton's largest call centres (some of whom had been featured giving "testimonials" in the video) gave presentations which emphasized the rewarding nature of customer service work and the opportunities presented by working in a dynamic, information-technology driven industry. They identified the qualities that a good customer service representative should have as communication skills, willingness to work flexible shifts, a people-oriented personality, and the ability to work in a team environment. Later, the general qualifications for employment at call centres were laid out by a representative of the local business association. These were identified as a high school diploma and basic keyboarding skills. Bilingualism and some customer service experience were also considered helpful, and could be indicated on the form.

The "Job Fair" revealed that the work of representing call centre jobs as highly desirable, career-oriented opportunities was not only done by the provincial government; municipal governments, local Chambers of Commerce, the industry association and the firms themselves have all been actively involved in the ongoing construction of a certain image of call centre work. In addition to participating in these types of events, the firms reinforce the idea of this work as "professional" through such things as the enforcement of fairly formal dress codes, despite the fact that employees are never seen by customers.[24] Many of the larger companies spend a significant proportion of the two to three week training period educating employees in the firm's "philosophy" and policies. Employees (even those working through temporary agencies) were given opportunities to compete for prizes that were usually corporate merchandise of one type or another. Opportunities to advance within the firm are held out as the "carrot" to new employees; one interviewee reported that she had been interviewed by a woman who had started with the firm as a teleservice representative, and told her that she had been promoted six times. The clear message the employees are to receive, despite firm organizational strategies which appear to indicate the contrary, is that they too will be promoted and that teleservice is merely the first step in a career with the company.[25]

The successful "professionalization" of call centre work within New Brunswick is in sharp contrast to the situation elsewhere, as revealed by the views of call centre employees interviewed in Toronto and Winnipeg.[26] Particularly in Toronto, they referred to the work as a marginal, temporary stop-gap until something better came along. In New Brunswick, while the jobs tend to occupy the same marginalized place in a firm's organizational structures, most employees I spoke with, apart from several university students, approached the job as a permanent position. Several younger call centre employees reported that they had picked teleservice as their chosen career. The seriousness with which New Brunswick call centre employees approach their jobs is bolstered by the fact that most of those who work at the centres have at least some post-secondary education, including some with two year degrees from newly minted community college courses in teleservice. Some have paid $1,400 for a 35 week course offered by a private firm that boasts of placing 90 percent of its graduates directly into local teleservice jobs. While these courses may serve only a limited training function even for inbound call centre employment, where most workers are hired with no previous experience and are on the job after about two weeks of training, they do provide another avenue through which prospective workers can be socialized and funneled into these positions. It would appear that the most important function of employee training, in-house, in community colleges or in private firms, is to encourage new employees to see themselves and the work as serious and important; to give workers a sense of themselves as professionalized participants in the larger corporate world, the boundaries of which extend well beyond the province of New Brunswick.[27]

Life on the Line: Accommodation and Resistance in Call Centre Work

I have suggested that New Brunswickers' attitudes and actions in responding to the influx of call centre work are also an important aspect of how the global search for productive labour unfolded itself in this part of the Maritimes. Companies who located to New Brunswick found the workers initially to be eager, determined and uncomplaining.[28] The interviews I conducted with employees generally supported this view. Many were very pleased to have obtained what they considered to be a good job in a call centre. Even when they expressed concerns in confidential interviews with this researcher, they were often qualified in their criticisms of their employers. One women who does shift work for a firm that provides financial services expressed concerns about the ease with which a company might exploit the reasonableness of its employees:

> I love my job. Like, what are you going to say. But mostly people are happy. But I guess I think companies owe - I think people are going more than half way. The employees are good people, you know, they don't want the sun and the earth. There are just some things that would be fairer. They wouldn't say that I don't think. So, I have been sitting on the fence watching, but people are pretty happy - I think the potential is there to abuse the situation.

In her own workplace, she is one of a significant number of part-time employees who never know from week to week how many hours or what shifts they will be asked to work. Employees are routinely sent home partway through a shift if a centre is slow, even though many of them commute quite significant distances. Similar workplace practices were the impetus for the unionization of a telefundraising centre in Toronto in 1996, yet unionization was not an alternative publicly embraced by the call centre employees I spoke with in New Brunswick.[29]

Among some workers, reluctance to complain might stem as much from a fear of reprisal as a general attitude of acceptance. Most call centres that were not unionized made no secret of their hostility toward the possibility. Although many might agree that unionization could improve conditions, one employee observed, "They're so afraid of that word because immediately they think they are going to lose their job if they talk union at all."[30] Although job security was identified as an important issue by New Brunswickers, only those few who have gained permanent employee status at one of the three unionized centres reported that they felt that their jobs were secure.[31]

Although it is clear that New Brunswickers were happy for the influx of jobs and reluctant to do anything that might jeopardize them, few anticipated what coping with the day to day demands of the work would require. Service jobs which involve almost constant interactions with customers require very well developed interpersonal communication skills, yet these skills are rarely recognized as such. In addition to the written scripts discussed in an earlier section, the performance of these jobs requires employees to enact "emotional scripts" which reflect gendered social expectations. Arlie Hochschild, in her influential study of flight attendants, identified the performative, gendered, and largely invisible work done by service workers as "emotional labour" (Hochschild 1983; Wharton 1993). Emotional labour is a useful term because it brings into focus one of the least visible ways in which women's social roles in the private sphere are both extrapolated into workplace expectations and personalized, so that they become part of job requirements, yet not identified as "skills" (Hall 1993; Jenson 1989; Poynton 1993). While approximately 80 percent of call centre workers in New Brunswick are women, everyone who works in a call centre has to develop ways of managing the "feminized" emotional and interpersonal demands the jobs placed upon them (Belt, Richardson and Webster 1999; Duffy and Pupo 1992; Jenson 1989; 1996).

Telephone work may be more challenging than other types of service work because of the "narrow bandwidth" of the method of communication. Call centre workers must have the ability to immediately communicate a friendly, helpful and professional demeanor in a few spoken words. The work involved in projecting friendliness over the phone appears to be quite similar to that described in studies of waitresses and flight attendants, where a key component of the job is the ability to continue to smile regardless of how you feel or how others treat you. One call centre employee said that they were told to smile while they were speaking to customers on the phone because it would make them sound friendlier. She said that she believed that it did work, and if she was having trouble with a particular caller, would silently ask herself whether she was smiling.[32] Not only must workers be able to sound friendly on the phone, they must continue to be friendly as unhappy or upset customers complain and criticize, enacting the script of the deferential "servant" over the phone. Although it might seem less likely, there also seems to be a component of scripted flirtation in call centre work just as there is in waitressing. One young woman who was the top salesperson in a telemarketing centre, when asked to share the secret of her success, admitted that she used a different tone of voice if the caller was a man. Her sales pitch for men was higher, more singsong, and definitely more flirtatious, while her pitch for women was lower, firm, and businesslike. The two tone approach had also worked to dramatically improve the sales of one of her female friends at work who had formerly been having trouble making quota.[33] Although the call centre jobs are attractive to potential employees because they are perceived as office jobs and because they pay better than minimum wage, many workers find that the demands of the jobs raise their stress levels beyond what they are prepared to accept. In comparing her own work experiences, one interviewee ranked telemarketing below waitressing because of the stress level, despite the better pay. She no longer worked as a telemarketer, but had gone to the media to publicize working conditions among telemarketers in her city. "I would rather stay on my feet for eight hours a day and work waitress work than sit there for four hours and be stressed out the way I would be stressed out." In describing the job stresses, many workers refer to the confined nature of the work, the repetition, the monotony. One woman, who had worked for a couple of years at call centres while going to school, explained why she could not imagine herself returning to phone work as follows:

> I'm burnt out on phones. The thought of tethering myself to another desk, to be stuck there for eight hours, only being able to move within a ten-foot radius, for eight hours, doing the same thing every 90 seconds...I don't think I could do it anymore. I just don't have the patience to handle it.[34]

Keeping the customer happy is as important a part of the telephone workers' job as the teller, the waitress or the retail salesperson. However, it can be much more difficult, particularly where someone has been on hold for 10 or 15 minutes. Teleworkers refer to angry callers as "irates." How well one deals with "irates" can be a key component in performance evaluations as well as in an individual's ability to cope with the work over the longer term. Employees seem to vary significantly in how effective they are at managing "irates," as well as in the extent to which the calls "get to them." Those workers who could establish a degree of emotional distance between themselves and the caller appeared to be the least likely to experience the jobs as overwhelmingly stressful. Since evaluations are generally based on talk time as well as quality or outcome (usually "conversions," meaning sales), it is important for callers to "get control" of a call and deal with the problem in as short a time as possible, while still leaving the customer with the impression that they are important. One interview subject shared a handout distributed to employees at her workplace that provided tips on how to reduce talk time by getting control of a conversation and keeping it, which included asking specific questions and politely but firmly refocusing callers attention back to the matter at hand if they had a tendency to stray.

Not all call centre workers were happy to rely on the employers' scripts and tips for dealing with customers or potential customers. Some identified with the people they were calling and were reluctant to pressure them into a purchase or a reservation. One woman who worked selling insurance for an outbound telemarketing firm said that she told management when they put her on a "campaign" that she felt was not a good deal, that she would not work as hard to sell that particular product. She was a top performer elsewhere, and had good relationships with her superiors, so she felt that she could do this without putting her job in jeopardy.[35] Others simply managed the dilemma by resisting silently, refusing to cross certain self imposed lines to make a sale, even if it meant that they would have poor performance records. Over time, this might mean that they would earn significantly less money, or even lose their jobs. In larger urban centres like Toronto, many telemarketing employees simply move on to another firm.

While the outbound centres relied almost exclusively on quantitative performance indicators, in the inbound call centre environment there could be a significant amount of variation between firms. In the effort to implement a more customer service oriented form of work organization, some have chosen to base all, or a significant component, of their employee evaluations on the results of (qualitative) customer satisfaction surveys rather than on numbers of calls serviced in a given period or other (readily available) quantitative measures. Employees subjected to exclusively quantitative measures of productivity had a harder time understanding or learning how to improve their performance. They are often less motivated to do so, because they perceive that the standards are unfair or arbitrary,[36] and would be more likely to engage in acts of resistance, including work slow down, using up sick days, or subversion of the monitoring system.

Rather than being empowered by their workday access to the information highway as they might have imagined, call centre workers more often find themselves disempowered, and even dehumanized by it. One call centre employee described her relationship to the technology in terms of Heidegger's notion of the "standing reserve," that is, "things that are not even regarded as objects, because their only important quality has become their readiness for use" (Heidegger 1977). As she put it, "you are standing waiting until that call comes in to use you to make money. And you are simply another part of that machine."[37] Increasing the amount of authority a worker is given to solve customer problems seems likely to increase both their level of job satisfaction and reduce their inclination to subvert the system, while those who can't do anything for irate customers except transfer them to a supervisor may, out of frustration, be less inclined to try to learn ways to deal with upset callers. More autonomy allows the worker room to accommodate her own goals and aspirations, her sense of herself as a professional worker, to the demands and stresses of the work. On the other hand, the limited autonomy and highly quantitative productivity indicators in most call centres tend to undermine the "professionalization" approach that had been so successful in bringing employees to the centres in the first place. Despite this apparent contradiction, most firms studied in New Brunswick (with a few exceptions)[38] continued to prefer hierarchical forms of work organization and high levels of employee monitoring and control to the risk of granting more autonomy and flexibility to employees, despite the likelihood that employees would be better able to utilize the skills they have, and be more productive and more satisfied at work.

While New Brunswickers seem less willing to take their chances on finding another position that might be marginally better than teleworkers elsewhere, there are more alternatives for experienced teleworkers as the number of firms located in the province's three small urban centres increases. It may be that the hyper-mobile telemarketing culture of Toronto will yet be replicated in New Brunswick in the future. However, for the time being, the major ways in which employees accommodate themselves to call centre work in New Brunswick is through the notion of "professionalization" that I discussed above. In marked contrast to other urban centres, where telework (especially telemarketing) is held in such low regard that workers are embarrassed to reveal what they do for a living, having a call centre job in New Brunswick is still a very desirable thing. This may stem from the contrast between inbound and outbound centres. A greater proportion of centres that have located in the province are inbound, and tend to pay better wages, hire full time employees and offer benefits and some limited opportunities for advancement. These are the types of jobs that New Brunswickers imagine when they think of call centres, and in the current economic climate and low cost of living in the province, they can be described as "good jobs." While many call centres in the province don't offer these "good jobs," even those working at other centres imagine that they will have an opportunity to move up from one to the other.

However, the call centre story in New Brunswick is young yet. While many of those I interviewed there said that they imagined themselves working at the call centre for a long time, none had actually been doing the work for more than three years. Even those with "good jobs," after a couple of years, appear to start having difficulties with the work. One woman whom I interviewed in April of 1997 told me that she was on the edge of quitting her job, although it paid $14/hr, because of the "constant negatives" that make up her working day. Six months later, when I spoke with her again, she was still working at the same job, but still on the edge of leaving. She had been a frequent user of sick days and often went home early when she was having a difficult time with the work. She said that the "money was a trap" that kept her in the job despite the growing signs of stress that she was observing in her own life. After being refused a period of unpaid leave, she was seriously considering taking a stress leave, even though she feared what her family and friends will think about a 23 year old who can't "handle it."[39]

Even though the approach of most New Brunswickers to surviving call centre work appears to incline towards more accommodation than explicit resistance, there may be a point at which this tendency will shift. The work appears to become more difficult for people over time, and employers' expectations and demands will likely increase in the future. Either way, more pressures on employees will likely result in more people finding their coping skills stretched to the maximum. The qualities of New Brunswickers that make them such an attractive local labour force, their serious attitudes towards the work, the eagerness to perform well, the low turn over rates, and reluctance to unionize may gradually shift as New Brunswickers learn that the call centre jobs are not all that they were promised to be.

Conclusion

The first two sections of this chapter examined the role of strategic decisions on the part of the provincial government and restructuring firms which have converged in the emergence of a growing local specialization in the provision of telephone services in New Brunswick. I argued that the emergence of this market was created through the initiative of the provincial government in both constituting, through external marketing efforts, the province as a "desirable site" for call centre operations and simultaneously producing, by internally promoting the call centre jobs, a local labour force which was attractive to firms. Firm relocation decisions, in my assessment, were driven in large measure by their belief in the existence of this labour force. I then went on to suggest, in the third section, that the role of the workers themselves also had to be taken into account. While the provincial government and the firms were the participants in the initial negotiations that led to the arrival of call centres in the province, in order to understand the unfolding dynamic of call centre restructuring, one must see it as the product of ongoing negotiations between firms and their workers, conditioned by the social and political climate of the province.

I have only begun to tell this story here. Further research needs to be conducted on the emerging tactics of employees as they adapt to the conditions of work in the call centres. There is some evidence of increasing rates of turnover at call centres in the province which present the most stressful working conditions. I've suggested that people may not be able to perform at a high level in these types of repetitive and monotonous jobs over extended periods of time. The use of stress and sick leave in those workplaces that have such benefits may also increase as employees begin to feel more secure in their jobs. Over time, the strategies and responses of workers will play an increasingly important role in the evolution of the "call centre" market here. This role will be particularly important given the findings of this chapter regarding the double-edged nature of the story surrounding the emergence of the call centre phenomenon. While the valorization of the call centre work as "professional" has brought workers into the labour force and imbued them with new levels of optimism and aspirations about their future, many will end up being disappointed by their inabilities to advance or the limited skills they acquire in the job. On the other hand, while firms are currently pleased with the high levels of productivity their new workforces are displaying, it may only be a matter of time before employees, encouraged by their ability to move between centres, begin to make greater demands in terms of wages, working conditions or shifts. At this stage, in trying to assess the impact of call centres on the province of New Brunswick, it is difficult to come up with either a wholehearted critique or endorsement. The eventual outcome of developments here, like other sites where global processes meet local actors, will depend on a longer trajectory of locally based struggles and accommodations.

Thus, while the changes in New Brunswick are clearly driven by familiar structural global processes, such as the centralization of high-profit activities and decentralization of routine functions by firms and the increasing segmentation and flexibilization of labour, this chapter aims to illustrate how local histories and cultures also play an important role in the process of change currently "taking place" there. In this way, this account of call centres in New Brunswick leavens hegemonic accounts of globalization with the particularities of local history and the agency of workers and communities struggling to retain or recapture opportunity, security and even prosperity on the current shifting economic terrain. It illustrates the uneasy accommodation in a particular locality of a number of strands of the current transformation, the implications of new telecommunications technologies, firm level restructuring, the changing role of government at all levels and the accommodations and resistances of the local labour force, without ascribing any of them a determining role. Rather, the story is the amalgam of tactical responses to the uncertain conditions of globalization simultaneously pursued by governments, firms, and workers.

Notes

1. This chapter draws on interviews and field work conducted for a larger case study of the emergence of the New Brunswick call centre industry over the past several years. A mail survey of companies which had relocated to the province was conducted between May and July of 1996, and site visits to eight call centres were made during that time. In addition, semi-structured interviews with ten call centre managers and thirty employees were conducted between May 1996 and July 1997. Several follow-up interviews were also conducted in December of 1997. The research was supported by the Canadian Institute for Advanced Research in the fall semester of 1996. The Law Foundation of New Brunswick and the University of British Columbia Hampton Fund also provided assistance.
2. Jane Jenson suggested this helpful wording to me.
3. A recent half-page advertisement placed in the *Globe and Mail* by the Government of New Brunswick cites a Deloitte and Touche Nacore 1995 Benchmarking Study, "It is not uncommon to achieve labour cost savings of more than 20 percent and real estate cost savings of more than 33 percent by back-officing."
4. One interview participant suggested, however, that the databases are only as reliable as the franchisees. Much information on the database that she worked with (for a centre that supported a number of hotel chains) was inaccurate, out of date or incomplete.
5. I will discuss further the ways in which individual employees adapt to both the monitored and scripted nature of their jobs in a subsequent section.
6. Personal interview with call centre worker, Fredericton, NB, July, 1996.
7. Personal interview with union representative, St. John, NB, June 12, 1997.
8. Personal interview with Brian Freeman, Acting Director, Information Highway Secretariat, Department of Economic Development and Tourism, May 16, 1997.
9. New Brunswick was one of the first Canadian jurisdictions to introduce a mandatory workfare programme. Alan Freeman, "New Brunswick Hits the Books After Years of Hard Knocks," *The Globe and Mail*, January 16, 1993.
10. Some referred to the experience of their parents; others had followed media coverage of a few recent, bitter and unsuccessful strikes. The two year strike of refinery workers at the Irving plant in St. John, ending in 1996, was notable both for its length and the outcome for the workers, all of whom were replaced.
11. I owe this useful analogy to Zuboff (1988).
12. The slogan is borrowed from a half page advertisement placed by the province of New Brunswick in the *Globe and Mail* (national edition) in January, 1998.
13. Students from NBWorks, the workfare programme, and the NB Community College were invited to the opening of the United Parcel Service Centre in Fredericton. The Premier was reported as having said to them, "I want you to know that all the hard work that you have made to upgrade your skills is going to give you a chance at a job. I want you to go back to your classes and tell others that there is hope out there." and "Thank Yous All Around as NB Lands UPS Jobs," *Telegraph Journal*, January 12, 1995.
14. By 1999, call centres employed approximately 9,000 people in the province, according to the Department of Economic Development and Tourism, personal communication, October 20, 1999.
15. Personal interview with Brian Freeman, Department of Economic Development and Tourism, May 14, 1997. Freeman joined the Department of Economic Development and Tourism in 1989, at the same time as Kevin Bulmer, whom he credits with the suggestion

that the province might have an economic development "driver" in the telecom sector. He advised that Bulmer had come to government from NBTel.

16. Meagher, David, "$28 Million Aid to Call Centres," *The* (Fredericton) *Daily Gleaner*, May 1, 1996.

17. "We have never really been able to compete with the other provinces in terms of money because we have never had as much. So, usually we try to put as much on the table ... enough on the table so we will not be thrown out of that game and that the rest of our competitive advantage will allow us to win. But, most of the competitiors, we could beat ... jurisdictions with more money." Interview with Frank McKenna, December 29, 1997.

18. Brian Freeman advised that there was no specific programme in place for loans (i.e., number of dollars per job created) but that the loans were part of an individualized process of negotiation with a firm considering relocation.

19. A search of revisions to provincial statutes and regulations in the areas of employment standards, labour, occupational health and safety and taxation between 1990-1995 conducted by a UNB law student working as a research assistant on this project in the summer of 1996 revealed no other significant changes that would benefit call centre operations.

20. The idea of the imagination as functioning in this constructive way, as work rather than play, comes from Appadurai (1996: 31): "The image, the imagined, the imaginary – these are all terms that direct us to something critical and new in global cultural processes: *the imagination as a social practice* . . . the imagination has become an organized field of social practices, a form of work (in the sense of both labour and culturally organized practice), and a form of negotiation between sites of agency (individuals) and globally defined fields of possibility."

21. "Premier Challenged on Job Creation" *The Daily Gleaner*, August 2, 1995.

22. In an interview with CBC Radio May 27, 1997, Premier Frank McKenna acknowledged the difference in wages and working conditions among the call centres, in particular, the contrast between inbound and outbound centres, and commented that the province was focussing its efforts on "moving up the food chain" in its efforts to attract more investment in inbound centres, and particularly, technical support bureaus which would require a more highly skilled workforce. He later confirmed this observation, and added that it was necessary to provide work for people of "all skill sets," so the fact that call centres presented a range in remuneration levels and working conditions didn't seem to him to present a problem. Personal interview, December 29, 1997.

23. Two call centre employees whom I interviewed subsequently (December 1997) reported that they had been hired 6 and 9 months after attending the "Job Fair" (one was in Moncton, the other attended a similar event in St. John, NB) In both cases, the employee was contacted for an interview by a temporary agency which provided employees to one of the larger centres in their respective cities. Both hope that they will eventually be hired on by the firm. Personal interviews, December 1997.

24. One twenty year old man showed me a dress code protocol which precluded him from wearing his earring to work, despite the fact that he worked a graveyard shift, along with only two other employees two nights a week.

25. The significance of the collective construction of a "professionalized" attitude towards low skilled work is developed in a very interesting study by Leslie Salinger (1997) which contrasted the attitudes towards work of two very different immigrant Latina domestic worker cooperatives. In one of these cooperatives, both the value of the work done by the women and their perceptions of themselves as workers were effectively transformed through a dynamic of professionalization which characterized the groups operations.

26. Personal interviews were conducted with 40 call centre employees in Toronto and Winnipeg in June and July, 1998 as part of a forthcoming Status of Women Canada report (Buchanan and Koch-Schulte 2000 forthcoming). For a preliminary discussion of the comparative views of teleworkers on the nature of their jobs, see Buchanan (forthcoming 2000).

27. Incidentally, an instructor at a community college course designed for call centre work advised that basic North American geography was one of the subjects that their course included, and added that she had been quite amazed at the lack of basic geographic knowledge displayed by some of her students.

28. An employee at an outbound centre in St. John reported, "They cannot believe the quality here in Canada and they are amazed at the quality of people here at this call centre. Our accuracy rate is fantastic, just phenomenal compared to the other ones. They rate us against the other call centres and we're number one and we've only been in business here for six months. We're beating call centres that have been in business 2 and 3 years." Personal interview with a female call centre worker, June 13, 1996, St. John.

29. I spoke with five employees and former employees of the unionized Toronto centre in October 1996. Several specifically identified the practice of sending slow performing callers home early as the key factor in mobilizing workers to organize, although many other workplace practices were also unacceptable. When asked how she was able to convince her fellow telefundraisers to sign union cards, one organizer claimed she relied on skills she had acquired raising money for charities at the company. "We're telemarketers, right? We were using telemarketing techniques to sign people up! What better people. It got to the point where there were so many people we were signing up that we had almost like a script. . . We used good selling techniques, so we would explain the situation to people, tell them how urgent it was, make them feel as if they were involved in something special, that's another technique. Tell them this is the first telemarketing centre in Canada to have an organizing drive." Personal interview, November 18, 1996. Shortly after the unionization drive, the company opened a second (non-union) centre in New Brunswick, which was closed in the spring of 1998.

30. Personal interview with call centre worker, St. John, June 13, 1996.

31. Incidentally, this meant that gaining access to employees for interviews was quite difficult. For example, the union representative at one workplace who was assisting me in contacting workers for a confidential offsite meeting had difficulty finding individuals who were not afraid they might lose their jobs. In the end, only four workers (out of a workforce of several hundred) attended the confidential meeting in a private home, three of whom were union representatives.

32. Personal interview with call centre worker, April 1997.

33. Personal interview with 28 year old woman, April 16, 1997. Another young woman interviewed in Toronto, July 1998 reported that she was particularly successful in sales to men, due to the effects of her low husky voice. In fact, her boss at the telemarketing centre where she worked had told her she "should do phone sex." She quit one week later.

34. Interview with 22 year old woman, St. John, December 23, 1997.

35. Personal interview with telemarketing worker, St. John, November 4, 1996.

36. For example, all of the performance evaluations in one fundraising centre studied were based on the amount of money brought in during a shift. This was despite significant variations in returns produced by the lists of phone numbers forwarded to individual callers by the predictive dialler, over which the callers had no control. Similarly, in the service bureaus, the use of quantitative indicators to measure productivity, such as the

measurement of time a caller spent on "not ready," (not available for new inbound calls), could be frustrating for employees. Quantitative indicators excluded time spent after a call resolving a customer's problem.

37. Interview with call centre employee, Toronto, Ontario, November 18, 1996.

38. For example, one firm as part of a more general management restructuring, had expanded the authority of front line customer service representatives to issue cash refunds or rewards to unhappy customers to $200 without the need for authorization from a supervisor. Previously, a refund for the same amount would have had to have been authorized by several levels of management. The same firm claimed to be increasingly relying on customer satisfaction surveys to evaluate productivity of their employees, although quantitative measures were also available to them. Interview with Human Resources Manager, Moncton, November 22, 1996.

39. Personal interview with call centre worker, December 1997.

References

Appadurai, Arjun 1996, *Modernity at Large: Cultural Dimensions of Globalization*, Minneapolis: University of Minnesota.

Appelbaum, Eileen 1993, 'New Technology and Work Organization: The Role of Gender Relations,' in Belinda Probert and Bruce W. Wilson (eds.). *Pink Collar Blues: Work, Gender and Technology.* Carlton, Vic: Melbourne University Press.

Belt, Vicki, Richardson, Ronald and Webster, Juliet 1999, 'Smiling Down the Phone: Women's Work in Telephone Call Centers,' unpublished.

Buchanan, Ruth (forthcoming), 'Life on the Line: Survival Strategies of Teleworkers in Canada,' in Frank Munger (ed.), *Low Wage Ghetto: Work, Hope and Poverty at the Margins of the New World Order,* London: Sage.

Buchanan, Ruth and Koch-Schulte, Sarah (forthcoming), *'Gender on the Line: Technology, Restructuring and the Reorganization of Work in the Call Center Industry,'* Policy Research Series, Ottawa: Status of Women Canada.

Clement, Andrew 1992, 'Electronic Workplace Surveillance: Sweatshops and Fishbowls,' *The Canadian Journal of Information Science,* 17 (4): 18-45.

Castells, Manuel 1996, *The Rise of the Network Society*, Cambridge: Blackwell.

Duffy, Anne, Glenday, Daniel and Pupo, Norene (eds.) 1997, *Good Jobs, Bad Jobs, No Jobs: The Transformation of Work in the 21st Century*, Toronto: Harcourt Brace and Company Canada.

Duffy, Anne, and Pupo, Norene 1992, *Part-time Paradox: Connecting Gender, Work and Family*, Toronto: McClelland and Stewart.

Economic Council of Canada 1990, *Good Jobs, Bad Jobs: Employment in the Service Industry*, Ottawa: Ministry of Supply and Services.

Heidegger, Martin 1977, *The Question Concerning Technology and other Essays*, New York: Harper and Row.

Hall, Elaine J. 1993, 'Smiling, Deferring and Flirting: Doing Gender by Giving "Good Service",' *Work and Occupations*, 20 (4): 452-471.

Hochschild, Arlie Russell 1983, *The Managed Heart: Commercialization of Human Feeling*, Berkeley: University of California Press.

Jenson, Jane 1989, 'The Talents of Women, the Skills of Men: Flexible Specialization and Women,' in *The Transformation of Work: Skill, Flexibility and the Labour Process*, Stephen Wood (ed.), London: Unwin Hyman.

--------- 1996, 'Part-time Employment and Women: A Range of Strategies,' in *Rethinking Restructuring: Gender and Change in Canada*, Isabella Bakker (ed.), Toronto: University of Toronto Press.

Meagher, David 1996, '$28 Million in Aid to Call Centres,' *The [Fredericton] Daily Gleaner*, 1 May.

Poynton, Cate 1993, 'Naming Women's Workplace Skills: Linguistics and Power,' in *Pink Collar Blues: Work, Gender and Technology*, Belinda Probert and Bruce W. Wilson (eds.), Carlton, Vic: Melbourne University Press.

'Premier Challenged on Job Creation,' 1995, *The Daily Gleaner*, August 2.

Sabel, Charles 1996, 'Bootstrapping Reform: Rebuilding Firms, the Welfare State and Unions,' *Politics and Society*, 23 (1): 5-48.

Salinger, Leslie 1997, 'A Maid by Any Other Name: The Transformation of "Dirty Work" by Central American Immigrants,' in Lamphere, Ragone and Zavella (eds.), *Situated Lives: Gender and Culture in Everyday Life*, New York: Routledge: 271-291.

Sassen, Saskia 1991, *The Global City: New York, London, Tokyo*, Princeton NJ: Princeton University Press.

--------- 1996, *Losing Control?: Sovereignty in an Age of Globalization*, New York: Columbia University Press.

--------- 1997, *Informalization as a Systemic Trend in Advanced Market Economies*, (unpublished).

Shalla, Vivian 1997, 'Technology and the Deskilling of Work: The Case of Passenger Agents at Air Canada,' in Duffy, Anne, Glenday, Daniel and Pupo Norene (eds.), *Good Jobs, Bad Jobs, No Jobs: The Transformation of Work in the 21st Century*, Toronto: Harcourt Brace and Company Canada.

Storper, Michael 1997, *The Regional World: Territorial Development in a Global Economy*, New York: Guilford Press.

Wharton, A. 1993, 'The Affective Consequences of Service Work: Managing Emotions on the Job,' *Work and Occupations*, 20 (2): 205-232.

Zuboff, Shoshana 1988, *In the Age of the Smart Machine: The Future of Work and Power*, New York: Basic Books.

3 Globalizations Past: From Lahaina to London in the 1820s

SALLY ENGLE MERRY[1]

Globalization is generally described as a phenomenon of the last two decades. It is characterized as rapidly transforming the world through the global transfer of signs and symbols as well as capital and labour. In this short space of time there has been a rapid expansion of global capital markets and the geographical fragmentation of production and the creation of transnational urban centers linked to one another and increasingly separated from their hinterlands (Sassen 1994; 1996). An increased flow of people and information has followed a transformation in the technology of transportation and communications. The twin effects of mass migration and the expansion of electronic media have created a rupture in the work of the imagination, transforming the way selves and worlds are conceived, as new resources and stories for the making of these selves become available. The diasporic social worlds created by mass migrations reshape the possibilities of modern subjectivity (Appadurai 1996: 3-4). At the same time, a new emphasis on human rights and the practices of international intervention in sovereign states, while still limited, may foreshadow a more powerful transnational community and some redefinition of the meanings of sovereignty (see Lyons and Mastanduno 1995; Donnelly 1995).

Many facets of contemporary globalization, such as the dispersion of productive processes and the rapid circulation of ideas and images around the globe, are unprecedented. The acceleration in communication and transportation produces the remarkable time/space compression of contemporary globalization (Harvey 1989). But there have been global movements of population, capital, and signification in the past. The nineteenth-century radiation of exploration, commerce, evangelism, and labour migration from Europe to much of the rest of the world was also a form of globalization. Although it differed in many ways from the globalization of the present, there are some intriguing parallels. The emerging liberal consensus of neoliberal economics, weak or minimalist states, liberal democracy, and the rule of law which this volume identifies as characteristic of late twentieth-century globalization replicates nineteenth-century commitments to capitalism, progress, and the rule of law. Although nineteenth-century globalization took place under the banners of "the civilizing process," Christianity, and white racial supremacy, rather than modernization, development, or democracy, both nineteenth century and twentieth century justifications are creatures of the market, driven by demands for unregulated commerce and capitalist expansion.

Just as today, the rule of law was a core idea promoted by European imperialists. The rule of law became a marker for the seductive idea of "civilization": that complex set of signs, practices, and forms of bodily management which could confer sovereignty upon a monarch with brown skin even when white masculinity seemed the essential badge of rule. For the Europeans, the "uncivilized" peoples they encountered in much of Asia, Africa, and the Pacific lacked a legitimate system of law. Yet, when European settlers clashed with Europeans from other nations in these places, sometimes they were forced to use the local legal regimes. Such conflicts reveal the dynamics of nineteenth-century globalization and the beginnings of a global structure of sovereignty based on a European framework. They also emphasize the importance of local struggles for the construction of a global social order.

A fight between British sailors and American missionaries over access to the sexual services of Hawaiian women in the 1820s is one dramatic instance of a local conflict with global implications for sovereignty and the expansion of the rule of law. This dispute was ultimately settled by the intervention of the Hawaiian *ali'i,* or ruling chiefs. Fueled by national rivalries, the battle juxtaposed American Christian morality to British demands for prostitutes. One striking feature of this incident was the extent to which local events were played out on a global legal stage stretching from Lahaina to Boston to London. In the long run, the incident was one step toward the Hawaiian Kingdom's achievement of sovereignty in the European system.

In the European order of sovereignty established by the Treaty of Westphalia in 1648, sovereignty depended on internal supremacy and external independence, although in practice there were significant variations in internal supremacy (Fowler and Bunck 1995: 36-7). Legitimacy of internal control was also important. The central determinant of sovereignty was recognition by other sovereign states, particularly powerful ones. For non-European peoples, the number of states required was larger (Fowler and Bunck 1995: 58). Moments of crisis provided particular opportunities to assert the supreme power to decide, one of the marks of sovereignty (Fowler and Bunck 1995: 38). Thus, acquiring sovereignty under the Westphalia system required acceptance by the international community of a state's domestic political supremacy, even if its control was not absolute in practice. But sovereignty was not easily accepted for peoples who were not European.

At the Congress of Vienna in 1815, for example, the five great powers agreed that they were responsible for maintaining order in international relations through their own rules and institutions and had the right to intervene in Africa, Asia and Latin America (Lyons and Mastanduno 1995: 6-7).

There are signs that the Westphalia system is now changing in the post-war and post-cold-war periods. The United Nations provides a way of recognizing a far wider set of states as sovereign and provides an arena for these decolonized states to participate in negotiating the rules of international relations (Lyons and Mastanduno 1995: 7). At the same time, the international community has begun to deny recognition to states with extraordinary violations of human rights, such as apartheid South Africa, and to intervene within sovereign states in cases of extreme violations, such as genocide, to conduct war crimes tribunals or offer humanitarian or military aid. However, this intervention also requires extensive justification, taking place collectively and in accordance with general norms and procedures (Fowler and Bunck 1995: 62; Lyons and Mastanduno 1995: 8). As Donnelly (1995) points out, human rights violations alone rarely produce interventions.

During the first half of the nineteenth century, while the Westphalia system still reigned, the Hawaiian *ali'i* ended up adjudicating the conflict over prostitution between American missionaries and British whalers in the harbours of Hawai'i. The chiefs of the highly centralized Hawaiian state were able to assert their legal authority over British and American citizens within Hawaiian territory while the British and American contestants were forced to accept that sovereignty. Through events such as this one, a new world order of European-style sovereignty gradually spread around the globe. The Hawaiian *ali'i* also became more interested in adopting a European-style legal system. Analyzing such moments of encounter provides insights into the micro-processes of contest and negotiation that constituted sovereignty and constructed global orders in the nineteenth century as in the present.

European acceptance of an indigenous legal order's authority over them was an unusual event in the early nineteenth century. European powers were convinced of the superiority of their own national legal systems and believed, following prevailing nineteenth-century models of social evolution, that societies which lacked a rule of law were at the stage of savagery or barbarism. In these "uncivilized" areas, conflicts among Europeans and between Europeans and their non-European trading partners raised questions about which law should apply to whom and who was entitled to apply it. In many cases, indigenous political and legal regimes governed the territories in question but European citizens refused to recognize their authority or accept their law. Moreover, in areas with mobile nationals from more than one

European country, each often demanded to be governed only by the law of his own nation, rejecting the law of other European nations as well as that of chiefly and tribal social units.

Thus, this dispute between an American missionary and a British whale-ship captain in the Kingdom of Hawai'i in the 1820s exposes the process of negotiating indigenous legal authority and sovereignty in non-European spaces. As the participants talked about how to settle this problem, conflicting ideas about law emerged, some of which had a global reach. Ultimately, the conversation was about civilization and savagery; about the rule of law and national pride. This was a local conflict with global ramifications, but one which took place at a vastly slower pace than contemporary conflicts.

The Conflict Over The Sex Trade

In the early nineteenth century, Hawai'i was a highly stratified chiefdom based on a complex subsistence economy of taro and sweet potato farming, fishing, and animal husbandry. While most of the people worked the land as commoners, or *maka'ainana*, a small chiefly class of *ali'i* surrounded by an extensive system of tribute and ritual protections and prohibitions controlled the land. *Maka'ainana* worked the land under the *ali'i* who held rights to that land. Patterns of conquest and succession led to redistribution of lands within the chiefly class, although the *maka'ainana* were not generally evicted in these land transfers. Chiefly rank and distinction was enunciated in a system of *kapu* (tabu) which demarcated various statuses, including that of men and women, separating and governing their relations to one another. Local communities of commoners were governed by systems of rules focusing on respect and reciprocal obligations maintained by patterns of collective enforcement and vengeance (Kame'eleihiwa 1992; Kamakau 1961).

Captain Cook's "discovery" of the islands in 1778 initiated trade. They became convenient watering and restocking sites for the merchants engaged in the China trade and the fur trade on the North West Coast, many of whom were based in New England (Sahlins 1992). By 1820, the *ali'i* were deeply in debt to merchants who supplied them with generous quantities of silks, porcelains, and clothing in exchange for promises of sandalwood harvested from the mountains, available in ever dwindling amounts. The introduction of guns spawned devastating wars which unified the islands under a single paramount chief by the early nineteenth century while the ravages of introduced diseases and rum decreased the population by three-quarters in the first forty years after contact, according to reports to a missionary touring the islands in 1823 (Ellis 1969). In 1819, the ruling chief, Liholiho, declared that the *kapu* on men and women eating together was broken and in effect dismantled much of the religious/political system undergirding chiefly authority.

The first contingent of New England missionaries arriving in 1820 interpreted the abolition of the *kapu* system as an act of God, reinforcing their belief in their mission to the heathen. These missionaries, predominantly Congregational, brought with them a stern moral code condemning all sexual activity outside marriage, strong drink, gambling, and other forms of play and bodily display such as dancing, surfing, and swimming. They demanded rigid adherence to the Sabbath as a day of rest and set high standards of social and sexual conduct as the threshold for membership in their churches. Many expressed very derogatory opinions about the Hawaiians, complaining in their voluminous letters and journals home about their licentiousness, indolence, and child-like behaviour (e.g., Bingham 1847; Grimshaw 1989).

By the 1820s, the Hawaiian Kingdom included three major groups of foreigners: merchants, missionaries, and whalers (see Merry 2000). The merchants were the first to arrive and had become an established community by the 1820s. They served as ships' chandlers for the traffic between China, New England, the fur seal regions of the Pacific Northwest, and Europe, and as intermediaries in the sandalwood trade. During the first two decades of the nineteenth century, the *ali'i* sent their followers, *maka'ainana*, into the forested mountains to gather sandalwood which they traded to the merchants for European and Chinese goods and ships. As the supply of sandalwood dwindled, however, the *ali'i* fell increasingly in debt to the resident merchants who badgered them for repayment while continuing to extend credit (King 1989). Although most of the merchants were Americans, a substantial number were British. The two groups were frequently hostile and in competition with each other for the favour of the chiefs. Each nation had a resident consul who managed relations with the merchants and the chiefs. In 1826, an American gunship arrived demanding repayment to the US merchants.

The second group was the American missionaries from New England. These missionaries quickly became influential with the ruling chiefs who saw the benefits of writing and hoped that the new god, Jehovah, would bring the Kingdom back to a state of righteousness and check the appalling decline in population (Kame'eleihiwa 1992). The most powerful chiefs had their own teachers among the missionaries to instruct them in Christianity and reading and writing. The missionaries soon began to advocate new laws based on

Christian teachings which included stringent regulations of sexual behaviour in accordance with their notions of sexual sin. By the late 1820s, the missionaries' enthusiasm for encouraging the chiefs to enact the Ten Commandments as the law of the land had engendered considerable opposition from the foreign merchant community in the islands as well as from many of the powerful Hawaiian *ali 'i* who were not attracted to the rigid morality which condemned adultery, rum selling, prostitution, and gambling.

The third group was the whalers. Whaling in the Pacific began to expand in the 1820s, peaking in the 1840s. As whaling in the Pacific developed, a pattern of three to four-year voyages from home ports in New England and Britain evolved, with seasonal stops in Hawai'i and other Pacific ports for refitting, restocking, and transshipping whale products back to home ports (e.g., Garner 1966). Sex and drink were in great demand among whale-ship crews. This burgeoning industry strengthened the resident merchant class and at the same time brought large numbers of British, American and other captains and seamen from around the world to the ports of Hawai'i during the fall and spring of each year for about six weeks of shore leave, including patronage of grog shops and brothels.

By 1825, some of the most powerful *ali 'i* had converted to Christianity. The missionaries, now prominent advisors to the *ali 'i,* pressed them to stop the sex trade between visiting seamen and the Hawaiian women who flocked to the port towns during the shipping season. Although the Honolulu chiefs were not enthusiastic about the missionary prohibitions, sharing the view of many resident merchants that the sex restriction was harmful to trade, on the island of Maui the powerful chief, Hoapili, imposed a *kapu* or restriction on women going out to ships anchored in the port town in Lahaina. Many whale-ship captains and crews were infuriated. The crisis that ensued reveals the difficulties posed by the kind of legal vacuum the British and Americans considered the Kingdom to represent. It shows that this local conflict was aired in a global world of public opinion, one which judged by the standards of the Christian mission, the Enlightenment, and the rule of law.

The conflict was exacerbated by a statement from the mission, published in an American missionary journal, that a whaling captain had purchased a Hawaiian woman to go with him on his ship, naming the captain and accusing him of slavery. Slavery was punishable by death in London. The charge spread from Hawai'i to Boston to London and back to Hawai'i again. The British Consul accused the missionaries of libel and threatened to take the American missionary who leveled the accusation back to London to provide evidence in a trial. The American threw himself on the protection of the Hawaiian *ali 'i* for guards against the whale-ship crews and to avoid being taken to London. The *ali'i* themselves were divided between those more sympathetic to the British merchants and those more sympathetic to the American missionaries, but they ultimately decided to support the missionary.

Thus, the conflict stretched from Lahaina to London. The accusation of slavery was considered in terms of British law, while information about the accusation was exchanged through American newspapers and missionary publications. The whale-ship captain retaliated that the missionary was guilty of libel but he could not prosecute him in a place like Hawai'i, given its legal system. The conflict was settled in Honolulu by an assertion of sovereignty by the Hawaiian Kingdom over the resident British and American merchants. This was accepted joyfully by the missionary and reluctantly and angrily by the British Consul and the whaling captain.

The Confrontation (1825)

In 1825, Captain Buckle of the British whale-ship Daniel, a previous visitor to the islands, arrived in Lahaina to discover that his crew no longer had sexual access to Hawaiian women. Buckle confronted the missionary in Lahaina, William Richards, demanding the repeal of the law (Williston 1938: 36-8). Richards, a 32-year-old New Englander in Hawai'i only two years, was a graduate of Williams College and Andover Theological Seminary. He had been an ordained minister since 1822 (Williston 1938). According to the Hawaiian historian Samuel Kamakau, Buckle tried to test the new restriction by allowing his men shore leave (1961: 280-3). The men waited until dark to go and tear down the house and beat up Mr. Richards, but the chiefs and their people guarded him night and day. Richards wrote Captain Buckle complaining of this abuse and requesting him to prevent it. Buckle replied that if Richards would give women to his men there would be peace in Lahaina. Richards would not consent.

Richards describes the assault in a letter he wrote to his fellow missionary Hiram Bingham on October 7, 1825. A copy of Richard's letter was sent on to the secretary of the American Board of Commissioners of Foreign Missions (ABCFM), Jeremiah Evarts, in the Mission Rooms in Boston.[2] In his letter to Evarts on October 28, 1825, Levi Chamberlain, the business manager of the mission, describes the incident and quotes Wm. Richards' letter to Bingham of October 7.[3] In it Richards said that his house in Lahaina had been surrounded by 20 English sailors armed with knives and that about 40 men from the ship Daniel had threatened his and his wife's lives if he did

not consent to females going on board their ship. He refused, of course.
Chamberlain quotes Richards' letter to Bingham:

> The American ships do not molest us, and some of them have gone so far as to
> tell the Chiefs to guard us. The end we cannot foresee. If our lives will promote
> our great and good cause, and there should be none but these partly enlightened
> people to tell the circumstances of our death, you may rest assured that we die
> rejoicing in the belief of the final triumph of our cause and rejoicing in the hope
> that we have done with trouble and with pain (ABCFM n.d.[a]).

Chamberlain adds that one of the sailors stabbed at a "native" who was
guarding the gate. He says that the Hawaiian chiefs had immediately called out
armed guards who protected the house and person of Mr. Richards until the ship
departed the harbour. Thus, in Chamberlain's account, Hoapili assumed authority
in the situation and protected the American against the British assault. As
Richards' account further on below indicates, however, at first he himself had to
employ men to protect himself and his family and only later, after some pleading,
did he succeed in getting Hoapili's official protection. Apparently Hoapili did
not immediately see his role as protecting the foreign missionary from another
foreigner.

By the end of the season (the period of time in which the whale-ships
remained in Hawaiian ports refitting and preparing for the next several months
of the hunt), Levi Chamberlain reported to J. Evarts that the campaign against
women going out to whale-ships had been successful. On December 10, 1825,
he wrote that since the departure of the ship Daniel under Captain Buckle, there
had been no molestation nor any instance of insult as there had been during a part
of the past season.

> The restrictive measures adopted by the chiefs to prevent females frequenting the
> ships as formerly, if insufficient to effect *all* that was desired, were by no means
> unsuccessful or useless. Multitudes were prevented going on board, and a
> degree of *disgrace* became attached to the practice, though before regarded
> *honourable*. Several individuals who were detected going off secretly were
> brought before the chiefs, and punished. In passing among the vessels in port,
> I have been gratified to see them free from women. During no former season
> has such a pleasure been allowed us, but in passing through the harbour, or
> going on board a ship, we have been offended with the sight of a dozen of more
> half naked females, in the chains, lounging on the windlass, resting on the
> bowsprit, creeping out of the forecastle or steerage, and, I should be happy not
> to say, in some instances, even out of the Captain's state room (ABCFM n.d.[b]:
> 59-63).

Chamberlain's letter incorporating Richards' account was sent to Boston sometime after October 1825. The journey around Cape Horn lasted at least six months at the time. Parts of this account were published in the July 1826 issue of the ABCFM's journal, *Missionary Herald* with details of the attack and allegation of slavery attached to Buckle's name. This account was in the form of a letter from five members of the Hawaiian mission, including Bingham and Chamberlain. Richards mentioned the purchase of the woman in his own letter but did not label the transaction slavery. The letter includes quotes from Richards but is not his creation. In it, Buckle is accused by name of enslaving a woman by purchase.[4]

The riotous crew of the whale-ship Daniel, Captain Buckle, having the countenance and example of their master, purchasing for a stipulated sum of money, a female slave, and carrying her as the inmate of his cabin during his late cruise, were, on their recent return to Lahaina, enraged at the tabu, prohibiting females from visiting the ships, and, after repeated insults and threats to Mr. Richards, left the ship in a body, and landed in three boats under a black flag, and, armed with knives, surrounded the house of Mr. Richards with the most abusive threats, and seemed determined, as Mr. R. writes, to have his life, or his consent for females to go on board – the former of which he would have surrendered first (Bingham *et al.* 1826: 208).

Nationalism is important: American ships do not molest the American missionaries, according to these writers, only the British ships, even though the Americans are also displeased by the *kapu* on women in ships.[5]

In February, 1827, the *Missionary Herald* published parts of William Richard's journal including his own account of this incident. In the preface to his letter, the editors of the *Herald* note that the brutality of this assault warrants its becoming known "in the four quarters of the globe," requiring them to expose "to public reprobation, wherever civilized man is to be found, deeds so atrocious, – the missionaries and their patrons feel impelled to avail themselves of this painful remedy" (Richards 1827: 40). Publishing details of this attack is, they claimed, strictly a matter of self-defense against lawless violence. Thus, the editors pick up the theme of the earlier publication that missionaries are at risk from foreign violence, warranting extraordinary measures of censure on the global stage. The case must be presented to the "civilized" international community.

In Richards' own description of the incident on October 5, 1825, he notes that he employed armed men to guard his house after the first confrontation rather than relying on the support of the chiefs (1827: 40). Thus, it appears from this more detailed account that chiefly protection was not immediately forthcoming but had to be negotiated. Richards first tried to persuade Captain Buckle to restrain his men by sending him a letter, which he did Oct. 6, but Buckle wrote back that he would not control his men unless Richards lifted the *kapu* on women boarding ships. Richards says that he held out little hope for Buckle's change of heart because Captain Buckle had earlier taken one of their best pupils on board as his mistress for six months. The girl's chief, Wahine Pio, sold her for $160 even though she had entreated Richards to be released. The next day, when an armed group of sailors surrounded the house, the chiefs provided guards and agreed to arm them, overturning their previous refusal. By this time, Richards had apparently successfully persuaded the chiefs to see him as a subject warranting their protection. The confrontation and threats from the sailors lasted four days, but Richards reports that the guards and other "natives" stood by him. He heard from American whale-ship masters that Captain Buckle had supported his seamen in all their endeavours and even promised them arms if necessary. This full and detailed account was published in the February 1827 *Missionary Herald*.

Buckle's Return (1827)

By late summer 1827, news of the publication of this story arrived back in Honolulu, almost two years after the incident. The *New York Observer* had published some portion of this account and a copy of the article was brought to Hawai'i in August or September. Stephen Reynolds, an American merchant resident in Honolulu, reports in his chatty private journal on August 4, 1827 that he read in the *New York Observer* a missionary account of the ship Daniel's crew assailing Mr. Richards at Lahaina in Autumn 1825. "It is there stated Captain Buckle had bo't a Female Slave, the Season before to carry in his ship!!!" (King 1989: 193). Buckle himself arrived in Hawai'i again in the fall of 1827. According to Kamakau, Captain Buckle received a letter in October 1827 from a brother in England saying that a story had appeared in the papers there telling of his improper action toward Mr. Richards and how he purchased a woman of Maui. Buckle was furious that an account of this incident had appeared in the newspapers (1961: 280-283).

Levi Chamberlain wrote a long letter to Rufus Anderson, head of the ABCFM in Boston, on September 14, 1827. describing the excitement the mission's statements about the conduct of Captain Buckle of the English whaling ship Daniel and her riotous crew had caused when they reached Honolulu.[6] He describes his interview with the British Consul, Charlton. Charlton represented the interests of the powerful British nation in Hawai'i and hated the American mission. He was infuriated by the accusation against Buckle and wanted to use this incident to force Richards to back down or to travel to London, a journey lasting between six months and a year. Charlton told Chamberlain, in Buckle's defense, that:

> it must be proved that Captain Buckle purchased a female *slave*, as he has been accused of doing by one of the missionaries. You have charged him with committing a high crime, but by the laws of England it is *piracy*, and my instructions are very explicit on that subject. [emphasis in original]. [7]

Chamberlain replied that it could indeed be proved that Buckle paid for a Hawaiian female whom he took on board against her wishes to accompany him on a cruise. Charlton countered that it could not be proved that the woman was taken contrary to her inclinations:

> and if it cannot be proved, as I think it cannot, were I in Captain Buckles' place, I would prosecute the Society [the American Board of Commissioners of Foreign Missions, housed in Boston] of a *libel*!

Thus, Charlton mobilized British legal categories such as libel to threaten suit against Richards. Charlton also claimed that the account of the riot was very greatly exaggerated. The American Consul, Jones, supported Charlton, siding with the merchants over the missionaries. He said that publishing such things was very improper and made the missionaries no friends but, on the contrary, many enemies. In Chamberlain's letter he says that he replied that it is proper for the missionaries to communicate their circumstances to the Society [the ABCFM] which chooses what to publish. He heard later that Mr. Charlton wanted to send him to England as a witness against Captain Buckle because he [Chamberlain] had said that the fact of Buckle purchasing a slave could be proved. Clearly, the threat of British legal authority both legitimates Charlton's position and raises the spectre of great inconvenience to the missionaries by requiring them to take the long journey to London. As Chamberlain writes:

> This circumstance is in itself too trifling to mention, but it serves with others to show what a spirit of hostility exists in the heart of this man against the missionary cause. I do not believe he has authority to remove an American missionary from his work 18,000 miles to bear testimony to such a charge in an English court of justice, nor on the charge of *piracy*, nor have I heard anything further respecting one of the missionaries being forced from his labours to follow him as a witness, – but ill will enough exists on the part of some to send every missionary and every one who favours and patronizes the missionary farther than the ends of the earth, if that were possible. But we must be careful

what we say in a *public* manner of public characters, though we may claim the privilege of communicating freely and confidentially with our patrons on any subject connected with our work.

There is clearly an important transnational arena of public opinion of great importance at this period, although it moved vastly more slowly than the same arena does today.

William Richards wrote a long letter to the mission in Boston on December 6, 1827 giving his account of the conflict set off by the New York *Observer* story (ABCFM n.d.[c]). The foreigners saw the account that Captain Buckle purchased a slave only in a newspaper, he says, but the source was a joint letter from the [mission] station. They suppose him the source and claim to be most offended that he has charged Captain Buckle with engaging in the slave trade which is punishable by death both in England and America. Richards continues that many of the natives believe that because of his letters, Captain Buckle will hang as a slave dealer as soon as he arrives in London. Clearly, local discussions of this incident also locate it within a global legal terrain which is assumed to reach from London to Lahaina.

In his December 6, 1827 letter, Richards says that he first received a letter from Chamberlain in Honolulu on November 2 saying that there was excitement about his communication to the Board regarding Captain Buckle, and that nothing is talked of but *make o ka haole* – death of the foreigner (Richards' death). The Consul met with the chiefs yesterday, Chamberlain continues, and "grievously accused" some of the members of the mission. The merchants said that Mr. Whitney was king of Kauai, Mr. Bingham of Oahu, Mr. Richards of Maui. These accusations reflected the merchant community's unease about the growing political power of the American missionaries in the Kingdom. Chamberlain notes that all the foreigners took the part of Captain Buckle and concludes, "I fear he will do some mischief, but let us confide in the Lord, and after taking such measures as prudence will direct, leave the event with him."

The Chiefs' Council in Honolulu (1827)

In early November, Richards sailed from Lahaina to Honolulu to answer the charges of Charlton and Buckle that he had made libelous accusations against Buckle. The Hawaiian chiefs viewed the conflict as one between foreigners and were reluctant to intervene, but Richards sought to pull them into the conflict with his request for their protection, as he had earlier with his request for protection by Hawaiian soldiers. On November 13, Richards received a letter from the British Consul, Charlton, who was also in Honolulu. He provides an exact copy in his December 6 letter to Boston:

> A statement having been made in an American newspaper (said to be a copy of your journal), that Mr. William Buckle, master of the Daniel the Fourth of London had purchased a female slave at Maui for 160 dollars. As the purchasing of a slave is by the law of Great Britain declared to be piracy, and my instructions regarding slaves are very explicit, I have to request that you will confirm your statement upon oath; that the offender may be brought to justice as Mr. Buckle is now in this harbour (ABCFM n.d.[c]).

Richards says that he replied to Charlton that he did not make a statement in a newspaper nor did he ever say that Buckle was guilty of engaging in the slave trade (The word "slave," indeed, had been employed only in the letter from the mission as a whole, not by Richards himself). Nor had he seen the newspaper story.

The following day Richards received a letter from Charlton along with the newspaper itself. Although many of these individuals lived in the same small town, they communicated via letters, many of which were laboriously recopied into letters home. The newspaper itself was apparently precious evidence to be passed from hand to hand. Richards did not find the word "slave" in the newspaper story.[8] Charlton asked for the newspaper back as soon as possible so that he could send a copy to the British Secretary of State by way of China on the ship Tantan. Charlton said he wanted to bring Buckle to trial in England if this statement were correct, and wanted Mr. and Mrs. Richards to identify any of the crew who used threats or violence against them. Richards notes in his letter that the newspaper account was taken from the *Missionary Herald* of February 1827, which he had not yet received, but that it agreed well with his copy of the letter which he sent to Boston. Reynolds, the American merchant in Honolulu, reports in his journal on November 19, 1827: "Charlton and Buckle called on Mr. Richards, about the Publication in the Public Newspapers relating to Captain Buckle's purchasing a Slave – result I have not heard" (King 1989: 204).

This conflict was clearly between the foreigners and the terms of debate were Anglo-American laws about piracy and libel. But both sides turned to the *ali 'i* and asked them to intervene. The foreigners complained to the chiefs about the missionaries' accusations and wanted to meet with all of them. The *ali 'i*, however, were divided among themselves about how to respond to this conflict. Some had loyalties to British or to Americans, some to merchants or missionaries. They sought advice about the implications of British law for this problem. Kamakau reports that John Young, the politically prominent Englishman who had served the previous king Kamehameha since the late eighteenth century, was asked his opinion and said, "England is very big to offend; a libelous letter is very wrong" (1961: 280-3). Boki, the governor of Oahu and a prominent pro-British *ali'i* informed the young king and the powerful regent Ka'ahumanu of this judgment. They decided Richards must be wrong and wrote to the chiefs of Maui telling them to allow Captain Buckle, Captain Clark, and the British Consul to take Richards away (Kamakau 1961: 280-3). Richards' biographer, a law professor writing about his grandfather, says that some chiefs and some white residents joined in saying that it was wrong to make this known in America (Williston 1938: 40). The *ali'i* decided that the best course was to let foreigners take up the matter with foreigners.

But the most powerful *ali'i*, Ka'ahumanu, who had converted to Christianity and adopted the American missionaries as her priests, wished to save her teacher Richards, although it was not clear how she could do so (Kamakau 1961: 280-3). She called a council of all chiefs to decide if it was right to give up Mr. Richards to the rage of the foreigners or if it was their duty to protect him. They met for two days without a decision. Richards, who spoke Hawaiian fluently, met with them in council. Reynolds reports in his journal that on November 26, 1827, Mr. French and Captain Ebbets, two prominent American traders, went with many others up to the chiefs' council to hear Mr. Richards make his defense, but Richards failed to appear until many of the chiefs had left (1989: 205). Richards' version, detailed in the December 6, 1827 letter to the ABCFM, is that he acknowledged to the chiefs that he had written the letter about the incident (ABCFM n.d.[c]). The chiefs said, "But writing the letter was no crime, and we all know that Loaki was sold." But Boki, the pro-British *ali'i* who governed the island of Oahu, said that the chiefs could not protect him. Richards replied that when he arrived four and a half years ago, the chiefs asked the missionaries to stay as their teachers. At that point, he came under their laws and control. But Richards offered to leave if the chiefs wanted him to. Here he is arguing that the chiefs have sovereignty over him and are responsible for him and therefore must protect him in this conflict.

The *ali'i* were ready to turn Richards over to the foreigners with Boki's support even though Ka'ahumanu was reluctant, when David Malo, a Hawaiian student of Richards', asked the chiefs a critical question: "In what country is it the practice to condemn the man who gives true information of crimes committed, and to let the criminal go uncensored and unpunished?" (Malo 1898). Ka'ahumanu agreed. The next day, when the British Consul, Buckle, and others came and demanded that Richards be punished, Ka'ahumanu said she had made up her mind and refused (Williston 1938: 40). According to Kamakau, Ka'ahumanu supported Richards, but by this decision made enemies of Boki and

Manuia, another pro-British *ali'i*, as well as the British Consul and the foreign merchants. The two captains, Buckle and a second involved in a similar conflict named Clarke, became her worst enemies. It is significant that Malo's question locates the Hawaiian Kingdom within an international community of states which shares certain ideas of justice and procedure.

Richards includes in his letter to the ABCFM in Boston a letter from Buckle dated November 28, 1827, copied in full.[9] The letter gives Buckle's view of the incident. Buckle says that the missionaries have duped the public by their accounts of missionary sufferings and privations and by their flattering accounts of missionary labour. He locates his position within another global public opinion than that of the missionaries, one which celebrates the spirit of inquiry in the world and an enlightened community duped by missionaries. The tale of the Daniel's crew (told in Buckle's imperfect history):

> has no doubt answered your purpose well, such a narration is well calculated to call forth the charities of the fanatical community, and no doubt has been the cause of taking bread from the mouths of many a half starved child, to enable the deluded [illegible] to contribute his proportion for the relief of the poor persecuted missionary.

As far as the incident with the people of the Daniel:

> Conceive of it nothing more than a sailor's frolick and the less that was said of it the better, indeed there are some gentlemen who were at Lahaina at the time who knew nothing of the transaction till they heard of it at this place. You must have been deceived by your own fears when you saw black flags flying pistols and daggers brandishing and heard such dreadful threats. Your eyes and ears must have been as much deceived as were those of your valiant guard when he mistook the harmless Mr. Stewart for one of the dreadful assassins and so boldly presented his firearms through the window even at the expense of arousing you from your sweet sleep.
>
> But this story is too ridiculous longer to enlarge upon. For your own sake and the cause in which you are engaged, it were better it had not come before the publick. Such things are calculated to do much injury and no good.
>   . . . Your letter to the Board is a base libel. Were we in a land of civilization, redress might easily be obtained. Here we can obtain none – I have a right however even at this place to demand of you a contradiction of the charges alleged against me in your publication: you know they are false and if you are activated of Christian motives, you will not hesitate to comply with my request.

I wish you well and hope that in your future dealings with mankind you will be more careful to remember the Ninth Commandment.
Signed, William Buckle

Thus, Buckle asserts again that the missionaries are guilty of libel, but lacking the courts in a "land of civilization," he is helpless to win the justice he deserves. Note that like Malo, he situates his claims in an international community of civilization and law. He also deploys the language of Christianity to criticize the missionaries and their hypocrisy.

Richards continues his letter on December 17, 1827, noting that Buckle is coming to Lahaina, where he himself is now, but is not worried because Hoapili's loyalty has been tested. Hoapili wants to get some large cannon from Honolulu for Lahaina to defend it. Richards concludes that there is no termination of the issue: "Indeed there is scarcely a possibility of any termination or even a suspension of our difficulties with the foreigners while we have so much success among the Natives." He adds that the British Consul and Captain Buckle threaten to prosecute the editor of the *Herald* for a libel and also to publish a contradiction of the facts noted in his letter. He also sends a copy of Hoapili's letter to Ka'ahumanu giving an account of the firing on Lahaina by Captain Clarke in 1827, a similar conflict over the sex trade.

The Global Context of Local Conflict

Hawai'i's indigenous rulers seized control over the situation as they did in many other conflicts among foreigners even though they were uncertain about the relevance of British laws and courts. The power to decide lay with the local rulers despite their lack of knowledge of European rules and procedures. Yet, the entire debate was carried out on a global terrain of information exchange and in terms of the dominant legal categories of the "civilized world." As the *ali'i* took control of the conflict and rendered a decision, they took a step toward asserting sovereignty in this European world order. When Richards, Charlton, Jones, and Buckle accepted the *aliis'* decision, they nudged the creation of Hawaiian sovereignty forward. Since sovereignty depends on the recognition of sovereign status by other sovereign nations based on the capacity of a country to control its internal affairs, the Hawaiian assertion of authority in this crisis was one small step in that direction.

Clearly, American and British rivalry created the space for this assertion. The local conflict was globalized while global tensions between Americans and Britons, missionaries and merchants were localized. The fight over the *kapu* on women going out to ships was part of a larger struggle for power between two factions of Hawaiian *ali 'i*, one led by Boki which was tolerant of the sex trade and one led by Ka'ahumanu and Hoapili which was opposed. Foreigners were clearly part of this struggle, the merchants on Boki's side and the missionaries on Ka'ahumanu's. Boki's group was sympathetic to the British, Ka'ahumanu's to the Americans. Boki had visited London in 1824 and liked English royalty, who lived like high-ranking chiefs. Many of those who shared his views had accompanied him to England. On the other hand, several of the ruling chiefs, including Ka'ahumanu, decided that the missionaries from the United States constituted their best resource. The tension between the US and Britain was intense after the Revolution and the War of 1812, exacerbated by Britain's growing naval power. Opposition between devout and less devout Christian merchants and whale-ship captains was important around the world. Missionaries tried to persuade the whalers to abstain from whale-hunting on the Sabbath, for example. Christian captains were sometimes willing to do so while other captains felt that whaling should take place whenever whales appeared. Pious captains were more willing to control their crews' sexual exploits than others. Thus, local conflicts were framed by global politics while global rivalries played out in the local situation.

One of the intriguing features of this conflict is the speed of information flows and the technology for communicating it. It was not unusual for writers in Honolulu to send two copies of letters to New England, one via Cape Horn and the other via China and the Cape of Good Hope in the hope that at least one would arrive. Richards copied letters from others to send to the Mission Rooms in Boston. As the conflict intensified in Honolulu, concerned parties passed around what was apparently the only copy of the offending newspaper, noting whether or not the word "slave" had been mentioned. This is a conflict in a global legal arena, but the patterns of space and time are vastly different than in the present. Indeed, it was two years between the initial incident and the confrontation over its publication.

This conflict takes place within the context of a transnational legal community situated in England, the United States, and on ships traveling around the globe. It takes place on a global legal stage which places London at the centre, 18,000 miles from the conflict. The case indicates both the uncertainty of global legal regulation of the early nineteenth century and the dimensions of time and space by means of which national law was deployed. The Hawaiian *ali 'i* were drawn into this legal community despite their lack of knowledge of its rules and practices. The battle between the missionaries and merchants over prostitution and grog was long standing, reenacted in many harbours around the globe including those of New England. It was part of a deeper conflict about the relative merits of commerce and Christianity in promoting the global civilizing project. Captain Buckle himself deployed the language of the Enlightenment and the spirit of inquiry on his behalf, characterizing the religious alternative as retrograde and deceitful. In the long run it was commerce, rather than Christianity, which came to dominate the emerging shape of that part of Hawaiian society that was connected to the global society.

The Kingdom of Hawai'i responded to this and similar conflicts by adopting a new legal system, form of government, and court structure between 1825 and 1850. In this period, the king and chiefs adopted a constitution, a system of courts, and a criminal law code modeled after Anglo-American laws and courts. By this means, they were able to claim authority over the merchants and foreign businessmen settled in the islands. However, once the Kingdom had adopted this new legal system, it needed people who knew how to run it. Former American missionaries, including Richards, and American and British lawyers were employed to this end. American lawyers were needed to deal with the complicated commercial conflicts among resident foreigners (Nelligan and Ball 1992). By the mid-1850s, the Kingdom of Hawai'i had the legal and political structure of a European nation and had been recognized as independent by the US, England, Belgium, and France. At least for the moment, this strategy preserved its independence (see Merry 2000).

Conclusion

This incident reveals the negotiation of sovereignty in European terms through the resolution of crises resulting from nineteenth century globalization. The referent for this negotiation was a national legality, located far away in London. Both Americans and Europeans demanded respect for their nation's law and claimed its exclusive authority over them as a measure of their own honour and that of their nation. Yet, despite claims for judgment through national laws, both the Americans and the British turned to the local political/legal authority – the Hawaiian state – to settle the conflict. Buckle reluctantly accepted this decision, backed up by the military force of the Kingdom. In this conflict, both the Americans and the British accepted the authority of the Hawaiian state, taking a step toward creating its sovereignty in European terms by recognizing its authority to decide conflicts within its territory among foreigners. Despite the global discourse and exchange of information within which this incident took place, its resolution was localized.

The long-term consequences of this and other local conflicts was the transformation of the Kingdom itself in concert with European/American standards of civilization and the rule of law. It was necessary for local powers to reconstitute themselves in accordance with the European system of sovereignty in order to protect themselves from imperial takeovers and the appropriation of land and resources. The Hawaiian Kingdom managed this challenge to its authority by adopting a legal system based on an Enlightenment declaration of rights.

The idea of the civilized nation drove the transition in Hawai'i, paralleling the situation Keyman describes in Turkey during the Kemalist period (this volume). In Hawai'i, as in Turkey, the nation was constructed in terms of civilization and modernity. The Kingdom of Hawai'i sought recognition as a sovereign state through the use of legal transplants: by adopting legal codes, legal institutions, and legal procedures from one society to another. These transplants were often carried out in the name of civilization and from the desire to achieve recognition as sovereign by global society. They characteristically were understood as the adoption by so-called "savage" societies of the legal systems of so-called "civilized" ones. This strategy helped to deal with demands by intransigent resident Europeans that they be governed only by their own legal systems. Yet, the process of legal transplantation ultimately led to a loss of control of the legal system itself and to the criminalization of the population. Everyday activities such as consuming alcohol and its indigenous equivalents or having multiple sexual partners rather than a single enduring one were redefined as crimes: as drinking, adultery, and fornication. And, in Hawai'i, this also meant a radical redistribution of land in fee simple ownership which transformed the political system and opened the door to massive alienation of land from commoners to foreign sugar planters (Merry 2000).

The process of legal transplantation was widespread during the imperial era and continues today, exemplified by the Turkish adoption of the Swiss civil code in 1926 (Hooker 1975) and the adoption of an American legal system by the Federated States of Micronesia (Tamanaha 1993). Legal transplantation is another aspect of globalization. It brings with it new institutional structures of power, new cultural practices, and new identities and categories of personhood constructed by law. Although it is no longer done in the name of civilization but instead modernity, development, or human rights, there are clear continuities with the earlier ideas of the civilizing process. In the early nineteenth century, the dominant force for change was the market. The state was incorporated by the market: merchants continually deployed the law of their nation-states to expand their trade. Even though the law appears to have regulated the market for sexual services in Hawai'i in the 1820s, its effective control was short-lived. By the 1840s, the sex trade was booming and restrictions on foreigners' sexual access to Hawaiian women virtually gone. Court records show few prostitution cases during these peak years of the whaling trade even in the port cities. Again reminiscent of contemporary globalization, the market trumped efforts at legal regulation, smoothing the conditions for commerce and the movement of capital rather than suffocating them.

Notes

1. I am grateful to the National Science Foundation, the National Endowment for the Humanities, and the Canadian Institute for Advanced Research for support for this research. I appreciate helpful comments from all the other contributors to the volume, and from the editors, Boaventura Santos and Jane Jenson, in particular.
2. Stephen Reynolds, a resident merchant in Honolulu, reports in his journal from October 2, 1825 that he heard that the crew of the ship Daniel, under Captain Buckle, went on shore and threatened the missionary with destruction because girls were not allowed to go on board as usual (King 1989: 108).
3. Chamberlain to Evarts, October 28, 1825 (ABCFM n.d.[b]).
4. Kamakau notes that Buckle had previously purchased a woman named Leo-iki whom he took with him to Oahu (1961).
5. The letter points to the irony that they had originally thought it necessary to have more than one missionary working together in order to protect them from the "natives," but now the "natives" are protecting them from "lawless foreigners" and their violence (Bingham *et al.* 1826: 208).
6. Chamberlain to Rufus Anderson, September 14, 1827, ABCFM 19.1 (2) #70.
7. Only the first account, written by Bingham *et al.* used the word slavery; Richards simply referred to the purchase of the woman.
8. Perhaps the *Observer* story was based on the 1827 account in the *Missionary Herald* rather than the 1826 one. The existence of two slightly different accounts might be the cause of this confusion.
9. Apparently Richards knew Buckle from previous visits to Lahaina.

References

ABCFM n.d.[a], Volume 1, Houghton Library, Harvard University, Cambridge.
---------- n.d.[b], Volume 2, Houghton Library, Harvard University, Cambridge.
---------- n.d.[c], Volume 3, Houghton Library, Harvard University, Cambridge.
Appadurai, Arjun 1996, *Modernity at Large: Cultural Dimensions of Globalization*, Minneapolis: University of Minnesota Press.
Bingham, Hiram 1981 [1847], *A Residence of Twenty-One Years in the Sandwich Islands*, Rutland: Charles E. Tuttle Co.
Bingham, Hiram, Blatchely, Abraham, Chamberlain, Levi, Ruggles, Samuel, and Loomis, Elisha, 'Outrage of a Whale-ship's Crew,' *Missionary Herald* 07/1826: 208-9.

Donnelly, Jack. 1995, 'State Sovereignty and International Intervention: The Case of Human Rights,' in Lyons and Mastanduno (eds.) 1995, *Beyond Westphalia: State Sovereignty and International Intervention*, Baltimore: Johns Hopkins University Press, pp. 115-147.

Ellis, William 1969, *Polynesian Researches: Hawaii*, Rutland: Charles E. Tuttle Co.

Fowler, Michael R. and Bunck, Julie M. 1995, *Law, Power, and the Sovereign State*, University Park: Penn State University Press.

Garner, Stanton (ed.) 1966, *The Captain's Best Mate: The Journal of Mary Chipman Lawrence on the Whaler Addison 1856-1860*, Hanover: University Press of New England.

Grimshaw, Patricia 1989, *Paths of Duty: American Missionary Wives in Nineteenth-Century Hawaii*, Honolulu: University of Hawaii Press.

Harvey, David 1989, *The Condition of Postmodernity*, Cambridge: Blackwells.

Hooker, M.B 1975, *Legal Pluralism: An Introduction to Colonial and Neo-Colonial Laws*, Oxford: Clarendon Press.

Kamakau, Samuel M. 1961, *Ruling Chiefs of Hawaii*, Honolulu: Kamehameha Schools Press.

Kame'eleihiwa, Lilikala 1992, *Native Land and Foreign Desires*, Honolulu: Bishop Museum Press.

King, Pauline N. 1989, *Journal of Stephen Reynolds I: 1823-1829*, Ku Pa'a Incorporated, Honolulu, HI and Salem, MA: Peabody Museum of Salem.

Lyons, Gene M. and Mastanduno, Michael (eds.) 1995, *Beyond Westphalia: State Sovereignty and International Intervention*, Baltimore: Johns Hopkins University Press.

Malo, David. 1898 [1951], *Hawaiian Antiquities (Moolelo Hawaii)*, 2nd Edition, Honolulu: Bishop Museum Press.

Merry, Sally Engle 2000, *Colonizing Hawai'i: The Cultural Power of Law*, Princeton, NJ: Princeton University Press.

Nelligan, Peter J. and Ball, Harry V. 1992, 'Ethnic Juries in Hawaii: 1825-1900,' Social Process in Hawaii 34: 113-163.

Richards, William, 'Outrage of the Master and Crew of the English Whale-ship Daniel,' *Missionary Herald* 02/1827: 39-43.

Sassen, Saskia 1994, *Cities in a World Economy*, Thousand Oaks: Pine Forge Press/Sage.

Sassen, Saskia 1996, *Losing Control: Sovereignty in an Age of Globalization*, New York: Columbia University Press.

Tamanaha, Brian 1993, *Understanding Law in Micronesia*, Leiden: E.J. Brill.

Williston, Samuel 1938, *William Richards*, Cambridge: Harvard Law Library.

PART II
MOBILIZING WITHIN
GLOBALIZATIONS

4 Dismantling State Regulations, Remaking Public Rights: The Dispute for Social Regulation in Brazil

MARIA CELIA PAOLI

A decade ago Brazil seemed on its way to a broader democracy, based on extending the definition of citizenship to include active participation in public life and collective decisions. Traditionally, state power in Brazil included the power to promote social change and impose it on a "thin" civil society. But in the 1980s a variety of social movements – and in growing numbers – struggled around claims to individual rights and an autonomous associational life. As a result, a politicized public life started to appear, with spaces for the expression of social conflict as well as for contestation of power relations and their transformation. More than 10 years later, however, Brazil now resembles its previous authoritarian past, unable or unwilling to accept any kind of organizational mediation between government and individual citizens. Now the celebrated complex of citizenship values that emerged out of social movement practices in the 1980s is under attack. The current order of the day is privatization of social life, the result of dismantling public services (and thereby returning responsibility to the "privacy" of the family or the community) and labour market regulations (and thereby returning responsibility to the "privacy" of the firm).

The government justifies its dismissal of this emergent political public life with two arguments. The first is a "realist" claim. The government warns that dissent or even real political debate is a luxury which an "emergent country" forced to implement economic reforms in accordance with global imperatives can ill afford. It cautions that opening up political debate will only lead to an identification of false alternatives. These are condemned in advance because the government is supposedly simply doing what any country faced with a fragile currency and the pressures of globalization must do. The second argument involves an appeal to Brazil itself to understand its wayward ways. Since Brazilian politics have proven to be just like Brazilian society – described as culturally backward, nostalgic for traditional social patterns and preoccupied with local problems – the task of modernizing must fall to the government. Only it has a sufficiently broad vision to manage the country's insertion into the new global economy. This idea goes along with the notion that there is one and only one technocratic recipe to bring the country into line with rest of the world. This discourse and these two arguments are paradoxical. A limited state can not achieve these goals. Rather, their realization requires, for one thing, that the state intervene is a significant way . . . in order to end its own regulatory role. It also must be an active state in order to ensure equality and provide legal protection from private arbitrariness. And finally this recipe for globalization requires that the state intervene in order to impose freedom, albeit a freedom modelled on the rules of the market economy according to which citizens deprived of social services are expected to "maximize" their advantages.

Organizing Against Globalizations

Thus far, the result of such politics has been the erosion of social rights, via reforms usually introduced piecemeal and before any substantial public debate can occur. The boundaries of social citizenship, already bureaucratically controlled and precarious, have been shrunk further. There has also been erosion of established values and beliefs; people feel less that they belong to a recognizable social group or order. The importation and domestication of globalization's neo-liberal economic policies has had devastating effects in a country such as Brazil, already riven by so many deep social inequalities.[1] The policies have caused unemployment to rise, the informal labour market to swell in size, already dramatically large income gaps to widen, and poverty and social exclusion to climb. Increasingly visible daily violence provides evidence of this public neglect, at the same time as increasing fear and paranoia among the middle and upper classes widen the distance between them and the popular working classes.

Despite this, the Brazilian story is more than a tale of woe. Something more exists than disguised authoritarianism in the political economy, and more than misery, violence and social resentment in civil society. There **is** political debate. As elsewhere, counter-hegemonic social forces contest the proposed model of technocratic reason. Therefore there is a lively controversy over the basic principles and policies, the criteria to be used to organize labour relations and social policy.

On the one hand, there are those who seek a "workable" set of minimum rights which could be flexible enough to meet the imperatives of neo-liberal economics and globalized markets. On the other hand, there are also those who seek a fair or just set of rights, so as to halt immiseration, reduce unemployment and stop the erosion of social bonds. This debate over rights and interests is conducted among a wide variety of voices, such as employers, corporations, unions, ordinary working people, staff of state governments and the federal government, lawyers and judges, economists, and not the least the media. Disputes even get into semantics; there is contestation over the meaning of words such as "solidarity," "community," "citizenship," "civil society," not to mention the many meanings of the mysterious "modernization." This debate is never simply a normative or a "theoretical" one, however. There have been practical experiments, particularly local attempts to establish collective practices of negotiation and social partnerships that, although small-scale, are important for the broader political debate.

The effect of this contestation is that the political scene is one of conflicting visions, even if it appears to be "non-political." Self-organized social groups, negotiating with local and state-level authorities, oscillate as they act as mediators between individuals and the state. Some of these organizations are primarily service providers in poor neighbourhoods, delivering health care, including preventive care for women and children, education for poor and street children, basic nutrition and housing programmes. They have little interest in being involved in "politics." Other groups find, however, that they cannot remain on the margins and are drawn into on-going negotiations of citizenship and its forms, between democratic collectivities acting together in the name of building a common life and government. In this second category of community group and this second form of "community," actions go beyond social creativity. They become public and political interventions and inventions, creating a site where political compromises are built. There are gains and losses on all sides, as a real political process moves towards a more collective rationality.

The City of Porto Alegre, in the state of Rio Grande do Sul, provides an example of the creation of such a political public space. In the city of 2 million, spending decisions are taken via a "participative budget." Acting together individuals and local groups decide what public investments the city will make. This process is an excellent example of a politicized public life. It is so not because it achieves perfection in its decision-making processes or because its model is fully operational: rather, it is a good example of how to deal with diversity and conflicting interests. As its inventors and proponents describe their budgetary preferences, all participants are compelled to make their claims public and argue for them; choices are not based on hidden bargains behind closed doors. These negotiations push all parties to strive for an ancient political virtue, that of the common fair measure, even if they are not equals in wealth and power. By participating in this budgetary process and constructing their city, they act as equals in a political process.[2]

The rest of this chapter explores the possibilities of as well as the limits to production of political alternatives via such local democratic initiatives. To be fully realized, such extensions of democracy require that political space be widened and peopled by citizens prepared to engage in deciding the shape of their common world. All this implies reaffirming the role of self-organized movements and associations which, through the very process of building bonds of participation among themselves, succeed in creating public forms and ideas that link individuals to public life and to the state. In doing so they are creating themselves as mediators who permit the expression of social life in anticipation of new configurations of politicized public life.

The enemy of this kind of democracy is clearly the privatization of social life currently promoted by state policy in response to globalization. One such privatization is personified by the image of the liberal individual proud of his personal autonomy from the state and whose only bonds to others are via legal contracts. But such privatizations are also personified by individuals who have been abandoned by retrenchment of state social services, whose life is of no meaning to others, isolated by his or her needs and lacking even a citizenship contract. Such an individual is "excluded." He or she may be young, a migrant or old. She may be a woman in any of these categories. He or she may be working in the informal economy, surviving on casual earnings, or unemployed. In any case these excluded unquestionably live in either a "pre-contract" or a "post-contract" situation, one that is a direct result of neo-liberal economics and deregulation policies generating privatized social relations (Santos 1997).

The analysis here is based on assessment of such experiments in democracy in the recent history of the labour movement. It relies on secondary research, based on work whose original intentions were different (Siqueira 1994; Oliveira 1994; Cardoso and Comin 1995; Bresciani 1997; Arbix 1997; Campos 1998). The following pages present a reading of this material in the light of a concern for the political significance and social meaning of labour's new negotiating practices in the context of deregulation of labour markets, restructuring production, unemployment, an expanding informal labour market, and exclusion.

Three Legacies for the Political Culture of the Public Space

The Brazilian labour movement faces a particular challenge in the creation of new public democratic spaces and political meanings. It must overcome the historical legacy of the way social and labour rights were established in Brazil. Labour was a "pariah" in early modernization projects (Paoli 1992). No genuine regulated labour market was established; there was a "private labour social order" (Simão 1963: 63).

Under the first liberal republican order (1890-1930), the private matrix of authority, which had dominated in the previous three centuries of slavery, continued. Liberalism was, in other words, profoundly limited; employers retained private power as proletarianization and industrialization went forward. If the labour movement entered into a social contract it was in the context of private, almost personal, dominance; it had no public channels for the expression of claims. Generations of urban and industrial workers experienced lives permeated by personal bonds and police violence (Hall 1983). The incipient labour movement was represented as a pariah, in the sense that it had no recognized political legitimacy and the modernizing middle and upper classes were profoundly hostile towards workers, whom they saw as contributing to social disorder (Paoli 1992). The legacy of these views is still recognizable in the ways that poor workers in the informal labour market must submit to employers while the opportunity to work is presented as a personal favour. The risk of dismissal is always "deserved" because working people supposedly lack the requisite moral qualities.

A second representation of working people and the labour movement was part of the "enlightened" civil dictatorship between 1930 and 1945, termed the Vargas era. This regime gradually constructed public policies addressing health, education, housing, culture, the urban environment, and so on. Corresponding public bureaucracies were constructed. Two pieces of labour legislation, regulating labour contracts, working conditions and industrial relations, were passed at the time and remained in effect until 1998. One law regulated the right to work, legislated an 8-hour day, weekly rest periods, set minima for working conditions, wages and pensions, and limited women's and children's work. The second recognized unions and their right to organize. Their form and responsibility were strictly limited by the state, which designated unions as "advisory and technical agencies," supposed to help governments in the "solution of problems related to class interests." In this corporatist vision unions were an "organic force, co-operating with the state." In this way ordinary workers became citizens via their organizations (the unions), while new rights and institutions were created to adjudicate conflicts in industrial relations. The most important of such institutions was a specialized branch of the judiciary, the Labour Courts, which had a legal monopoly over all individual as well as collective labour disputes.[3]

The model was one of "tutelage," with the central idea being the need for public institutions to "protect the weak." The state would, therefore, oversee relations between labour and capital. Limited as unions were by legislation and state institutions, the labour movement had no autonomous voice, nor was there any space in civil society for autonomous organizing. Indeed, even the liberal idea of an individual with the civil rights of citizenship received little validation in this vision. The model was not one of a "public," composed of individuals with civil rights and able to act in the name of and responsible for his or her actions. Instead, the core idea was of the nation integrating its people via interventions to protect the weak and to generate a fairer distribution of wealth.

A kind of welfare state did come out of this representation of labour-capital and state-society relations. But it was an authoritarian and bureaucratic version, which rooted the political legitimacy of an omnipresent state in a large bureaucratic apparatus supposed to address inequalities.

With the installation of this idea of citizenship, Brazilian society has developed a political culture founded on an expectation that governments were responsible for producing social justice and for managing inequalities. Governments were judged good or bad according to these criteria, while the very notion of citizenship and rights depended on such expectations. The result was that the notion of citizen was intrinsically linked to the notion of "meeting needs" rather than freedom to act, to organize or to make claims politically. The state and its institutions are barely separable from civil society. This regime and its legacies account for the fact that collective actions and conflicts were interpreted as threats to social order, activists labeled as resentful and menacing, and repression by the police seen as an appropriate response to mobilization.[4]

A third model characterized the years between 1978 and 1988. The presence of renewed labour and social movement actions was a major political novelty, given the previous pariah and tutelary traditions. Unexpectedly, militancy and labour organizing appeared in the automobile industry, with campaigns against state interference and judicial oversight of internal union matters and industrial relations more generally. The unions, which sought autonomy in bargaining with employers, spoke the language of collective rights and citizenship. They called for democratic decision-making, a role in deciding policies addressing inequality and privileges, and community as well as workplace participation. If realized, all this would have generated new political spaces for democratic politics. These mobilizations produced offers to local and state governments of a new kind of "partnership," actively to invent new modes of social regulation and foster democratic qualities.

In my view, the 1980s, in Brazil produced for the very first time something that might be labelled "civil society." By this term I mean the capacity of social forces to create for themselves a realm of action and ideas in which they have the power to give a public political face to their organizations. Taken together with the massive mobilization of social movements in the popular sector that occurred in these years, and despite their fragmentation and localized character,[5] we can say that Brazilian society was acquiring capacity and creating space for conflict resolution that included both state and civil society.

It is in this realm that economic globalization has its major impact. Poorly paid, unskilled and precarious forms of work are driving workers back into isolation and away from collective action for social development and common political action. In other words, economic restructuring creates more than mounting poverty. It also contributes to the erosion of recently invented ideas and practices about the equality of citizens and their membership in a common society composed of all Brazilians. The poor, or the "excluded", are increasingly consigned to a "world of deviance." They are assigned the status of an underclass, treated as permanent outsiders. At same time movements' collective actions are termed obstacles to the flexible political decisions imposed by a globalized economic logic and political logics that are more technocratic than democratic. Politics becomes a private matter of elites and technocrats, whose tasks become to dismiss, disorganize and silence the people, who are in turn categorized as "losers" in the new global economy.

With this picture of modern Brazilian democracy and its citizenship regime, we can begin to trace the ways in which conflicts over rights now involve a displacement of legal guarantees and commitments to democratic forms of conflict resolution. If organized movements still possess a capacity for democratic invention, then the debate about regulation and rights is ultimately a struggle for democracy and about the boundaries between public and private power.

Reshaping Social Rights

By the early 1990s, many Brazilians had come to realize that capital accumulation was rapidly changing shape, and that such changes went well beyond technological adjustments. Governments began to seek new strategies for positioning their economies in these circuits, while employers called for greater "flexibility" in financial transactions and markets, in capital mobility and in labour relations. This last dimension was by no means the least important of the three.[6] In addition, the country had its first elected federal government after 25 years of military rule. A kind of movement for democracy was abroad in the land, and political actors sought to define "democracy" in their preferred way. The goal was to establish a solid basis for economic modernization and political modernity by adjusting the domestic economy to the world economy, and to maintain democratic forms.

Within the labour movement this moment generated two experiments. The first involved the establishment of sectoral "chambers," or negotiating tables. This was done in the automobile industry and generated a tripartite negotiation among multinational producers of cars, the federal government and that of the state of São Paulo, and the national trade union organization, the *Central Unica dos Trabalhadores* (CUT, translated as the Unified Workers' Organization). At first the negotiations had been only between representatives of governments and producers, despite the fact that plant closures and therefore job losses were looming on the horizon. A trip by union representatives to the United States in 1992, to discuss plant closings with General Motors, was decisive in provoking the subsequent inclusion of unions in talks about the automobile industry in the state of São Paulo.[7] As soon as the negotiations became tripartite the process changed scope and meaning. It became a space to negotiate new norms and regulations for the whole sector, with the idea being that these negotiating tables provided a space for some democratic discussion of industrial policy. Some gains were made by governments, which feared loss of tax revenue if plants closed, and unions obviously seeking to avoid job losses.[8] Negotiations were institutionalized for two years, from 1992 until 1994, and they inspired others to imagine that they could create similar public spheres of discussion.[9]

As Oliveira writes (1993a; 1993b; 1994), the model was powerful because it managed to create a **common measure** by which results might be judged, a result of the public recognition and acceptance of the voicing of divergent and conflicting private interests. In the model, the somewhat paradoxical reciprocity altered the confrontational nature of class conflict, without taming it. The "convergent antagonism" of which Oliviera writes actually redefined the line separating public and private, and built new and clearer rules for access to public funds. It dismantled a long tradition of secret negotiations in which personalistic pressures on public officials blurred the frontiers between public and private. In a word, the political invention and use of such negotiating tables undermined the image of the state as an entity ruling above the interests of classes or groups. For a time these negotiating practices lifted the legally defined control of unions by the state and limited the freedom of companies to translate their own interests into public policy.

All this was, of course, formally illegal. It provides an example of the co-existence of different "modes of production of law and social power" (Santos 1995). The legal monopoly of the Labour Courts remained formally intact. This continuity accounts for the ease with which subsequent governments have been able to dismantle this audacious experiment in power sharing. There was no public outcry when the Minister of the Economy called government officials out of the chambers, away from the negotiating table. Without the presence of the government it became impossible to come to any agreement about crucial matters such as taxation. Therefore, in the absence of the third party, one of the others – the employers – resumed bilateral and private negotiations with the state (Arbix 1997).

When the same Minister became President of Brazil, the preference for a centralized decision-making structure became even clearer. By then concerns about currency stability and other macro-economic policies were used to justify the return to technological expertise and "efficiency," and the princely virtues of a centralized and non-participatory administration.

Nonetheless pressures for a plurality of forms of law and power re-emerged in the same industry, this time in the more private space of plant floors of automobile factories. Decisions about restructuring production, increasing flexibility, technological change, and out-sourcing all involved negotiations between workplace organizations and management. The most powerful of the organizations representing workers are the "plant committees." These elected bodies are composed of union members who are workers in the plant. They are chosen by their co-workers, from among the members of the metalworkers union which federates the various craft and categorical unions in the plant.[10] The other organization is an official one – the Committee for Prevention of Labour Accidents (CIPA) – reflecting workers' constitutionally defined rights to workplace safety. The members elected to this CIPA tend to be chosen for their prominence in the plants' internal politics, and therefore despite its bureaucratic nature the organization also occupies meaningful political space.

Recent research shows that workers count more on these institutions, and their union representatives within them, to manage technological change and restructuring than on official judicial routes to representation (Cardoso and Comin 1995; Campos 1998). As Campos' most recent study found, workers plainly relied on plant committees for direct contact with management about matters such as hiring and firing (60 percent versus 11 percent using the judicial route); introduction of new technologies (ditto); wage increases (58 percent versus 4 percent), overtime (55 percent versus 17 percent) and scheduling work (43 percent versus 15 percent). Asked if management of technological unemployment, one of the most dramatic workplace issues, should be pursued through the Labour Courts, 85 percent of the autoworkers questioned answered with a resounding negative. They much preferred a collective contract, which would bring more efficient discussion and "good and understandable" norms. Asked about the actual role of plant committees, most workers defined them as being there to strengthen the power of working people and to act as equals with management in negotiations (59 percent), while 34 percent saw their role as being to "disrupt the power of legal dispositions over unions." Nevertheless, even if "workers themselves agreed that internal plant committees have already acquired a broad legitimacy to intervene in the course of industrial restructuring" they maintained a commitment to stronger unions (Campos 1988: 99).

These recent developments in a major wing of the labour movement raise the question of whether such practices can be extended beyond individual plants and the role of unions in this. Plant committees exist in part because of efforts by the government in the 1980s to displace union power and limit the visibility of one very active union in society and politics. Thus, the ambiguity of the autoworkers' plant committees is that employers and governments initially promoted the institution as way to legitimize "free negotiations" within each company or plant, and thereby to deregulate and privatize labour relations. Campos shows that the newly invented plant committees appeared to metalworkers as another arena of struggle that complements the other work of the union. They saw them in relation to the other tasks and representations undertaken by the national-level union. In this way, their plant-level experiences become institutionalized into a broader set of relations. In doing so they are also refusing to accept that labour law or other regulations exclude negotiations, debate, and participation.

Negotiations within this new model, even if restricted to a single plant, can still be represented and experienced as part of a larger process of renewal.

This experiment contradicts the assertion of many, especially economists in the Brazilian context, that "unions are dead," irrelevant in an era of economic globalization, and that value can only be generated by markets. Such claims downplay, even ignore experiments such as this one, just as they also ignore the importance of dissent and mobilization to achieve true democracy, an achievement that depends on moving beyond formal arrangements and investing broader social practices.

The second experiment occurred between 1992 and 1994, when the CUT proposed to replace the traditional Labour Code (within which the Labour Courts function) by what it called a "national system of labour relations" (Siqueira 1994). These would have established national-level collective bargaining and contracts. The proposal was accepted for consideration by the Ministry of Labour, which set up a national forum to debate the project, composed of employers, unions, academics, lawyers and others. Nevertheless, when the new government came into office the project went the same way as the chambers; it was abandoned.

The original idea promoted by the unions was that the time had come to establish another public social contract for Brazil, one that would set unions free from the state and the judiciary. Autonomy of negotiation and action would replace judicial oversight and control. They saw such practices as basic and necessary conditions to underpin mobilization and empower ordinary Brazilians with rights of citizenship, including accepting workplace organization, the right to strike and alternatives for settling industrial conflict. As a union leader said, they sought to secure "less law and more negotiations, less of a judicial monologue and more of plural dialogue aimed at defined goals, less solutions and more shared administration" (quoted in Paoli 1997).

For the proponents of this reform, the experiments with sectoral "chambers," or tripartite negotiating tables, and the plant-level dispute resolution show that unions can do better by relying on their own organizational base of action than on closed legal systems for conflict resolution. Moreover, rather than seeing labour relations as fragmented experiments, they propose them as models which assert the potential public role of the working class.

What is the Future of Labour Movements, Regulation and Politics?

These experiments in Brazil and among organized workers suggest the following conclusions about the capacity of labour movements or other social movements close to them, organized in non-governmental organizations (NGO), to claim space for new practices and ideas. These had the democratic virtue of making a place for dissent and democratic outcomes. Some of practices were accepted for a short time by government and they were institutionalized, even incorporated into local governing structures. Nonetheless, the Brazilian state does not seem about to share its legal ordering principles with pluralistic and negotiated social regulations.

Many reasons might be invoked to account for this lack of capacity to attain such a result, among which we might list powerful economic pressures to adopt neo-liberal privatizing economic policies or the government's inclination to avoid at any price any risk to its policy of currency stability and other reforms. Beyond this, however, we might reflect on the legacy of political authoritarianism and social neglect, which hides or downplays the capacity of some groups to engage in inventive democratic practices. In other words, and certainly paradoxically, the very presence of a tradition of "non-democracy" helps to reinforce the adoption of an exclusionary modernity.

The result is that in Brazilian society, the very power to name and identify democratic possibilities remains, even more than before perhaps, a matter of political contestation. The legitimacy of the traditional concentrated, state-centric decision-making and judicial authority is fragile and the prerogative of the state to interpret society and define routes to its future is reduced, as more and more people recognize that the government is not really interested in seeing them participate. Media-led public opinion seems to be preferred to a politicized civil society, and the administration of society to democratic practices. The management of economic life is presented as an administration of the necessary, by technocrats with their data and technical solutions. As the French philosopher Jacques Rancière writes: "Government's wisdom today is nothing more than the knowledge of the automatic formulas for the great world belly of wealth . . . It is enough to show the common people the laws which govern needs, which have only one centre and one way of operating" (1996). There is nothing to be discussed, and therefore nothing to be contested.

"Adjustment" and "economic equilibrium" thus become justifications for limiting critical thought. Everything is subordinated to "realistic" assumptions and a "consensus" about the new order, thereby marginalizing social conflicts that might produce alternative histories. In labour relations, more specifically, the mandatory vocabulary includes concepts such as productive restructuring, lean production, flexible production, re-engineering, out-sourcing, downsizing and deregulation. These words impose their presence, becoming a monologue of experts and crowding out dissent and conflict, thereby removing alternative visions and proposals.

When, however, the "small bellies" (to return to Rancière's imagery) start to talk as thinking beings and demand the right to generate their own futures, they obviously are trying to put politics back into place. At such moments, the closed logic and seeming consensus of debates moves beyond the imposed terms and implicates more than the limited number of actors deploying them. Then it becomes possible to see that there is nothing inevitable in today's narrow patterns of capital accumulation and that the global game may have more than one centre and one way of being played. At such times the experts' monologue about the "inevitable logic" of globalization can be revealed for what it is: a sophisticated way to re-impose old and well known forms of domination.

Notes

1. The 1996 official statistics establish an economically active population of 100 million people, of which 22 percent are industrial workers. Only 49 percent of these workers are protected by labour standards. There are approximately 20,000 unions, an increase from the 14,000 present under the military dictatorship. However, only a fifth of these are really active. The informal labour market encompasses fully 32 percent of the workforce, which has no access to welfare programmes or protection by labour law. As for the distribution of wealth, Brazil wins the international sweepstakes for income concentration and inequality: the richest 20 percent of the population keeps 32 times more wealth than the poorest quintile. In Canada, for example, this difference is only 7. The richest quintile has an average of 10 years of schooling, while the poorest has barely two years. All this exists despite the fact that the rate of economic growth is high, but not translated into social development. By some measures, Brazil ranks with the poorest non-industrialized countries of Africa as well as Latin America.
2. This interpretation owes much to the work of Hannah Arendt (1981). On the idea of the participatory budget see Genro and Souza (1997). Tarso Genro is a former mayor of Porto Alegre.
3. This meant that labour disputes were not resolved through collective bargaining. Although the Labour Code provided for such a mechanism, it directly conflicted with the power of the Labour Courts.
4. An example of the consequences of this labour relations regime was the May-June 1995 strike of petrol workers. They struck state-owned Petrobrás, demanding that the federal government respect the terms of a previous wage settlement, which had itself resulted from the direct intervention of then President Itamar Franco, overturning a decision of the

Labour Court. The strikers also opposed privatization of the company. President Fernando Henrique Cardoso launched an aggressive campaign against the strike in the media, where workers were represented as corporatist, privileged, subversive, anti-modern, and anti-consumer. He pressed the Supreme Labour Court to declare the strike illegal and finally sent the Army to occupy the plant. This was an act of very traditional Brazilian authoritarianism. Petrobrás later dismissed 59 leaders of the strike, that ended with no gains for the workers.

5. This renewal of the labour movement took place at the same time that a multitude of social and cultural "new movements" appeared, representing women, blacks, urban dwellers, Indian nations and forest people, environmentalists, landless peasants, and others. Each demanded "particular" rights, but each also spoke the more general language of "rights" and citizenship. Together they managed to enlarge the political vocabulary and democratic repertory of the country, including the legitimacy of popular participation in public affairs (Paoli 1992; 1995).

6. Employers associations invited experts from the US and Japan to provide well remunerated courses to Brazilian managers, employers and owners of small firms. A sampling of newspapers in 1992-93 finds someone speaking every week about "total quality," entrepreneurial initiative, business imagination, and so on (Paoli 1997). New management systems, based on the Japanese model, had been implanted in industrial plants and banks.

7. The firms involved were Ford, General Motors, Volkswagen, and Mercedes-Benz, all of which were located in the contiguous cities of São Bernardo de Campo, Santo André, Diadema and São Paulo. Fiat, which is located elsewhere, did not participate in this institution.

8. Despite a context of economic crisis and mounting inflation, the negotiations produced results such as: lowered taxes on corporations in exchange for maintaining or expanding employment; less cheating on taxes and therefore more revenue for governments; better wages and social provision for workers; lower priced cars for consumers (Arbix 1996; Guimarães 1994).

9. Chambers were imitated in the civil construction sector (Silva 1996) and chemical industry.

10. Brazil's unions are organized by branch; even white collar employees belong to the metalworkers union in the automobile branch. Only one union per branch may exist in a town or municipal district. In the case analyzed here, a single union represents all the multinationals listed in Note 7, as well as small plants and businesses in the area. This resulted from the successful unification politics across four neighbouring municipal districts pursued by the metalworkers union of São Bernardo de Campo in the 1980s. With this unification, the whole industrial sector could negotiate as one.

References

Arbix, Glauco 1997, 'A câmara banida,' in Arbix e Zilbovicius (eds.), *De JK a FHC: A Reinvenção dos Carros*, São Paulo: Scritta.

Bresciani, Luis Paulo 1997, 'Os desejos e o limite: reestruturação industrial e ação sindical no complexo automotivo brasileiro,' in Leite, *O Trabalho em Movimento*, São Paulo: Scritta.

Campos, André Gambier 1998, *Modernização ou fragmentação? O sindicato dos metalúrgicos do ABC nos anos 90*, Dissertação de Mestrado em Sociologica, Universidade de São Paulo.

Cardoso, Adalberto, Comin, Álvaro 1995, 'Câmaras setoriais: modernização produtiva e democratização das relações de trabalho na indùstria automobilistica brasileira,' in Castro, Nadya (ed.), *A maquina e o equilibrista*, São Paulo: Paz c Terra.

Genro, Tarso, Souza, Ubiratan 1997, *Orçamento participativo: a experiência de Porto Algre*, São Paulo: Fundação Perseu Abramo.

Guimarães, Ivan 1994, 'A experiência das câmaras setoriais,' in Oliveira and Oliveira (eds.), *O mundo do trabalho: crise e mudança no final do século*, São Paulo: Paz e Terra.

Hall Michael 1983, *On widening the scope of Latin American working-class history*, IFCH/Unicamp.

Oliveira, Francisco *et al.* 1993a, 'Quanto Melhor, Melhor: O Acordo das Montadoras,' *Novos Estudos* 36.

--------- 1993b, 'Carta aberta ao Ministro Fernando Henrique Cardoso,' *Folha de São Paulo*, 02/05/93.

--------- 1994, 'Interview,' *Revista Plural* 1.

Paoli, Maria C. 1992, 'Citizenship and Inequalities: The Making of a Public Space in Brazilian Experience,' *Social and Legal Studies* 1.

--------- 1995, 'Movimentos sociais no Brasil: em busca de um estatuto político,' in Hellmann (ed.), *Movimentos sociais e democracia no Brasil*, São Paulo: Marco Zero.

--------- 1997, 'Práticas e representações sobre a cidadania do trabalhadores na crise dos direitos sociais e trabalhistas: Brasil, anos 90,' Relatório de Pesquisa apresentado ao CNPQ, Agosto.

Rancière, Jacques 1996, *O Desentimento*, São Paulo: Editoria 34.

Santos, Boaventura de Sousa 1995, 'On Modes of Production of Social Power and Law,' in Santos (ed.), *Towards a New Common Sense*, London: Routledge.

--------- 1997, 'Uma exigência cosmopolita: entre o précontratualismo e o pós-contratualismo,' in Oliveira & Paoli (eds) *Os Sentidos da Democracia*, São Paulo: Vozes.

Silva, Ana A. 1996, *Cidadania, conflitos e agendas sociais: das favelas urbanizadas aos foruns internacionais*, Tese de Doutoramento em Sociologia, Universidade de São Paulo.

Simão, Azis 1963, *Sindicato e Estado*, São Paulo: Difel.

Siqueira, José Francisco 1994, 'Contrato Coletivo de Trabalho no Brasil,' in Oliveira and Oliveira (eds.), *O Mundo do Trabalho: Crise e mudança no final do século*, São Paulo: Scritta.

5 Gendered Politics in Transition: South Africa's Democratic Transitions in the Context of Global Feminism

GAY W. SEIDMAN

In early 1993, about a year before South Africa's first democratic elections, South African audiences were stunned when the evening news showed footage of the negotiations that lay at the centre of the transition process. The surprise had nothing to do with race: after all, democratization in South Africa was primarily about opening the political process to the country's black majority, and any South African would have expected black negotiators to be full participants. Rather, the visual shock came from the negotiators' gender: fully half the negotiators were women. Almost without public discussion, all 26 parties involved in the process had agreed to include women in their negotiating teams. In a country with a long and multi-cultural tradition of male dominance, the fact that women played so prominent a role in designing the new constitution – and continue to be prominent in democratic politics in the present – represents a startling break with politics as usual.

Most discussions of South Africa's democratic transition in the early 1990s focus almost entirely on the opening of political participation to all races; for most of the twentieth century, the country's black majority was excluded from citizenship on racial grounds, and the shift to universal adult franchise in 1994 marked a monumental change. But the racial opening is not the only remarkable aspect of the transition: through the democratization process, and in the construction of new democratic institutions, concerns about gender equality have been surprisingly visible. An explicitly gendered democratization process, in which activists inserted gender issues into the political arena during the construction of the new state, has affected the character of democratic institutions, and has important implications for the gendered character of citizenship – for men and women's participation in the public arena, and for the construction of institutions and policies that may, in turn, reshape gendered citizenship in the future.

What explains the prominence of gender issues in South Africa's democratic transition? General discussions of democratization generally focus almost entirely on internal dynamics. Some authors limit their analysis to the dynamics of the actual negotiations; other writers include some analysis of the local political context, looking at the interaction of social actors in the democratization of society. But in order to understand how gender issues rose to such prominence in South Africa, we must also consider how broader international dynamics affected the way local actors conceptualized citizenship and democratization, and at how international dynamics offered new ideological possibilities and material resources to groups which might otherwise have been unable to affect local discussions. Only by considering the influences of global dynamics, pressures, and resources can we explain why some South Africans began to incorporate concerns about gender inequality in their understanding of democratization, how they were able to introduce those concerns in the broader transition, and how those concerns have been institutionalized in the framework of the new democratic state.

Gender issues were by no means the only aspect of South Africa's transition that was altered by international discussions; changing international discourses reconfigured local political coalitions, both among elite actors and within oppositional social movements. Increasingly, theoretical discussions of democratic transitions recognize that the international context constrains and shapes internal political processes. "Transnational cultural flows" have probably always played a part in the spread of democratic aspirations (Reuschemeyer, Stephens and Stephens 1992: 74), and negotiators for both authoritarian regimes and oppositional movements have regularly looked around the world for examples that might reveal new rhetorical and institutional possibilities (Markoff 1993). In the late twentieth century, in a rapidly changing global environment, ideas and resources spread rapidly, so that what Keck and Sikkink (1994) call "transnational issue networks" frequently influence domestic political debates – redefining issues, providing information and ideas, and providing material resources and sometimes moral leverage to activists in specific national contexts.

But in discussions of democratization, transnational flows of ideas and resources are generally treated as a backdrop for local affairs. By contrast, the South African case suggests that in order to understand the unusual prominence of gender concerns in the late twentieth century, the influence of the international feminist movement must be treated as an independent dynamic, which has both changed the attitudes of local actors toward gender politics and provided resources with which local actors can influence the gendered character of the new state. I argue in this paper that analyses which ignore international influences are incapable of explaining why oppositional activists and authoritarians alike in South Africa began to take gender issues seriously in the 1990s – seriously enough to include consideration of gender inequality in the way they structured negotiations, the constitution, and parliament itself.

This argument should not be interpreted as suggesting that feminism can be dismissed as a new form of western cultural imperialism, however. Gender ideologies have long been a site of international intervention: colonial authorities regularly argued that their intervention in colonized societies was partly an attempt to free women from the oppression they experienced in traditional indigenous households (Chatterjee 1989). In the late twentieth century, this dynamic has become even more pronounced: the international flow of ideas and resources has become a basic element in local debates involving gender equality (Chowdhury *et al.* 1994: 15; Mohanty 1991: 7-11). But it is important to note that gender issues are not simply raised by outsiders: as the South African case amply demonstrates, by the mid-1980s women activists around the world were beginning to bring feminist concepts and analyses to bear on concrete situations. While previous structural changes – new educational and labour force participation patterns for women, changing household patterns – created new possibilities for women to participate in politics, a new repertoire of feminist theory, and feminist discussions of earlier democratic transitions, helped democratic activists in many settings rethink gender issues. Thus, because of their contact with international feminist currents, women activists who had previously been relatively silent about gender inequality grew increasingly concerned about including gender issues in the construction of new citizenship, and raised these concerns within the framework of local organizations. After first demonstrating how international influences strengthened feminist voices within the South African transition, I go on to look at how South African feminists have sought to build feminist concerns into new state institutions, in ways that might allow the new state to address gender inequalities as it institutes new policies in the future.

Negotiated Transitions: A Place at the Table

In the 1980s, discussion of democratic transitions tended to focus almost entirely on the negotiation process itself, on the moment when authoritarian regimes began to give way to regularized, relatively open political processes. Often relying on game-theory metaphors, transition analysts sought negotiating strategies most likely to produce democratic outcomes and full civilian rule (O'Donnell and Schmitter 1986; Przeworski 1991; Slabbert 1992). But analysts spent relatively little time examining who was doing the negotiating, or how specific individuals became the arbiters of new democracies (Cumings 1989); since most negotiators were male, this approach tended to assume that all important players would be men. Few of these game-theoretical studies asked how the new state would deal with gender issues, or wondered whether this even mattered to the character of new democracies.[1]

But the South African case demands greater attention to the gendered dynamics of the transition – and particularly, to the ways in which women's voices were included in the negotiation process. Initial secret discussions between the authoritarian (white-supremacist) government and the democratic opposition were indeed almost entirely male, but during the 1990s, that pattern changed rapidly.

This shift, it should be noted, did not occur because of principled decisions by the anti-apartheid opposition. When all political parties were unbanned in 1990, the African National Congress included some women in its negotiating team, but gender issues were not raised in negotiations – despite the ANC's rhetorical inclusion of gender equality as part of its democratic aspirations (ANC 1990). The anti-apartheid movement's silence on gender issues hardly reflects the absence of gender inequality in South Africa. While South Africa's system of racial discrimination gained international notoriety, apartheid also involved systemic gender discrimination. For blacks, urban residence permits depended on formal-sector employment; gendered labour markets left most black women working in the informal sector or unemployed, faced with a choice of waiting for migrant workers' remittances in impoverished rural areas, or living illegally near towns. Women of all races faced some degree of state-sanctioned discrimination: legislation from tax codes to pensions recreated women's subordination by assuming their dependence on male breadwinners (Kemp, Madlala, Moodley and Salo 1995; Ramphele 1989; Walker 1990; Segar and White, 1992).

During the next five years, however, women activists grew increasingly visible. Women activists across the political spectrum began to argue that gender issues should be taken up during the transition, insisting that women's voices be heard – although generally acknowledging that those voices were multiple and often contradictory (Fouche 1994: 79). An activist in the Africanist Pan African Congress, for example, argued that since "women are universally discriminated against . . . it becomes necessary that the rights of women should be defined, enshrined in the constitution of a liberated Azania" (Mothopeng 1992: 49); the black consciousness organization AZAPO committed itself to anti-sexism in 1993 (Moodley 1993). Women activists in the largely-white Democratic Party concluded, "The status of women in society must be improved both on the grounds of democracy and justice. The period of transition is the moment to tackle this. Very seldom is there an opportunity to remake society and to let this opportunity pass without improving the status of women would be a dereliction of responsibility" (Bonnin 1992: 44). By late 1991, gender issues had been explicitly brought into the process. Most officially-appointed negotiators were still male, but all parties had agreed to the creation of a Gender Advisory Board, to consider the "gender impact" of negotiated agreements. Although this Board was not itself present at negotiations, its commentaries began to raise questions about an abstract discourse of democracy that ignored gender completely.

Soon, the Advisory Board was replaced by more direct involvement of women in the "elite-pacting" process. Negotiations between the government and the anti-apartheid opposition broke down completely in 1992, largely over on-going violence in black townships. When talks were reconvened, ANC women activists decided that the Gender Advisory Board was inadequate. Instead, they sought to ensure that women's voices would be heard inside the negotiating chambers. In March 1993, in a little-publicized event, women ANC activists demonstrated at the negotiation chambers, blocking talks until women were literally given places at the table. Amazingly, all 26 parties participating in the negotiation process accepted a gender quota. Fifty percent of each two-person team had to be female; thus, half of the negotiators who finally accepted a provisional constitution and set the elections in motion were women – a composition that had real implications for the kinds of institutions created under the new constitution.

Women negotiators were not united on most issues. As one activist asked, "Who do the women now in the talks really represent? Many are loyal to their parties, not to women. And many of those parties are not gender-sensitive at all. So can we really say that women are represented in the talks?" (Mthintso 1993). Yet despite their political differences, during the final constitutional negotiations the women negotiators managed to form a separate women's caucus which could find unity on some issues (Finnemore 1994). Most importantly, the women's caucus insisted that the new constitution assert the principle of gender equality over that of respect for customary law, consciously allowing millions of African women married under customary law to use the new constitutional framework to demand greater equality within the household. The women's caucus thus sought a democracy in which domestic relations as well as relations in the public arena could come under state scrutiny (Albertyn 1994a and 1994b; Segar and White 1992). The caucus' two other major successes were the creation of a special body to ensure women's participation in the 1994 election process, and the inclusion of an advisory committee to scrutinize the gender implications of new policies in the new government structure (Manzini 1994).

Although the women's negotiating caucus made few other concrete proposals, its real achievement was to insert visible gender concerns into national debates. By South Africa's first democratic election campaign, in the first part of 1994, most political parties had expressed at least a rhetorical commitment to gender equality. Putting it politely, a leading ANC activist – later appointed to a cabinet post – concluded, "Gender consciousness has become one of the national priorities in South Africa" (Mabandla 1994). Speaking rather more bluntly, another leading ANC activist told a reporter, "Suddenly all the old men have woken up and realized that women are the majority in this country and that they need women's votes. It might be opportunism, but what the hell, we should make the most of it" (Gevisser 1994: 3).

Social Movements in Transitions

Why were South African women activists so willing to raise gender issues during the transition, and why were male negotiators apparently willing to listen? What had reshaped the gender dynamics around the negotiating table, and what did these changes mean for constructing a gendered democracy? In the midst of the process of redefining citizenship, why did South African negotiators decide to consider what redefined citizenship would mean for women as well as men?

To a much greater extent than game-theoretic approaches, theories of democratization which focus on the emergence of oppositional forces recognize that while broad structural processes shape the context in which social movements emerge, activists in social movements must interpret their constituents' interests in order to place them in the public arena. Rather than taking interests and goals for granted, therefore, much of the work done from this perspective looks at how social movements' goals change over time, in the process of creating a democratic opposition to authoritarianism, or during a negotiated transition (Alvarez 1989; Keck, 1992; Marx 1992; Seidman 1994).

This kind of approach – beginning by exploring the construction of oppositional collective identities – is particularly appropriate for analyzing the way gender issues were raised in South Africa. While democratic movements in most of the world have been led by men, the rank-and-file participants in community-based social movements have often included more women than men – from Argentina's Madres de la Plaza de Mayo, to Brazil's Movement Against the High Cost of Living, to South Africa's township civic associations. At the day-to-day level of collective mobilization, the gender of social movement activists almost certainly matters to the kind of concerns raised: several authors argue that while poor women's initial participation in grassroots movements may start from domestic concerns – concern for children or household incomes – participation in community-based organizations has sometimes led women to discuss and challenge gender inequalities within political movements, even to redefine political goals more generally, reconsidering the relationship between domestic inequality and broader political issues (Chinchilla 1991; Lind 1992).

The South African case may be especially revealing of the ways in which discourses around gender may be altered during democratic transitions. Until the late 1980s, activists in the anti-apartheid movement rarely raised gender issues publicly; when women were mentioned at all, it was usually as wives and mothers, seeking to strengthen women's domestic position, not to call for autonomous citizenship (Walker 1982; Gaitskell and Unterhalter 1989; McClintock 1993). Some activists rejected what they called "bourgeois feminism" as a new form of cultural imperialism; many others who objected privately to gender inequalities explicitly refused to discuss gender inequality, on the grounds, as a leading woman ANC activist said after the 1985 Nairobi conference on women, that "it would be suicide" to raise feminist concerns, for fear of splitting and undermining the anti-apartheid movement (Anon 1985).

By the early 1990s, however, this vision was explicitly challenged within the anti-apartheid movement, as the result of two linked processes. First, South African intellectuals began to discuss the ways in which apartheid had treated black women and men differently, and to consider how women's needs might thus differ from those of men during reconstruction. Feminist intellectuals, mainly women, began to argue that unless gender concerns were considered during the course of democratization, new political institutions would recreate and reinforce inequality; frequently, these intellectuals referred to feminist analyses of other historical cases of democratization, from China to Nicaragua, to illustrate their arguments (Hassim, Metelerkamp and Todes 1987; Hassim 1991; Horn 1991; Serote 1991). Although feminists within the anti-apartheid movement were always careful to consider the intersection of gender with inequalities of race and class in South Africa (Kemp, Madlala, Moodley and Salo 1995), they increasingly inserted concerns over gender issues into political debates. From the late 1980s, feminist ideas gained currency within the ANC: prominent activists began to insist that the democratic opposition should commit itself to ending gender inequality both in its internal structures and more broadly in South African society. Thus, for example, Frene Ginwala – the activist who feared that the "woman question" would be suicidal for the ANC – emerged as a leading feminist voice after 1990, demanding that gender issues be placed higher on the movement's agenda. After its unbanning in 1990, ANC slogans increasingly demanded a "non-racial, democratic, and non-sexist South Africa," and ANC meetings increasingly involved some discussion of what that goal might entail.

Second, gender issues began to be incorporated in the organizational forms of the anti-apartheid movement. In local meetings, anti-apartheid activists began to develop separate women's forums, hoping to increase women's participation. Women whose husbands objected to their political activities might feel more comfortable going to all-women meetings, it was argued; moreover, women might speak more freely if no men were present, and could thus gain valuable experience and confidence in public speaking. These forums, instituted in the late 1980s, represented the first explicit recognition within the democratic opposition that women and men might have somewhat different agendas. In a highly politicized environment, women mobilized within separate women's groups often analyzed their lives not only in terms of race and class, but also in terms of gender inequalities. Gender-specific organizational forms allowed, even encouraged, women activists to consider how their experiences differed from men; grass-roots mobilization created a new constituency for feminist concerns within the anti-apartheid movement – a new, explicitly gendered collective identity (Seidman 1993). New forms of mobilization within the democratic opposition – particularly, forms which encouraged women's participation – prompted a reformulation of anti-apartheid goals to include some consideration of gender issues.

Gender issues often provoked conflict within the ANC, challenging as they did the assertion of shared oppression which united the anti-apartheid movement. After a fierce debate, the 1991 national ANC conference refused to set gender quotas for leading ANC bodies. But leading women activists insisted that women should be included on all important committees, and by early 1992, this became organizational policy. By early 1993, when the ANC Women's League demonstrated against women's exclusion from national negotiations, they were simply carrying a principle that had been enforced within the ANC organizational structure to a new level.

Global Trends

This analysis, however, begs still another question: while changing forms of organization and discourse may explain why women raised gender concerns within the ANC, why did male activists acquiesce – and why did the other 25 parties represented in the South African negotiations accept the gender equality principle for their teams? The fact that democratic transitions in the 1990s occurred at a moment when intellectuals around the world were coming to view gender differences as socially constructed rather than biological was critical to the way women activists thought about gender equality: activists could draw on new theories, concepts and vocabularies, developed within a growing international feminist discourse.[2]

In South Africa, the impact of a global feminist movement was evident in two ways: first, through the ideas brought back to South Africa by returning exiles and students, and secondly, in the way resources were provided for groups and programmes looking specifically at gender inequality. South Africans visiting Europe and North America, either as students or exiles, were often introduced to new feminist ideas and publications. South Africans returned to participate in anti-apartheid oppositional groups with a new vocabulary of feminist theory, challenging earlier assumptions about the role of women in the democratic struggle, and about the nature of women's political aspirations. Activists inspired by feminist theories were often influential in deciding to create women's organizations. In the early 1990s, feminist ideas received additional support from returning exiles, who had been exposed to other feminist movements outside South Africa, and who returned to find, as one returnee put it, that patriarchy might be the one social institution shared by South Africans of all races (Berger 1991:1).

Drawing on feminist histories of other postcolonial and revolutionary experiences, women in the anti-apartheid movement increasingly insisted that postponing feminist issues for the sake of unity could erode opportunities for raising gender issues in the future. ANC activist Pethu Serote, for example, wrote:

> In earlier times it was almost taboo to talk about women's emancipation within the ANC. The subject was considered divisive. It was always argued that the national liberation struggle was supreme (an argument nobody disagrees with) and that the emancipation of women would come naturally and automatically with its triumph. History ... negates the second part of the statement ... When one builds a house one has to start at least by

digging and laying the foundation, and that's the stage we are at (Serote 1991: 6).

Drawing on international feminist discussions, activists infused South African discussions with new ideas about differences in the way women and men experience citizenship, while intellectuals described the way other countries' policies and institutions had attempted to redress gender inequality (Hassim 1991; Segar and White 1992).

It is important to note how much opposition these feminists faced within the anti-apartheid movement: women activists frequently expressed fear about voicing concerns about gender inequality, and described how women in the anti-apartheid organization were intimidated by male colleagues if they raised issues about internal organization. At a 1991 conference in Durban, the ANC was openly divided over a proposal to institute a quota system to ensure that women composed thirty percent of the ANC's national leadership. Despite Nelson Mandela's support for the proposal, delegates to the conference rejected it. But few prominent male activists were willing to admit publicly that they had not supported the quota, and opposition to the idea of gender equity within the ANC dissipated. Over the next few years, at the repeated insistence of women activists at all levels, the ANC gradually adopted a policy of including women on all committees – a policy that allowed activists to raise gender concerns in all internal discussions. Thus, the initial exposure of women activists to feminist ideas internationally – and the availability of international resources and support for feminist efforts within the anti-apartheid movement – gradually translated into policies that affected internal discussions in the ANC.

If anything, international influences have been even more important in the period since the 1994 elections, as new government officials, often working together with international donors, have promoted projects and strategies aimed specifically at addressing gender inequalities. The most obvious examples of this process have come since late 1995, when feminists in the new government used South Africa's participation in the United Nations' Fourth World Conference on Women in Beijing as a platform from which to articulate feminist concerns at home. The 45-person official delegation included cabinet ministers and deputy ministers, the Speaker and several members of parliament, civil servants from a range of departments, and activists from several non-governmental organizations dealing with gender inequality. On their return, these delegates publicized the conference's findings widely, shifting the basis of South Africa's commitment to addressing gender inequalities from a moral or ethical stance, to an internationally-recognized obligation (United Nations 1995). Even more pointedly, the Department of Welfare published a "Report on the South African Government's Commitments arising out of the Fourth UN Womens' Conference," which used the occasion of the Conference to underscore specific aspects of gender inequality in South Africa; moreover, the report drew attention to which government departments were best situated to address each of these concerns (Department of Welfare 1996). Through television interviews, widely-disseminated reports, and other forms of mass media, many of the delegates listed aspects of gender inequality discussed in Beijing, and then showed in detail how these broad trends worked out in South Africa. Deputy Minister for Social Welfare Geraldine Frazier chaired a "national post-Beijing planning committee"; by late February, 1996, she could go through the government departments, listing the specific targets set by each department in response to these concerns (Frazier 1996). Listing specific mechanisms, budgets, and time frames, she explicitly named departments she considered relatively serious about addressing gender inequalities – as well as those she believed were lagging behind. "It is time to implement our commitments," she concluded.[3]

In addition to changing the way local political activists understand and articulate their concerns, changing international discourses also affect the flow of material resources to countries undergoing democratic transitions. Although the process is difficult to document, most activists agree that western donor agencies made resources available to the anti-apartheid movement and the new government in support of feminist concerns. During the 1980s, anti-apartheid organizations relied heavily on foreign donors – reasonably enough, since they sought to mobilize people with few resources to spare for political campaigns. Projects aimed at black South African women may have received a more sympathetic hearing from donor agency personnel, themselves often influenced by feminist movements in Europe and North America. Anti-apartheid activists looking for outside help were frequently asked to consider the gender implications of their projects – a request often interpreted by South Africans to imply that donor funds required active efforts to include women in political organizations. Thus, for example, church groups funded projects designed to document the special needs of rural black women, at the suggestion of groups like the Catholic Institute for International Relief; the labour movement included campaigns to organize women as part of its national strategies from the mid-1980s, partly at the suggestion of foreign union movements; and a centre for legal studies and human rights developed a gender research project partly at the suggestion of the Ford Foundation. International organizations frequently requested women speakers rather than men, and the Dutch anti-apartheid movement went so far as to organize a special conference to introduce South African women activists to participants in the Dutch women's movement (Seidman 1993; Ford Foundation 1995).

Emphasizing the importance of international ideological trends and donor influence should not be interpreted as degrading the role of domestic activists. Especially in the 1980s, anti-apartheid activists devoted a great deal of time and energy to understanding the ways in which women and men experienced apartheid differently, and to addressing these differences within their organizations and strategies; moreover, through the 1970s, women were increasingly participants in the urban communities and factories which served as the basis for the anti-apartheid movement's constituency. International ideas alone cannot alter internal dynamics, but as local activists engage with and are influenced by new ideas and aspirations, local debates are likely to take new forms – especially if those external influences are accompanied by material resources which strengthen particular contestants in internal struggles.

Gendered Citizenship: Representation and Interest Articulation

A gendered perspective on democratization requires us to carry our analysis of democratization past the first elections, to look at the construction of new states, and at the ways in which new democracies redefine inclusion and citizenship. Feminist activists in South Africa argued that only a mobilized women's movement, with women representatives in parliament, could pressure the new state to implement new laws and to enforce rights granted under the new constitution. But they also sought to avoid a more subtle problem, linked to the character of citizenship itself. Instead of allowing the state to perpetuate gender inequalities by implicitly assuming that citizens are male – and thus, to maintain an existing set of gender relationships and ideologies – feminist activists sought to institutionalize discussions of gender issues at every level of policy-making. In the consolidation of democracy, feminists sought to insert some recognition of the ways that gender shapes the choices open to individuals, and to stress the need for policies which might undermine gender inequality. The South African case underscores the importance of considering the influence of the global context on how those identities and interests are defined. But all of this begs the following questions: what, if anything, does this case suggest about gendered citizenship, about an understanding of democracy that takes seriously the different experiences of women and men as citizens and subjects? What role have international feminist influences had on the consolidation of South Africa's democracy? If the point of democratization is not simply multi-party elections, but the construction of new institutions, what has South Africa's gendered transition meant for the construction of a new democratic state?

These latter questions may be especially important for feminists. Although there is little agreement over how women's interests should be defined, or over what kinds of institutions would best serve those interests, women's political participation is clearly affected by the state's willingness to enact policies that challenge, rather than reinforce, the domestic relationships that have tended to leave women subordinate. Feminists have certainly considered how state structures and policies affect women, but those discussions tend to be historical and critical, rather than prescriptive. There are relatively few discussions of what institutional forms might be best for women overall. This may be due to a general discomfort about asserting some universalized version of "women's interests:" given the wide range of women's experiences, there is no reason to think all women everywhere would have the same priorities in addressing women's subordination. Feminist theorists tend to treat interests as constructed and interpreted through specific collective experiences and institutions, rather than fixed (Berger 1991; Pringle and Watson 1992), so that representing "women's interests" in the state would require first knowing how a specific group of women understand and interpret their interests. If interests are shaped by, or at least interpreted through, a contingent process of collective identity formation and institutional frameworks, it becomes theoretically impossible to define an overarching set of institutions that would invariably be the best possible ones through which women could represent their interests.

In this section, I look at how feminist activists in the South African democratic opposition have approached two issues in the consolidation of democracy: the definition of women's interests through collective mobilization, and attempts to increase women's representation within new state structures.[3]

During the negotiation process, feminist activists sought to promote an explicitly gendered perspective on democracy and democratization. The ANC Women's League sought to legitimize feminist postures within the anti-apartheid movement, and to develop a vision of the concerns shared by women in different social positions.[4] In 1991, the Women's League began developing a non-partisan "Women's Charter," a set of demands which was to reflect the concerns of women across the country. The league launched a broader National Women's Coalition, seeking to discover and articulate

women's common concerns (Fester *et al.* 1992; Kemp *et al.* 1995). Made up
of some 70 women's organizations from across the political spectrum, the
Coalition was organized around the principle that women of different social
locations could find areas of common concerns and interest – although most
spokeswomen acknowledged that race and class shaped women's experiences
in fundamental ways, creating significant differences in how women would
rank priorities (Fouche 1994). These differences were not straightforward
reflections of the different experiences of black and white, rich and poor, but
also reflected the broad range of attitudes under the Coalition's umbrella. The
Coalition's unity was severely strained, for example, when members of
church groups disagreed with feminist activists over reproductive rights –
particularly, the right to legal, safe abortions (Makatini 1993: 19; Rumney
1994).[5] Despite the organizers' original intention to include all political
tendencies, coordinators acknowledged that within months, women from
conservative, largely white groups had tended to drop out, leaving mainly
activists from the anti-apartheid movement dominating the Coalition.

The Coalition's main goal was to develop some consensus around major
issues of gender inequality. Following a suggestion made initially by the
ANC (ANC 1990), the WNC embarked on an 18-month campaign to write a
"Women's Charter," which it hoped would serve as a kind of gendered bill
of rights. In addition to general discussions among activists, the Women's
Coalition led 203 focus groups with 1620 members and administered 2973
individual questionnaires, seeking to ascertain what women wanted from a
new state. Although most participants in the survey were already part of
women's organizations, and thus probably were already influenced by some
feminist ideas, the research report reflects a striking degree of agreement:
generally, respondents were concerned about giving women equal
opportunities in the world of work, and sharing burdens equally in the home.
While black and white women emphasized different concerns – for example,
black respondents frequently referred to the ways in which racial differences
overrode gender commonalities among women – the report detailed a series
of ways in which gender shaped women's life chances, from discrimination
in property, tax and inheritance laws, to exclusion from politics and jobs, to
the prevalence of violence against women (Women's National Coalition n.d.:
11-13).

Based on this research, the National Women's Coalition proposed a
women's charter to be included in South Africa's new constitution. The
charter is relatively general, but its proponents could reasonably claim that
its demands, which range from the assertion of women's reproductive rights
to demands for full equality at the workplace and in the home, reflect the

aspirations of a broad spectrum of women. The charter insists that women should be included in decision-making bodies throughout society, from traditional courts to policy-making bodies, and rejects gendered discrimination in law, education, and employment. It asserts the absolute right of women to control their own bodies, and calls for state efforts to protect women from sexual harassment and violence. Recognizing that women are concentrated in the informal sector and in unpaid work, the charter calls on the new state to take affirmative steps to improve women's access to formal jobs, to ensure all citizens have access to parental leave and child care facilities, and to create a system of medical, pension and welfare benefits that does not discriminate against citizens who have not worked for wages (Women's National Coalition, n.d.; Women's Charter 1994).

The women's charter campaign clearly succeeded in its explicit aim: it publicized gender-specific demands, detailing the ways in which women's experiences and access to resources differ from those of men. In the process, however, the charter campaign also attained an implicit goal, creating at least the impression of broad public consensus regarding gender priorities, building differences among women into a more generalizable set of principles. Many rural African respondents, for example, were concerned that husbands should not take all the proceeds from selling vegetables that the wife had grown (Women's National Coalition nd.: 99-100); in its more general summary, the charter's authors subsume this concern under the principle of granting women greater equality within the home. Similarly, the charter downplays issues that might divide women; whereas the research report includes black women's comments about white women's exploitation of black domestic servants, the charter discusses employment in the more neutral terms of equal access to employment and training for all South Africans.

Obviously, simply collating women's concerns into a charter will not lead to radical change in gender relations within most households. Most feminists realized that even if the charter were adopted in the new constitution, the legal innovation would not necessarily improve women's lives. A trade unionist who worked in the charter campaign, Dorothy Mokgalo, described a starting point: "We must use the Charter as a mobilizing document for women to know what rights they must fight for. At the same time, we must use it as a tool to protect women's rights once they are made law" (Mokgalo 1994: 34). Similarly, Nozizwe Madlala, an ANC feminist who became a new member of parliament, concluded that the most urgent task was "for women to organize themselves into a strong mass-based women's movement," which would monitor the new government's policies. "The struggle for emancipation depends on one key tool: organization. ... We cannot assume that the government will automatically be sympathetic to our demands as women. In fact, we will have to apply our united power to make sure the government heeds them" (Madlala 1994).

Nevertheless, politically-active feminists continued to focus more on the construction of a gendered state than on mobilizing grassroots support for feminist ideas and practices. While the notion of "women's interests" remained somewhat opaque, South African feminist activists were deeply concerned with ensuring women's representation within new state structures – with creating gendered institutions through which women could actively help shape new policies. Most South African feminist activists seemed more concerned with creating explicitly gendered institutions, than with outlining specific policies needed to redress gender inequalities. The discussion of how to construct gendered institutions took place on two levels. Feminists sought first to ensure that there would be individual women in decision-making bodies, and second, to ensure that state structures were designed to consider the impact of new policies on gender relations.

ANC activists viewed South Africa's first democratic elections as an opportunity to greatly increase the number of women representatives in national political office. Because negotiators agreed that the new electoral system would involve proportional representation, parties did not run individual candidates, but electoral lists. Responding to internal demands for gender-based affirmative action within the party, the ANC set a 30 percent quota for women on its electoral list – a decision reflecting political theorists' analyses of electoral systems most likely to produce a larger number of women in political office (Albertyn 1992: 2; Phillips 1991). Other parties appear to have considered gender issues important in attracting voters, and began to include more women as candidates on their lists (Gevisser 1994).

When the new national Parliament opened in May, 1994, it included 106 women, or 26.5 percent, out of 400 representatives, a dramatic change from the white controlled, almost-entirely-male parliament which preceded it; new parliamentarians almost immediately proposed the creation of a parliamentary day-care centre, as well as additional women's rooms. Most of these women insisted they were not going to parliament exclusively as representatives of women, but were active feminists. Frene Ginwala, the new Speaker of the House, was one of the ANC's leading feminist voices by the mid-1990s. Many new parliamentarians insisted that a top priority for the new government would be finding ways to challenge existing relations of gender inequality (Gevisser 1994: 3). Although the first cabinet included only two women out of 27 ministers, several more vocal feminists were added to the cabinet within the first two years of President Mandela's tenure, giving even greater visibility to feminist activists.

Largely as a result of proposals from the women's caucus during pre election negotiations, the new constitution required the creation of some kind of national gender commission in the new state. However, drawing on experiences from around the world – looking at the histories of feminist efforts to institutionalize gender inequality in countries ranging from Australia to Nicaragua – South African feminist intellectuals expressed concern about the ways gender issues are often marginalized. Feminist intellectuals argued that creating a Women's Ministry – the most common approach to addressing gender issues in new African states – would ghettoize women's issues, even though it would ensure cabinet-level representation and executive powers for the broadly-defined women's movement. Although some activists considered the Women's Ministry the easiest way to ensure that feminist voices would be heard in government, most pointed out that such ministries elsewhere have tended to restrict their vision to women's domestic roles: generally under-budgeted and under-staffed, they offer courses in nutrition, child care, and handicrafts, rather than addressing the underlying dynamics of gender inequality (Mabandla 1994).

Most South African feminists expressed some preference for a more multi-faceted approach: the government would create gender focus desks in all ministries, linked by a national commission on the status of women, which would then have some say in any policy that would affect the lives of gendered citizens (Albertyn 1992; Biehl n.d.; Mabandla 1994). Thus, for example, the gender focus desk in a ministry of development might insist on redesigning a job-creation programme, to ensure prospective workers included women as well as men. In the land reform ministry, a gender focus desk might make sure that land was available to women household heads, rather than allowing redistribution programmes to favour men. Reviewing departmental policies, developing appropriate strategies to ensure the integration of gender concerns in planning, coordinating training of staff in relation to gender concerns, and monitoring projects in terms of their effect on gender equity, these desks could permit concrete efforts to change the way policies were designed and implemented throughout government (Albertyn 1995: 25). By institutionalizing some discussion of the gender implications of all policies implemented by the new state, feminist activists hoped that gender desks would require policy-makers to consider how gender patterns affect citizens' lives. In theory, gender desks could ensure that the new state's policies do not exacerbate, and might even erode, the bases of gender inequality (Albertyn 1995). By early 1997, at least two departments – the

Department of Land Reform and, somewhat surprisingly, the Department of Intelligence – had apparently implemented this mechanism for policy review, and other departments had begun to make plans for creating similar structures under a new government policy (Department of Welfare, 1996). Similarly, the Justice Department had undertaken to review the country's family laws – including customary marriage, separation and divorce laws – to "encompass gender equality" (Sentle 1997).

From the point of view of many of the feminist activists involved in national policy debates, however, the most important new government structure seemed likely to be the national Commission on Gender Equality, which was mandated by the 1993 interim constitution, but for which parliament did not pass enabling legislation until 1996. As the peak coordinating body for all policies attempting to address gender inequality, activists viewed the Commission as a crucial lobby within government, whose members could pressure both political parties and civil service ministries to honour their rhetorical commitments. After much debate, appointments to the Commission were announced at the end of 1996. The twelve Commissioners included ten women, of whom several had already earned reputations as thoughtful and energetic feminists; in addition to individual histories of feminist activism during the transition period, several Commissioners had produced academic research on gender inequality and on policy options, while others had established reputations as vocal feminists within the ANC.[6] Moreover, the Commission's budget and statutory powers were clearly sufficient to ensure that the Commission could make significant interventions in national policy discussions in the future. Commissioners clearly expressed their intention to block attempts by other civil service ministries to undermine their status as an independent body.

Feminist activists have insisted that South Africa's democracy must be explicitly gendered. Building on the campaign which produced the women's charter – which began the process by defining a fairly broad consensus about the main mechanisms recreating women's subordination, and by legitimizing the idea that the state should deal consciously with gender inequalities – a relatively visible feminist movement recognized that unless new institutions were explicitly gendered, they would be unconsciously so. By seeking to ensure that women were visibly represented in new decision-making bodies, and that new institutions would explicitly consider gender issues when designing and implementing policies, feminists hoped to build the attempt to address gender issues into the structures of the new state. Thus, the fact that South Africa's democratic transition process was gendered – that a women's movement emerged and became engaged in negotiations during the transition to democracy – could have direct implications for the kind of democracy that will be consolidated over the next few years.

It is in the construction of democratic institutions which ensure that gender differences are considered in state policy-making that we begin to see how a new state might create a gendered citizenship which acknowledges and confronts the different experiences of men and women, and how these experiences affect the relationship between individuals and the state. If common gender interests cannot be defined objectively – if women in different situations interpret their gender interests in a variety of ways – then institutional mechanisms requiring officials to consider the impact of policies on real (gendered) citizens may be the closest any democracy can come to incorporating gender into the definition of citizenship. Gendered citizenship, then, would not so much include a specific package of rights or policies, as institutional mechanisms allowing, perhaps stimulating, the articulation of gendered democratic aspirations.

Conclusion

What, if anything, does the South African democratization tell us about more general processes of democratization? Three points seem worth stressing. First, understanding the ability to assert a gendered voice in the formal democratization process – to insist that special steps be taken to ensure women's participation in creating new state structures – requires looking outside the negotiation process, to look at how the agendas of oppositional movements are shaped before and during negotiations; it requires recognizing that negotiators arrive at the bargaining table with interests and goals, as well as strategies. An understanding of why gender issues might become important in the construction of democracy requires exploring the emergence and character of women's representation within the political opposition. In South Africa, women activists managed to mobilize a constituency sympathetic to feminist claims, and to assert the legitimacy of gender issues within the democratic opposition and the negotiation process. Once democratic aspirations had been redefined to include some degree of gender equality, feminist activists could use that new understanding of democracy to insist that negotiators design a transition process incorporating women's voices.

But those women activists were influenced by, and could draw on resources provided by, an international feminist movement. Thus, secondly, the South African case underscores the importance of considering how the international context shapes specific definitions of democracy, and the ability of actors within local movements to assert particular concerns as new democracies are constructed. In the late twentieth century, democracy is never defined in isolation: the international context of local struggles helps define possibilities and constraints. Without organizational and ideological resources to back feminist voices, South African women activists would probably have been less visible within the anti-apartheid movement and the transition process; indeed, many of them would probably have been less willing to articulate explicitly feminist stances. The success of anti-apartheid activists in articulating feminist issues as part of a larger political agenda – asserting the importance of gender issues in negotiations and inserting some consideration of how individuals' experiences are gendered in the construction of new institutions – can only be understood in terms of linkages to larger transnational cultural flows which provided crucial ideas and material support to groups representing women, and to activists raising gender concerns within the anti-apartheid movement. Thus, instead of simply focusing on internal organizations as vehicles of democratic aspirations, we need to consider the way international influences strengthen or weaken specific players in local debates, and how those influences redefine democratic aspirations.

Finally, a gendered perspective on the South African transition forces us to reconsider definitions of democracy. Markoff (1993) suggests that instead of treating democracy as an end-state, perhaps we should view it as a process: perhaps democracy is always democratization, as we learn to consider the demands for inclusion of newly-vocal groups, who believe existing institutions do not permit adequate representation of their interests. Instead of asking what role specific classes or groups play in democratic transitions, we would have to ask who defines democracy, as a goal and as a set of practices, for a particular society. During democratization, who designs the institutions that will frame political discussions, and how do they conceive the participants? Who articulates participants' demands? How do they understand the collective identities of constituencies, and how does that understanding shape the way interests are represented within the state? If we acknowledge that citizens lead their lives as men and women, discussions of democratization may move away from treating democracy as a defined state, to looking at how people – women and men, or other as-yet undefined collective identities – seek actively to give shape to their aspirations.

Notes

1. This gender-neutral vision seemed to blind observers to any possibility that women might have participated in the construction of democracy – to such an extent that a recent study of the South African transition decries women's silence, apparently overlooking the fact that women activists had literally forced their way into the negotiations (Adams and Moodley 1993: 182-184).
2. These ideas changed the way many activists around the world understood democratization. In Brazil, for example, returned exiles "introduced new ideas and feminist concepts into existing groups," Alvarez writes; one woman activist told her, "We suddenly 'learned' all of these new terms." (Alvarez 1989: 118).
3. A similar, although slightly less public, process occurred in relation to the International Convention for the Elimination of All Forms of Discrimination Against Women, which the South African Parliament ratified in December 1995; feminist non-governmental organizations, working with civil servants, incorporated discussions of South Africa's commitments under the convention into discussions of the implications of the Beijing conference for South Africa (CEDAW Working Group 1996).
4. A smaller group of ANC activists also formed a more explicitly feminist Commission on Emancipation during the transition period.
5. In 1993, about 300,000 women a year were estimated to have had illegal abortions, and nearly 36,000 women needed surgery yearly to remove the residues of these illegal operations in South Africa (Makatini 1993).
6. Some of the prominent feminists initially appointed to the Commission were Cathi Albertyn, Nomboniso Gasa, Thenjiwe Mtintso, Phumelele Ntombela-Nzimbande, and Viviene Taylor.

References

Adam, Heribert and Moodley, Kogila 1993, *The Negotiated Revolution: Society and Politics in Post-Apartheid South Africa*, Johannesburg: Jonathan Ball Publishers and the University of California Press.

African National Congress 1990, 'Statement of the National Executive Committee of the ANC on the Emancipation of Women in South Africa,' *Agenda* 8: 19-23.

Albertyn, Catherine 1992, 'Women and Politics: Choices in Structural Mechanisms to Empower Women in a Democratic Government,' paper presented to the Workshop on Structural Mechanisms to Empower Women in a Democratic Government, Durban, 4-6 December, 1992.

--------- 1994a, 'Two Steps Forward,' *Work in Programme* 95: 22-3.

--------- 1994b, 'Women and the Transition to Democracy in South Africa,' in Murray (ed.), *Gender and the New South African Legal Order*, Cape Town: Juta and Co., pp. 39-63.

Alvarez, Sonia 1989, *Engendering Democracy in Brazil: Women's Movements in Transition Politics*, Princeton: Princeton University Press.

Anon., 1985, 'The Nairobi Conference,' *Work in Progress* 38: 29-32.

Berger, Iris 1991, *Threads of Solidarity: Women in South African Industry, 1900-1990*, Bloomington: Indiana University Press.

Biehl, Amy, n.d., 'Structures for women in political decision-making: a comparative study', Gender Project, Community Law Centre, University of the Western Cape, mimeo.

Bonnin, Debby 1992, 'Challenge from Within: DP document on women's status', *Agenda* 12: 44-46.

CEDAW Working Group 1996, 'Implementing CEDAW In South Africa: A Resource Document,' Gender Research Project, Centre for Applied Legal Studies, University of the Witwatersrand: mimeo.

Chatterjee, Partha 1989, 'Colonialism, Nationalism, and Colonized Women: The Contest in India,' *American Ethnologist* 16: 622-633.

Chinchilla, Norma Stoltz 1991, 'Marxism, Feminism and the Struggle for Democracy in Latin America,' *Gender and Society*.

Chowdhury, Najma and Nelson, Barbara with Carver, Kathryn A., Johnson, Nancy J. and O'Loughlin, Paula 1994, 'Redefining Politics: Patterns of Women's Political Engagement from a Global Perspective,' in Chowdhury and Nelson (eds.), *Women in Politics*, New Haven: Yale University Press.

Cumings, Bruce 1989, 'The Abortive Abertura: South Korea in the Light of Latin American Experience', *New Left Review* 173: 5-32

Department of Welfare 1996, *Report on the South African Government's Commitments Arising Out of the Fourth UN Women's Conference*, Beijing 1995 (Department of Welfare, 1996).

Fester, Gertrude, Adams, Feroza and Horn, Pat 1992, 'Women's Alliance,' *Agenda* 13: 29-34

Finnemore, Martha 1994, 'Negotiating power,' *Agenda* 20: 16-21.

Ford Foundation 1995, 'Annual Report: South Africa,' New York: Ford Foundation.

Fouche, Fidela 1994, 'Overcoming the sisterhood myth,' *Transformation* 23: 78-95.

Frazier, Geraldine 1996, 'How Government Departments Plan to Implement Their Beijing Commitments,' Speech, Johannesburg: mimeo, 22 February 1996.

Gaitskell, Deborah and Unterhalter, Elaine 1989, 'Mothers of the Nation: a comparative analysis of nation, race and motherhood in Afrikaner Nationalism and the African National Congress,' in Yuval-Davis and Anthias (eds.), *Woman-Nation-State,* London: Macmillan Press, pp. 58-78.

Gevisser, Mark 1994, 'Crossing the line,' in *Work in Progress* supplement, *Great Expectations: Women's Rights and the 1994 Election*, April/May: 3-5

Hassim, Shireen 1991, 'Gender, social location and feminist politics in South Africa,' *Transformation* 15: 65-81.

Hassim, Shireen, Meterlekamp, Jo and Todes, Alison 1987, ''A bit on the side'?: Gender struggles in the politics of transformation in South Africa', *Transformation* 5: 3-31.

Horn, Patricia 1991, 'What about women's emancipation?', *Transformation* 15: 25-39.

Keck, Margaret 1992, *The Workers' Party and Democratization in Brazil*, New Haven: Yale University Press.

Keck, Margaret and Sikkink, Kathryn 1994, 'Transnational Issue Networks in International Politics', unpublished.

Kemp, Amanda, Madlala, Nozizwe, Moodley, Asha and Salo, Elaine 1995, 'The Dawn of a New Day: Redefining South African Feminism,' in Basu (ed.), *The Challenge of Local Feminisms: Women's Movements in Global Perspective*, Boulder: Westview Press, pp.131-162.

Lind, Amy Conger 1992, 'Popular Women's Organizations in Ecuador,' in Escobar and Alvarez (eds.), *The Making of Social Movements in Latin America: Identity, Strategy and Democracy*, Boulder: Westview Press, pp.134-149.

Mabandla, Brigitte 1994, 'Choices for South African Women,' *Agenda* 20: 22-29.

Madlala, Nozizwe 1994, 'Building a Women's Movement,' *Work in Progress* supplement April/May: 6-8.

Makatini, Linda 1993, 'Abortion as a Human Rights Issue,' *Agenda* 17: 18-22.

Manzini, Mavivi 1994, 'TEC Sub-council on the Status of Women,' *Agenda* 20: 106.

Markoff, John 1993, 'Waves of Democracy: Latin America in the 1990s,' in Von Mettenheim and Malloy (eds.), *Deepening Democracy in Latin America*, University of Pittsburgh Press.

Marx, Anthony 1992, *Lessons of Struggle: South African Internal Opposition, 1960-1990*, New York: Oxford University Press.

McClintock, Anne 1993, 'Family Feuds: Gender, Nationalism and the Family,' *Feminist Review* 44: 61-80.

Mohanty, Chandra 1991, 'Introduction', in Mohanty and Torres (eds.), *Third World Women and the Politics of Feminism*, Bloomington: Indiana University Press, pp. 1-47.

Mokgalo Dorothy 1994, interview, 'Woman on the Move,' in *The Shopsteward* vol.3.3, June pp. 32-34.

Mothopeng, Ellen 1992, Untitled paper, *Agenda* 12: 47-49.

Moodley, Asha 1993, 'Black woman you are on your own,' *Agenda* 16: 44-48.

Mthintso, Thenjiwe 1993, 'Interview with Thenjiwe Mthintso', *Speak*, July 1993.

O'Donnell, Guillermo and Schmitter, Philippe 1986, *Transitions from Authoritarian Rule: Tentative Conclusions About Uncertain Democracies*, Baltimore: The Johns Hopkins Press.

Phillips, Anne 1991, *Engendering Democracy*, University Park: Pennsylvania University Press.

Pringle, Rosemary and Watson, Sophie 1992, 'Women's Interests and the Post-structuralist State', in Barrett and Phillips (eds.), *De-Stabilizing Theory: Contemporary Feminist Debates*, Stanford: Stanford University Press, pp. 53-73.

Przeworski, Adam 1991, *Democracy and the Market: Political and Economic Reforms in Eastern Europe and Latin America*, New York: Cambridge University Press.

Ramphele, Mamphela 1989, 'The Dynamics of Gender Politics in the Hostels of Cape Town: Another Legacy of the South African Migrant System', *Journal of Southern African Studies* 15: 393-414.

Rueschemeyer, Dietrich, Stephens Evelyn H. and Stephens, John 1992, *Capitalist Development and Democracy*, Chicago: University of Chicago Press.

Rumney, Reg 1994, 'ANC Supports Legalized Abortion,' *Weekly Mail and Guardian* 20-26/05/94, p.3.

Seidman, Gay 1993, 'No Freedom Without the Women: Mobilization and Gender in South Africa, 1970-1991,' *Signs: Journal of Women in Culture and Society* 18: 291-320.

--------- 1994, *Manufacturing Militance: Workers' Movements in Brazil and South Africa, 1970-1985*, Berkeley: University of California Press.

Segar, Julia and White, Caroline 1992, 'Family Matters and the State,' *Transformation* 29: 61-73.

Sentle, Sepei 1997, 'The Justice Department is planning to scrap the laws that repress women in SA,' *Independent On-line* (Johannesburg).

Serote, Pethu 1991, 'National Liberation Equals Women's Emancipation: A Myth Totally Exploded,' *Agenda* 11: 5-6.

Slabbert, F. 1992, *The Quest for Democracy: South Africa in Transition*, London: Penguin Books.

United Nations 1995, *Summary Report*, Fourth World Conference on Women (Beijing, China), Johannesburg: Government Printer

Walker, Cheryl 1982, *Women and Resistance in South Africa*, London: Onyx Press.

--------- 1990, 'Gender and the Development of the Migrant Labour System c. 1850-1930: An Overview,' in Walker (ed.), *Women and Gender in Southern Africa to 1945*, Cape Town: David Philip, pp. 168-196.

Women's National Coalition n.d., *Campaign for Effective Equality*, Interim research report, Johannesburg: mimeo.

6 Global Forces, Life Projects, and the Place of Care: Conversations with Women in Project Head Start

LUCIE WHITE[1]

I'm from Mississippi too. That's why I'm here fighting. People have tried to get me to go up North, but I'm planning to stay here and make Mississippi a better place to live. And as long as we continue to go up North, and run away from the situation, we will never make it any better.[2]

Introduction: On the Edge of Hope

To many ordinary people, "globalization" is real. The world seems like it is really changing, in multiple but related ways. Just like the AT&T commercials tell us, people all over the world are getting more connected. Culturally distinctive lifeways are becoming less sealed off from one another. People, both rich and poor, are moving more freely between nations. Big companies are dividing up their activities and dispersing them across hemispheric boundaries. These processes are not entirely new. They are touching different peoples in very different ways. However, more and more people are starting to feel the dislocations that go with "globalization" in their own lives.

Yet at the same time that globalization is becoming real for more and more people, it is also a space of ideological and cultural contest. It is a collective mindscape, on which historically-grounded rhetoric, narrative, and imagery gets reworked through popular culture and broadcast through the voices of powerful public figures, all over the world. Like the grand finale of a summertime fireworks extravaganza, this explosion of words and pictures casts an unreal but insistent light on the day to day changes that global integration is making in common people's lives.

This volume collects essays on "globalizations" from an unusual group of academics. We have come together to document, analyze, and ponder the shifting space between what is real and what is spoken about "the global." Yet we have come together around more than a common set of scholar's questions. We have also come together around a common commitment to do our scholarly work in ways that enhance justice. We do not take up this commitment with the illusion that it will be easy to honor as we study globalization. Indeed, we share the view that the keywords of our common scholarly project – discourse, culture, ideology, power, history, and even the "real" – mark fields of contest rather than zones of certainty. Some of us do not say the word "globalization" except in the plural, in deference to the multiple threads of meaning that are tangled up in the conceptual field for which it stands.

That said, however, there are two fairly clear vantage-points from which we, as scholars, tend to place ourselves to do our common work. That is, we have come up with two places from which to get a good angle on the space between the real and the spoken about globalization. We have come up with two places that let us analyze that space in ways that further justice. First, we can place ourselves side by side with common peoples: those who are the consumers, the spectators, the exotic "indigenous" others, the dispossessed, the disappeared from the Cosmopolitan Scene. These are the locals, the ones who are said to lack the clout or connections to produce global trends, deploy global forces, or define what the global "really" means.

From this place, the scholar's first task is to listen. Her task is to get inside the talk of subaltern peoples, and then to trace, translate, record, represent, and perform the voices of resistance and hope that she hears. This scholar's task is both subtle and uncertain: she seeks to show, up close and with conviction, how people with little access to conventional forms of political and cultural power nonetheless take part in reproducing and thus transforming the meaning of "global forces" in their own lives. They do that work through the very act of surviving – of living over – these forces, as real people, who are enmeshed in all kinds of human attachments even as they yearn to be free.

The second vantage-point that we take as scholars is that of the discourse critic. From this position we attend to the language that common peoples use to make sense of their experiences of globalization. Where does their language come from? What basic notions shape its common images, storylines, and grammar rules? How are common peoples' ideas about the world shaped as they use it? To ask these questions, we use the methods of the linguist, the intellectual historian, the media sociologist, the cultural anthropologist, the rhetorician, and the literary critic. We go inside the imagined worlds where powerful discourse gets made. We seek to map how practices like collective remembrance, market transaction, artistic and cultural production, law, and politics interact to shape the discourses that are available to common peoples to give voice to their complex lived experiences of globalization.

Those are the two clear vantage-points from which we, as justice-seeking critics of the global, have typically done our work. This essay seeks out a third place from which to study the interplay between commanding images and storylines about global change and the ways of common people's lives. This third vantage-point is not located inside the spheres where powerful ideas about globalization are produced are diffused. Nor is this vantage-point located beside the paths that common peoples walk as they live their lives. Instead, this third vantage-point questions the conceptual separation between hegemony on the one hand, and marginalization on the other, that the other two positions take for granted.

This third vantage-point's hybrid methods seek to map out practices of domination and emancipation in the politics of globalization, without collapsing those complex but ordered patterns into two classes of persons: bad people with wealth and privilege, on the one hand, and good people on the margins, on the other. Let me explain. First, from this third position, we do not merely listen for the voices of ordinary people on the home grounds from which they feel, name, and thereby resist hegemonic images and narratives of the global in their own lives. Rather, we bring the discourse critic's methods into our practices of listening, displacing the idea that ordinary people are either passive consumers of dominant ideology, or self-possessed masters of their fates. We ask how common peoples subtly resist and rework the given language as they use it to give voice to their memories, activities, and aspirations.

Similarly, we bring the methods of patient observation and engaged, empathic listening to the spheres where powerful discourses are produced. We listen especially for unlikely moments in which common peoples, through their social movements, have insinuated themselves into those realms. We look closely at those moments, asking if they sometimes give rise to distinctively open-textured discourse rules, rules that do not merely allow common people to speak their own truths *through* the given language, but also authorize them to critique and revise the code itself. Thus, from this third location, we can track the real social and political histories out of which authoritative discourses are made. We can also track the ways that common people have helped to shape those discourses, both "on the inside" of realms of official power at times of intense social movement, and through their everyday practices of using their given languages, at times of quiescence.

Through this hybrid work, the justice-oriented scholar seeks not merely to map the space between the real and the spoken about the global. She also seeks hope for justice amid the powerful forces of globalization. Finding hope requires one to find the thin edge between what is actually going on and how it might best be imagined. It requires one to listen and critique with the ear of a magical realist, seeking out the very best that might have been, to enable more paths forward. This scholar will look for the unlikely moments when ordinary people have participated in shaping ideologically powerful discourses. She will look for the unlikely moments when ordinary people seize upon the gaps and ambiguities in authoritative legal and cultural texts, and fill out those spaces with strong, subversive social action. In addition to emboldening our hope that the global can indeed be spoken and experienced differently, such work can help us to theorize the ideological potential of grassroots social movements in the current era. What cultural texts have best enabled social movement of ordinary people in the past? How have social movements insinuated themselves into the histories through which those texts were produced?

I offer these three scholarly vantage-points as a back-drop for the essay that follows, which centres on a popular and successful social welfare programme in the United States: Project Head Start. The programme funds community-based religious and civic organizations to operate day-care centres for young children in poor neighborhoods. It was authorized by the United States Congress in the mid-1960s, as part of President Lyndon Johnson's War on Poverty. That programme's flagship statute, the Economic Opportunity Act of 1964, mandated that Head Start provide "maximum feasible participation" for the low income families served by OEO programmes. Subsequent federal regulations placed the formal governance of local Head Start programmes in the hands of elected parent boards. And the broad mandate of client participation created an opening for low income women to come together for services and activities that are directed toward their own, as well as their children's, well-being and development.

Head Start is uniquely successful among the federally funded United States social welfare programmes for the poor. It is also unique among them in its basic legal character. Most United States poor laws distribute meager cash or in-kind benefits to categorically qualified low-income persons under conditions that are stigmatizing, punitive, and isolating. The Head Start law, in contrast, is constitutional, rather than redistributive, in its basic logic. Indeed, the law is not merely constitutional. It pushes beyond the confines of formal liberalism, and wrestles with the constitutional terms that might secure a strong version of plural democracy.

First, let me name two key features of Head Start's law that make it unmistakably constitutional, rather than merely redistributive, in its linguistic and juridical force. The first is that rather than merely channeling money into individual hands, the Head Start statute establishes a new place for citizenship, in several senses of the word. It establishes a new order of street-level social institutions, designating the design of classrooms, governance bodies, and a civic space in which low income women and men can meet, interact, and deliberate. Thus, it creates a new law-ordained ground – real, symbolic, and imagined – on which low income people are called to come together, not just as clients, but also as citizens. The law's rhetoric sets the moral tone for this new place; its regulations lay out the precise contours of that new place's institutional shape; its funding formulas ensure that the place can be realized, in bricks and mortar and paychecks for the teachers and hot lunches for the children. Thus, the law marks a new place for caring and civic activity and sets the terms on which real people are empowered and expected to inhabit it. Second, Head Start's law is constitutional in that it explicitly configures the lawmaking powers and procedures within its domain, granting a large share of these powers to low income women.

Making new places and distributing law-making powers within them is a feature of any constitution. The law of Head Start goes on to imagine this place and configure those powers in ways that push beyond the limits of the dominant constitutional vision of the modern era, liberal legalism.[3] It does so in two important ways. First, Head Start's law challenges its low-income "legislators" and rank and file clients to act, as citizens of the programme, in a strongly pluralist way. Thus, Head Start's law requires and challenges each local parent group and policy council both to respect and to work into its day to day routines the multiple languages, moral norms, and cultural practices of all whom it brings together.

Second, Head Start's constitution charges its low-income legislators, teachers, and citizen-clients to place a higher value on the *practice* of care than the kinds of outcomes that can be produced and accounted for through the modernist disciplines of market exchange, bureaucratic control, and professional expertise. This charge challenges its citizen-clients to risk their own security in the hope that how they act together, rather than what they produce, will make for a better world. It creates a place of risk and of hope, a place where identities and boundaries are fluid, rather than fixed, as care demands. This charge creates a place where people who feel buffeted by powerful and confusing global forces can come together, not so much to resist those forces, but to make sense of them in ways that put at risk everything that had secured their power.

Head Start's unusual constitutional template was produced at a distinctive moment in United States political and social history. The programme was established at the height of the US Civil Rights movement, when African Americans and their allies came together to dismantle the regime of race segregation that replaced chattel slavery. In the first decade after Head Start was established, its national level bureaucracy included several African Americans who had been active in this movement. These people played important roles inside Head Start's bureaucracy, adding legislative and regulatory detail to the programme's open-textured constitution. These details enhanced the plural democratic possibilities in that founding law.

At the same time that they added important detail to the programme's legal framework, these unlikely bureaucrats played a second, equally important historical role. Empowered and coerced by the increasingly militant street-level Civil Rights and anti-poverty movements, they turned an unprecedented level of attention to the programme's grassroots activities. Indeed, they took several innovative steps to document the practices of effective local Head Start parents and teachers, and to bring wider attention to them. Many of those local voices were from African American women who had learned practices of caring and local self-governance within African American communities of resistance in the Deep South, and then migrated to Northern and Western cities in the decades after the Second World War. The culture, practice, and even law of the programme, on both the national and local levels, was deeply influenced by the voices of these African American migrants, particularly as amplified by the programme's national-level African American bureaucrats. Their efforts to facilitate cross-communication among local practitioners both strengthened local practice across the country and reinforced the law's rhetorical promise of local, plural democracy.

After a first decade of very high energy, in which the programme's unique legal template was both refined and animated, Head Start entered a more quiescent phase. Social movement subsided. Its constitution, which had been shaped during the Civil Rights movement, gained legitimacy through successful practice. At the same time, less ambitious experiments in ground-level plural democracy in other War on Poverty programmes were faltering in the absence of social movement and getting dismantled. By the early 1990s, Head Start centres were thriving in countless communities across the United States, including cities like Los Angeles that had drawn great numbers of Latin American migrants during the civil wars and economic dislocations of the 1970s and 1980s.

Immigrant women entering Los Angeles in these years present a harsh picture of lives caught up in global forces. Even in countries that were not at war, trends linked to a changing global economy – growing wealth disparities, dangerous and oppressive job conditions, increasing destitution, an erosion of hope – drove women North. Going North was a rupture: it tore women away from their families and communities. Yet at the same time, it was a strategy that women chose to pursue, precisely in order to care more adequately for themselves and their kin. They often followed the filaments of family networks across political borders, to join siblings, cousins, and children on the other side. Rather than assimilate themselves to a new home country, they reworked their idea of homeplace into cross-border circuits of caring, through which both family and the cash that sustained it continuously cycled back and forth.

As they made these journeys, women often found themselves caught up in a double-bind. At the same time that Northern cities invited Latina women's labour, those places also blocked these women's entry. Their presence inside the US border was criminalized. Their bodies were hunted down. Thus, the journey North placed women in a state of terror that magnified their sense of victimization to "global forces," while undermining their sense that the journey North enacted their will to care. Thus, both the experience of passage into the US and the political climate within US borders eroded their power to see the forces around them, and their own actions, in a hopeful, life-affirming way.

It was at such moments of moral stress that Latina women sometimes found their way to Head Start. Because of its unique constitution, the programme offered such women a sanctuary. It gave them a place of refuge, in the North, against the forces that seemed to assault them from all sides for seeking to care for their children. Not only did Head Start offer these women a moment's protection from immigration services raids, police helicopters, and interethnic rage. It also gave them some space to care for others and themselves without fear of reprisal. Head Start challenged them to care across differences of race, language, and ethnicity, as well as for their own. Thus, Head Start invited them to expand their sense of family and neighbours, defying, in their own caring practices, the boundary-drawing logic that drove the violence against them. Finally, it gave some women the chance to improvise new ways of participating as citizens, in their children's pre-school classrooms. And indeed, it is in such small improvisations that the best clues to the enigma of meaningful democratic citizenship in a new global epoch are likely to emerge.

Thus, in recent years Head Start programmes in border regions like southern California have given refuge to Latina women who have been drawn North in search of care. Head Start has offered such refuge because an earlier generation of migrants, emboldened by social movement and assisted by allies in the government, had brought their voices and practices inside Head Start's constitutional process. What follows are excerpts from conversations with two generations of Head Start women that helped me to see the programme, and women's place within it, in this way. The first excerpt, "Going North," recounts the journey of a young woman from her home in Mexico to Los Angeles in order to earn money to care for the mother and siblings she left behind. The excerpt ends with her connection to a Head Start centre in Watts. The second excerpt, "Before and After the Journey: Inventing Head Start's Law," traces how an earlier wave of migrants to Los Angeles, this time from the Deep South, gave the programme a constitution that, three decades later, would make such connections possible. The excerpts explore how common peoples can use law-ordained institutions like Head Start to enable hopeful life projects. They also explore how social movement can sometimes enable common people to influence the shape and culture of such institutions, so as to make such creative uses of their order a little more possible.

Going North

N. M. and I had finally found a quiet place for our first real conversation, in the space under the stairs that led up to the play-yard from the church's basement. Outside, the sun was blazing, which was rare in this part of Los Angeles except in the dead of winter. It hardly mattered to us, though, because the sun hadn't reached into the basement from the wide-open play-yard door. The children, including Ms. M.'s four year old daughter, Daniela, were out on the play-yard while the teachers and parent volunteers prepared the tables for lunch. Every morning, two men in their twenties, well aware of how lucky they were to be employed, would deliver two big metal trays of food – fried chicken and tacos and corn on the cob – to the Church of God, as well as the Education and Training Institute (ETI)'s[4] ten other sites, from the programme's central kitchen in Watts.

   N. M. had come North to find work and safety. Eventually, she had found her way to a temporary resting place in Project Head Start. All of the other women in the Head Start programme that N.M.'s daughter attends, like N. herself, could trace their families' origins to places that lay South of this city, Chiapas, or Honduras, or the Ivory Coast of Africa, by way of Alabama and then Saint Louis, or Chicago, or Detroit. Most of these women have not been as lucky as N. M. Their lives remain in transit. They move back and forth, South to North, in pick-ups, or second-hand cars, or Greyhound buses, or Amtrak trains, seeking work and safety, making home. For three decades, Head Start has been a place in common on these journeys, a place to find bearings, to raise voices, to wash dishes, to share a meal.

Head Start is the popular, federally-funded pre-school programme for low income children that was launched by United States President Lyndon Johnson in 1965. Since then, the programme has been marked by wide bipartisan support. By 1992, when I met with N. M., it was one of Lyndon Johnson's few social welfare innovations that was not at risk of extinction in an era marked by lots of talk about "new global pressures," steadily increasing wealth inequality, and social welfare retrenchment. The Head Start programme was left largely unaffected by these trends, perhaps because it is a small programme, which is more focused on making new public spaces for low income women to come together than on shifting cash in their direction.

The Head Start law and regulations funnel federal dollars to local non-profits and government entities to run pre-school and family support programmes that comply with strict regulatory requirements. These requirements include such unlikely features for a United States social welfare programme as open-door access for parents to their children's classrooms, a voice for parents in the local programme's basic management decisions, parent-directed educational activities, and a priority for parents to be hired as programme staff.

I was first drawn to Head Start in the early 1980s, while working in a legal aid programme in a rural county in a part of the American South a few miles from my childhood home. I worked with impoverished women with young children, the daughters of those sharecroppers, farm-hands, and maids who had not moved North in the 1940s or 1950s to escape Jim Crow. My job as a lawyer was to work the federal poor laws to get these women cash. In my first weeks in the job, I learned about Project Head Start. When I asked women questions about welfare, they would answer by talking about Head Start. They lumped all of the other social programmes, like income subsidies, Food Stamps, Medicaid Stickers and vouchers for day-care, under the heading of "welfare," and called them, simply, "the man." When they talked about Head Start, in contrast, their voices sounded different, less angry, less afraid.

As I got to know a few women better, I would go, on occasion, to their Head Start centre, to talk at a parent meeting or to attend a holiday party or to leave a message for a client who didn't have a phone. Eventually, several women asked me to be a "community member" of their policy council, the client-governance body that the programme was required to convene to comply with federal law. As I grew more familiar with the programme, I became more intrigued. The programme's aura of "success" is beyond dispute, as much among the low income women who use it, as among the wider publics who view it, like a kaleidoscope's glimmering mirrors, at the far end of a dark tube. Yet as I began to listen closely to the women who had drawn me into the programme, who know it, its contradictions started to jar me: a cast-iron legal framework, that renders "maximum feasible participation" in Fordist terms; the teachers' harsh voices, demanding an order from three and four year old children that seems at once to be wise, defiant, and defeated; the children's own ebullient voices, chanting their rote-learned letters as they fidget on the floor; and the women's sharp, wistful judgments of the programme's failures, judgments that confirm what they know about broken promises, and point toward something within them that eludes reason, a place where hope will not let go.

What secrets, I wondered, what kinds of insight about our practices of social policy design, would come forth through the stories of low-income women who had become involved in Project Head Start? In the mid-1980s, when I moved from my legal aid office in North Carolina into full-time law teaching in California, I could finally pursue this question in my own research. After reviewing Head Start's legislative and administrative history, I concluded that the insights I sought did not lie buried in government archives or social science data banks. Rather, what I sought to uncover lay dispersed among the thousands of low-income women who had sought refuge and found safety in Head Start programmes, on the ground. The knowledge I was seeking would come forth only as women were given the time to talk at length about their journeys toward the programme and their work within it, in the multiple contexts of their lives. Eventually, I took a year off from teaching to talk with women like N. M. about Head Start. I interviewed women in two Head Start programmes: the North Carolina programme in the county where I had worked as a legal aid lawyer, and the ETI Head Start, where N. M.'s child was enrolled. The North Carolina programme served about three hundred rural families, most of them African American. E.T.I Head Start served about seven hundred African American and Latino families in eleven sites that sprawled across South Central Los Angeles. On a first impression, these two programmes seem to be located in entirely different worlds. Most of the women in the North Carolina programme had never left the county. Most of the women in Los Angeles had come into the programme as exiles from civil war, economic destitution, or racial violence. Yet whether they came to Head Start before or after such a journey, the women in both of these sites shared certain fundamentals: very low incomes, multiple burdens on their time and energy, and a determination to find the space that they needed in order to care.

I had met N. M. a couple of times before our interview, at agency-wide parent meetings, and in Daniela's Head Start classroom, where she was a

regular volunteer. But this was our first sustained conversation. I talked to
N.M. right after she adjourned the January meeting of her site's parent group,
of which she was Chair. Her body still seemed to pulse with energy from a
task well done. She had grown up in a large landless peasant family in
Mazatlan. Neither English nor Spanish was her first language, but she had
seized both of these tongues with a fierce, gentle determination, and had
made them her own. At the parent meeting, she wove back and forth between
these two languages with the impromptu artistry of jazz. She spoke to me in
English, with her voice full and her vowels open and her hands repeating the
force of her words.

As a legal aid lawyer, I had sat in places like this with many low income
women, helping them fill out welfare applications or practice their testimony
for eviction trials or foreclosure hearings or disability reviews. But these
sessions were different. N. M. had not come to me with a problem.
Nonetheless, I would ask her intrusive questions, and then cut and paste the
transcript of her voice in an effort to speak my own. I knew that the project
was problematic, but so were our lives. To calm myself, I decided to
approach the interview as though I were taking a deposition. My carefully
scripted questions were tight and intrusive, damming up conversation just
when it started to flow. Only later in the conversation, when I could muster
up the will to be calm and watchful when my interlocutor was silent, would
I begin to hear her voice:

> My mother was a good mother . . . who was doing like father and mother at
> the same time. My father was always coming in and leaving out. . . . She
> used to work and she was taking care of us . . . It was kind of hard, over in
> Mexico. I don't know if you know a lot of people, you know, family, in
> Mexico. I was the lucky one that I could go to school, but the older ones
> couldn't go. We didn't have any money . . . The only money my mother
> could get was for feeding us . . . We had nothing; we didn't have clothes.

N. M.'s mother quit school in third grade, and then worked as long as she
could, doing laundry and cleaning houses. When she got too old to keep
working, she had to look to her children, four boys and four girls, to bring in
money for food. N. was the sixth child.

Her older brothers and sisters had to quit school when they were children,
like their mother. The boys went back and forth across the border to find
work. One of her older sisters found a steady job in an LA garment factory,
got married, and bought a home. N. went to work as early as she can
remember, cleaning rich people's houses and caring for their needs. But she

and her two younger sisters were lucky; they didn't have to drop out of school until they were teens.

What she most remembers about grade school was the girls whose families had money. The rich girls could see that N. was different – she didn't have money – from her clothes. She didn't get to participate in special activities, like folklore and sports. Other girls got chosen as chairperson for class events:

> They never put anybody like me ... They always put the rich kids ... I remember saying, "Oh man. If I could do that." ... I could never have done it. ... Over in Mexico, over in the school that I was in, you know, even though you were smart, the money counts. The money always counts.

For three years after she finished high school, she studied computers, on the advice of her mother, who had told her that computers were going to be in the future:[5]

> [My mother] was smart. She really likes to read, and I think she read about computers. I remembered that she was reading, always reading, always reading.[6]

But she couldn't find a job in computers, so she took a job in a factory that made tortillas. She went to work at five in the morning, and worked until four thirty or five in the afternoon. She made a hundred pesos, about five or six dollars, a day. The wage was good for Mazatlan, but the work was hard, and the owner was bad. In the mornings she had to feed the dough through cutting machines that had big knives:

> You have to stick your hand like this, be real careful, otherwise the knife that was cutting, it could cut your hands. ... I used to cut my fingers a lot.[7]
> You can't stop working, even if you cut your hands. You just ... grab something because you got to be faster. You had to be faster than that machine. Otherwise ... it'll be messed up. So, you didn't have the time to take care of yourself.[8]

In the afternoons, she would put the tortillas in the ovens. That part of the job made her burn her hands:

> Oh man, I can't do this job. No more. I can't do it ... [But] you know, you get used to it ... I have to keep going. I have to keep working.[9]

Her sister who had gone North to Los Angeles urged N. to do the same. It was "hard over there also," but if you were lucky, you could make a hundred pesos in less than an hour. For N., the main thing was helping her mother; the younger children had nothing, not even clothes. So in 1980, at age 19, she decided to go North:

Tell me what you remember from when you first arrived here?

Well, I remember, first of all, I didn't have my papers. You know, I, you know. So I was kind of scared, right? I was kind of scared to come over here to the United States. And when I was, when I got here I was still scared.

How did you make the trip from Mexico?

You really want me to tell you? [laugh]

Whatever you feel comfortable with.

Well, well, I think everybody knows that.

Her answers had aroused my lawyer's training. As a lawyer, I had helped many low income women prepare for welfare hearings before low level bureaucrats – tired-looking middle-aged women, white men with BAs in business who were going to night school to get better jobs. For the most part, these hearing officers were plain-spoken people, many of them union members, all of them fed up with speed-ups and lay-offs and salary freezes. Their lives were strung along the fragile borders of the suburbs, like laundry; they were doing their best to educate their children, and to keep their families white. I had become fairly good at winning these people over to a darker complexioned woman's plea to be excused from the welfare's stringent rules, either because she was sick, or because she lived in fear of a battering spouse, or because the car she used to drive her kids to day-care had broken down. Through trial and error, I had learned a tactic that could just about always win such hearings, hands down. It was simple: you had to coach the client to find the words to tell her story like a picture, in great detail. Then she had to speak it to the hearing officer, right in the eye. When it worked, the tactic would jar the hearing officer back into a private world – a world of things too close to remember, except through another's voice. After it was over, the officer could not explain why he had been moved.

Something that seemed like instinct pushed me to pose the gentle
questions that would draw forth Ms. M.'s words. Two fragments of vaguely
remembered reading came into my head at the same time. The first, from a
love poem by a Second Wave Lesbian poet, called all women into a "politics
of transliteration." "Like amnesiacs in a ward on fire," she had written, "we
must find words or burn."[10] The second, from Toni Morrison, searched for
the heart of darkness within this humanist plea:

> Consider the ways that Africanism . . . serves as a vehicle for manipulating
> love and the imagination as defenses against the psychic costs of guilt and
> despair. . . .
> We need to analyze the manipulation of the Africanist narrative (that is, the
> story of a black person, the experience of being bound and/or rejected) as
> a means of meditation – both safe and risky – on one's own humanity.[11]

My mind got caught for a moment. In this silence, Ms. M. continued:

> Ah, I was coming . . . I had two cousins over here, but they weren't legal,
> weren't here . . . My sister told them . . . "Try to help her over here. Don't
> leave her over there." Because it was dangerous, and you know, coming
> from across the border. . . . So they said ah, they said ok. . . . You know,
> they, we crossed the border. We crossed the freeway. It was hard.
>   Now that I was here, I remember I say, "Huh. Did I do this, man? Did
> I do this!" And now that I see it, I try to tell people not to do that. I say,
> "Man, do something else, but don't do that. . . . I was lucky. I was really
> lucky. Now that I see it, it had danger in it. I remember, I just keep . . .
> that's in my mind all the time. I remember the person that helped [me]
> escape. "You don't stop here. You see all these cars are coming. Let them
> stop, but you don't stop." And I didn't even know why he was saying that.
> I didn't even know the freeway. I didn't even know what the freeway was.
> So, they told me, you don't stop here. You make them stop, you run and
> run. You see a car coming, don't stop, you run and run and run. And I say,
> "Okay, okay." I remember I was so tired! I was so tired. Tired. I didn't
> even know were I was going. What I was going through. I used to have a
> skirt and my sister told my cousin to let me have pants. But they forgot to
> tell me. So I was wearing a skirt, I was wearing shoes like this. And I was
> running and running. And I was saying, "You go ahead. I can't, I can't go.
> I can't make it no more." . . . And . . . They grabbed [my] arms and said,
> "N. come on, come on." So I made it. . . . It was in the middle of the night
> . . . one o'clock in the morning . . . I was scared, so scared. . . .
>   . . . They used to have helicopters, horses, and motorcycles. The first
> night, the first week when I was here, I remember, in my sister's house, I

was eating and then ... the airplanes. [I used to] go under the table . . . When the airplane goes brrrr, I used to grab my sister . . . I used to be scared . . . I thank God for the Amnesty."[12]

After N. settled in at her sister's place, she started to take an evening English class. Then she found work, as a stock handler at a garment factory warehouse. At first she worked the floor; after three years, she became a supervisor. She was paid the US minimum wage.

She married a Salvadoran refugee who had started his own business. After the Amnesty, she had three children in three years, Daniela, Freddie, and Kevin. She developed high blood pressure during the fourth month of her last pregnancy. Kevin was born disabled. After his birth, she quit working in the warehouse, and started volunteering in Daniela's Head Start classroom. After she quit, her family lived on her son's disability benefits and her husband's job.

From N.M.'s first day at Head Start, she "loved" it. After a month of daily volunteering, the other parents elected her to chair their Parents' Committee. She presides over their monthly meetings, and urges other parents to get involved. This site has the highest number of hours of parent involvement in the ETI Head Start programme, in large part because the Head teacher in Daniela's classroom, Ms. F., works hard to help the Latina women, particularly those without papers, to feel welcomed when they come into the class. Several of the women who volunteer regularly in Ms. F.'s classroom come to Head Start after working all night in third-shift jobs. Other women volunteer in the classroom to seek respite from violence.

Before and After the Journey: Inventing Head Start's Law

Local Head Start programmes exist because of federal dollars and the dense web of federal laws, regulations, and performance standards that dictate exactly how that money must be spent. The programme seeks to improve the health and welfare of poor children through a plethora of discrete regulations, ranging from a requirement that they brush their teeth after their federally-funded breakfast, to requirements that their parents be offered instruction in parenting skills, and be visited in their homes by a staff member at least twice a year. Programmes are monitored by officials from the US Department of Health and Human Services. Funding can be withdrawn if a programme's level of compliance with federal regulations gets too far out of line. After reading the Head Start law and regulations, a legal scholar could rightly conclude that this network of street-level institutions would not exist but for Big Brother's iron hand.

The broad outlines of the programme's official history are straightforward. It was ostensibly designed by a group of early childhood experts who were drawn together by Lyndon Johnson. The first Head Start programmes were funded under the 1964 Economic Opportunity Act, and thereby were required by statute to ensure the "maximum feasible participation" of their clients in all phases of their activity. In the stormy years that followed Head Start's founding, it was touted by the Office of Economic Opportunity's chief Sergeant Shriver as the "good girl" of the War on Poverty. Its popularity provided some "political ballast," again to quote Shriver, that helped to keep the embattled community action agencies afloat in the face of attack by the white-dominated state and local political establishments that those agencies were seen to undermine.

Through the 1970s and into the 1980s, Head Start proved to be the single War on Poverty programme that thrived while others faltered. By the late 1980s, it was widely regarded as the "Crown Jewel" of the War on Poverty, to quote Jesse Jackson. Proposals to expand the programme to serve all poor children were seized upon by politicians seeking a quick fix for urban poverty. Lyndon Johnson biographer Robert Dallek has sought to untangle some of the passion that led Lyndon Johnson to wage his poverty war. Johnson ascended to the presidency at a moment of both chaos and opportunity, for one with his grandiose ambitions and half-hidden vulnerabilities. He was a child of Jim Crow Texas, a sensitive child, we are told, and he was white. He seized his moment, masterminding the back-room deals that restored the franchise to African Americans citizens and expanding the welfare state to provide health care for many of the nation's poor. Yet, these solid legislative victories were largely eclipsed, in the public's memory, by his wars.

LBJ announced his war for the poor with fanfare: it would vanquish injustice in that Other America, once and for all. Yet subsequent observers have dismissed this crusade as little more than a modern day poor law, chiding the poor to stop their idleness, while deferring to hidden market rules that gave those with the wealth all the power. LBJ's assault on poverty did not challenge the wisdom that viewed unemployment as the safety-valve against inflation, or that counted on union busting and race/gendered labour markets as the only sure way to keep our sweatshops at home. Rather, LBJ's War on Poverty targeted poor people and their neighborhoods. Its basic weapon was "democracy." By shaping their own social programmes and community development initiatives, poor people would have good reason to feel proud of their own achievements, even when their efforts failed to unstick them from the bottom of the bag.

But the most cynical observers of the War on Poverty's ideological premises may sell it somewhat short. For even if the Economic Opportunity Act can be viewed as a modern-day poor law, the War on Poverty, at least as it was understood and enacted in some communities, can also be understood as a project of liberation. It was a part of the movement toward freedom that was sweeping across the African diaspora in the 1960s, in both Northern and Southern spheres. The OEO's emphasis on poor people's participation in local institutions, in their own communities, evokes Gramscian, Africanist theories of hegemony and resistance in a neo-colonial world. According to these theories, colonial power gets implanted deep within the psyche of the colonial subject. Yet because that power pushes against the body's remembered wisdom, it is always unstable, always on guard. In such an order domination and resistance are everywhere together. Yet in order to get beyond episodes of violence, resistance needs some space of its own. It needs a home base, a free space, to pull itself together into a movement of liberation.

Further research into Head Start's legal history convinced me that these two master templates for the War on Poverty do not do justice to the complexity with which early Head Start activists enacted the programme's legal mandates at the grassroots level. As I dug deeper into the programme's federal legislative record, I recovered hundreds of testimonials from low income women, both parents and teachers, who had become politically active through their involvement in local Head Start programmes. These testimonials were interspersed between explanations of cost sharing formulas and expert testimony on the programme's behavioral and cultural goals. These women's testimony was undoubtedly scripted by the lawyers who worked for national Head Start advocacy groups. Yet taken together, these testimonials were more suggestive of African American conversion rituals than the bland prose of Washington lawyers. Indeed, in both their plot-lines and their rhetoric, these testimonials evoked Zora Neal Hurston's lyrical accounts of African American conversion rituals[13] and Albert Raboteau's reflections on the continuing force of those motifs in contemporary African American cultural practice.[14]

These official testimonials repeatedly addressed several themes. The most emphatic and persistent was about refuge. Women recounted how the Head Start programme gave them a place of safety in stressful, indeed, endangered lives. Curious, I thought, that such a space of refuge from what was often state-sanctioned violence could itself be constituted, in law at least, by the state's own hand:

> Starting to work with Head Start made me find my place.[15] ... I have a place to go. It's a place to get together ... to gossip and lose your tensions. You find out that other people have the same tensions as you ... you can get together and talk.[16]
>
> * * *
>
> I felt a sense of despair, with little self-esteem ... I thought my life was without meaning. One day I heard there was a Head Start class down the street, at a time when I had lost all hope of ever being anything but an outcast. ... I learned that I was not the only young mother or dropout. I started putting time in at the class. The teacher would give me work to do with the children. I remember picking up a book to read to the children and the fear I felt. I realized that I needed a Head Start.[17] ...
>
> * * *
>
> Twenty years ago, without speaking English, with a 4-year old child, I walked into a small classroom and immediately I felt very welcome. ... There is not the language barrier. It doesn't matter if we don't speak the language or we have an accept. There's always a place for us. ... These are the kinds of programmes that we need ... programmes that don't judge us. Programmes that have the opportunity to educate.
>
> * * *
>
> I encountered many friendly faces with smiles ... I did not need to be afraid of saying the wrong things ...[18] ... They were friendly and understood where I was coming from. It wasn't like walking into a bunch of strangers. ... They'll work with you instead of against you.[19]
>
> * * *
>
> When I came ... my self esteem was real low and I looked at myself as a little bud, but the flowers were wilting instead of growing. ... But as I got more involved in Head Start ... I got the Head Start feeling ...[20]

The second recurring theme in the legislative record was about how being in this place of safety gave some women a chance to hear their own voice:

> Before I entered the Head Start Programme, I was afraid. I wouldn't talk; my voice got shaky, and my knees would tremble ... and I couldn't talk in front of anybody. I was afraid to open my mouth. But my programme director pushed me. She told me I could do it ... and I kept trying. I kept getting up. She kept pushing me and I didn't stop trying. Today, I'm a new person ... I'm not afraid to talk anymore.[21]
>
> * * *

I began writing poetry. I was never interested in writing before, but the frustration of a bad marriage, a houseful of babies . . . needed a mode of expression. . . . The staff at Head Start found out about [my poems] and I gave them permission to print them in the Head Start parent Newsletter. . . . Head Start was there once again, providing outlets for my frustrated, creative urges. . . . Having a voice is one thing, but being able to express that voice is another, and having someone to listen when you express your opinion is the greatest success of Head Start. They listen![22]

The third recurring theme was about helping other women, how Head Start was a place where such helping was possible, and its value could be felt:

Ms. Boyd enjoyed her experience so much that she helped to recruit other parents so they could share the joy. "You feel good because you give yourself."[23]

* * *

I love getting the chance to help other people the same way I was helped.[24]

* * *

The moral support I got from Head Start down through the years has helped me to climb up the ladder. Many times it seemed like the next rung was missing or would break under the pressure - but I could always count on . . . Head Start to be there . . . I think the most important thing . . . [is] that through the support I have received, I have learned how to support others.[25]

* * *

Head Start helps you to get involved in your future. It's because of Head Start that I am training other people in assertiveness, leadership, and politics. Head Start has helped me to reach people, to encourage them. It makes me feel good to help others.[26]

The last recurring theme was about fundamental change:

If it had not been for Head Start . . . I might still be a maid. . . . Head Start gave me the first job I ever had that did not include pushing a mop . . .[27]

When I began my fieldwork in North Carolina and Los Angeles, I heard echoes of these themes in countless real-time conversations with Head Start women. In Los Angeles, Latina and African American women would come to their children's classrooms every day, to volunteer their time. Some would simply wash dishes from the mid-day meal, explaining that this was their way to take part in their children's education. Some would come to work with children who had been silenced by violence. They explained that this work made them feel better, and stronger, in their own lives. The multiple meanings that these women drew from their own work in the programme did not repeat the official language of the programme's laws. Rather, the meanings that they attributed to their work were negotiated through their own conversations with other Head Start women, often older women, who had themselves learned about listening and healing from elders, and were passing that wisdom along.

Gradually, as I talked with these women, I began to see my project, which had begun as an effort at "mapping" the sociolegal ecology of a welfare state programme, as history. My project was tracing a tangle of disparate histories – histories of a complex welfare programme in multiple ground-level enactments, of individual women and their peoples, and of America, as the programme projected it and these women remembered it. The project was also tracing my own history, as my own memories and fears intruded into theirs through my questions and my silences.

Over the course of our conversations, virtually every woman that I interviewed extensively, like N.M., remembered moving, moving North, and West, and back again, and again. They remembered anger, and fear, and silence, carefully plotted silences, and moments of peace and of healing, and the sealing of wounds. They told about wrestling the ground for citizenship out of almost nothing – the quiet space beneath a table or behind a stair, a sink full of dishes, their power to be silent in a meeting, or their work with a child too frightened to talk.

One of the women I interviewed while tracing the programme's "official history" was Bessie Draper. As the first national administrator of the programme's federally mandated parent involvement component, she was a central figure in shaping the federal regulations that were promulgated in 1970 to specify the activities that each Head Start programme would be required to provide to parents to ensure their participation. A middle-class African American woman who had grown up in Harlem, earned a bachelor's degree from Howard University, and then become involved in the civil rights movement in Saint Louis, Ms. Draper infused the programme's parent involvement component with two basic learnings from her own life. The first was that basic economic security must be guaranteed before participation rights can have any meaning. She explained through a story:

> Well, with poor parents who are trying to rear children in bad economic situations, one of the things you'd have to do is help them some – as an old politician from Saint Louis used to say – "help them put some meat on the table." . . . My experience as an employment counsellor taught me that . . . we had to provide counselling to help people endure in a very difficult

situation. While I was there . . . we received an application from a man who
. . . had a Bachelor of Science degree from Saint Louis University in physics
and was working as a freight handler at the Wabash Airport. . . . We had
a generation of blacks who had struggled to get their education, but had
never been able to fulfill their potential or use the skills the University had
given them. . . . Head Start was dealing with a population of parents who
had been turned off by the educational system, who had by and large been
unsuccessful because success is measured in this country by your economic
means.[28]

Draper's second learning was that the practical wisdom of the women
who were enacting the early programme at the grassroots level should be
drawn upon to give shape to parent involvement at the national level. To
achieve this, she convened a series of gatherings across the country in which
parents and teachers from local programmes were brought together to say
what they were doing, and to explain what they understood parent
involvement to mean. The people she gathered in these meetings were
women like Eula Boddie, from Los Angeles.

When I talked with Ms. Boddie in 1992, she had taught in Head Start for
thirty years. Ms. Boddie and the other women who shaped the LA
programme in its early years all had vivid remembrances of the teaching and
caretaking practices that they had brought with them from their communities
of origin in the South. In these longed-for communities, women described
how their mothers and grandmothers had devised grassroots practices –
institutions – for taking care of children, the elderly, and the infirm, for the
education and mutual sustenance of working men and women, for healing,
and for worship. Eula Boddie spoke about her own work in Head Start in the
following terms:

I came to Los Angeles in 1964. I came from Alabama. I had taught in
Alabama for about 18 years. So I knew something about teaching. . . .
Coming from a small town in Alabama, it was nothing but loving and care
and understanding, that's what I knew. So when I came here I brought that
with me. So I was appointed as a teacher. So I said, well, now Head Start
was just new. Nobody knew what you were going to teach. I said first
thing, you got to be honest. . . . They gave me eighteen children with
parents. So I said to myself what can I teach? So I decided to make me a
little book of what I was going to teach from the knowledge that I had. The
children knew nothing when I came here. The children didn't know a car,
a horse, zoo animals. They would look at me. They didn't know, and I was
just so surprised. So I said, I see what I have to do. You have to love

children, then you're going to get the parents. So I said, I see what I'm going to do. I'm going to start loving my children.[29]

She went on to explain at some length the ways that she enticed individual children to eat, to hug her, to listen in the classroom. She and other women from Alabama described how they drew upon their mothers' and grandmothers' resistance to Klan violence to inspire younger women in Los Angeles to stand up to employers and welfare officials.

Boddie's practices of working with younger women evoke the best practices of contemporary human development specialists, whose current buzz-words include collaborative, holistic approaches to intervention, identifying and seeking to enhance children's and families' and wider institutions' strengths, and the overarching metaphor of "ecology." These contemporary specialists, just like Ms. Boddie, work within a backdrop of theory in which the key themes include a ground of multiple, mutually embedded, infinitely complex, interacting human and social systems, and a stubborn belief in the force of living things to grow. They embrace a vision of best practice that is partial, local, gently ironic, well-timed, and wise rather than totalizing and transformative, that depends on the ear, the grain of the voice, the flow of the conversation, rather than the petrifying imperialism of objective knowledge. Yet unlike the contemporary experts, women like Ms. Boddie and Ms. Draper understand that the places and practices of healing must be sustained through a politics of struggle that can get the potatoes onto the table. They also know that the work of healing, done well, will nurture strong women's voices, voices that risk breaking the quiet of their masters' worlds.

In part through the persistence of Bessie Draper, something of these women's visions found its way into the constitution of the Head Start programme. Consider this excerpt from Head Start's parent involvement regulation. The author of this passage is uncertain. According to Bessie Draper's best recollection, she played a role in writing and editing this language. It came to her after listening to women like Eula Boddie describe the changes that were taking place in the local Head Start programmes that they created in the years before that law:

Many of the benefits of Head Start are rooted in "change." . . . These changes must take place in the family itself, in the community, and in the attitudes of people and institutions that have an impact on both. The success of Head Start in bringing about substantial changes demands the fullest involvement of the parents, parental-substitutes, and families. . . . This involvement of the parents, parental-substitutes, and families. . . . This involvement. . . should gain vigor and vitality as planning and activities go forward. . . . Successful parental involvement . . . helps bring about changes in institutions in the community, and works toward altering the social conditions that have formed the systems that surround the economically disadvantaged child and his family.[30]

Notes

1. An earlier version of excerpts from this essay was published as "On the Guarding of Borders" in 33 *Harvard Civil Rights-Civil Liberties Law Review* 183 (Winter 1998).
2. Excerpts from the remarks of an unidentified civil rights activist, from Hollis Watkins, Mass Meeting and Prayer, on Sing for Freedom: The Story of the Civil Rights Movement Through Its Songs (compiled by Guy and Candie Carawan, Smithsonian Folkways Records, 1990).
3. It might be noted that this liberal proceduralist version of constitutionalism has become normalized in the dominant legal culture of industrial regimes like the United States. And yet, its conceptual premises are belied by global trends. These questionable premises include the idea that a nation's territorial borders can be secured against the global flow of peoples, ideas, and wealth, and the consequent idea that legitimate political power is the exclusive prerogative of internally cohesive nation states.
4. The Education and Training Institute is a fictitious name.
5. Interview with N.M., p. 11, 596-597.
6. Id. p. 12, 606-614.
7. Id. p. 16, 860-879.
8. Id. p. 17, 893-929.
9. Id. p. 17, 923-927.
10. Broumas, Olga 1997, 'Artemis,' in *Beginning with O*, New Haven: Yale University Press, pp. 23-24.
11. Morrison, Toni 1993, *Playing in the Dark: Whiteness and the Literary Imagination*, New York: Vintage Books, p. 53.
12. Interview with N.M., pp. 21-23, passim.
13. See, e.g., Hurston, Zora Neale 1998, *The Sanctified Church*, New York: Marlowe and Company.
14. See Raboteau, Albert 1995, 'The Conversion Experience,' in *A Fire in the Bone*, Boston: Beacon Press, p. 152.
15. Stewart, Earnistine 1990, Head Start Reauthorization Hearing Before Subcommittee on Children, Family, Drugs, and Alcoholism of the US Senate Committee on Labor and Human Resources, 101st Congress, 2nd Session, p 103. Hereinafter "1990 Reauthorization Hearing."
16. O'Keefe, Ann 1979, 'What Head Start Means to Families,' US Department of Health, Education, and Welfare, quoting a parent from Kentucky, p. 25. Hereinafter "O'Keefe."
17. Malone, Lula 1990, Reauthorization Hearing, p. 97.
18. Prepared statement of Pauline Abu-Tayeh 1993, Oversight Hearing, p. 54.
19. Hale, Deloris 1990, Reauthorization Hearing, p. 108.
20. Norwood, Ms. 1993, Oversight Hearing, p. 61.

21. O'Keefe, quoting a parent from Alabama, p. 25.
22. Andrews, Myrtha 1990, Reauthorization Hearing, pp. 105-106.
23. Boyd, Eliza 1990, Reauthorization Hearing, p. 97.
24. O'Keefe, quoting parent from Alabama, p. 25.
25. Andrews, Myrtha 1990, Reauthorization Hearing, p. 106.
26. Blas Reyes 1990, quoted in 'Head Start Success Stories,' CSR Inc. Region V Head Start Training and Technical Assistance Resource Center, pp. 46-47.
27. King, Frankie 1984, Reauthorization of the Head Start Act, 1984. Hearing Before Subcommittee on Family and Human Services of the US Senate Committee on Labor and Human Resources, 98th Congress, 2nd Session, pp. 35-36.
28. Interview with Bessie Draper, pp. 4-5.
29. Interview with Eula Boddie, pp. 10-12.
30. US Office of Economic Opportunity, Transmittal Notice – Head Start Policy Manual 70.2, Instruction I-30, Section B-2, "The Parents."

7 *"Un Niño de Cualquier Color"*: Race and Nation in Inter-country Adoption [1]

BARBARA YNGVESSON

In a feverish stillness, the intimate recesses of the domestic space become sites for history's most intricate invasions. In that displacement, the border between home and world becomes confused; and, uncannily, the private and the public become part of each other, forcing upon us a vision that is as divided as it is disorienting (Bhabha 1992: 141).

It is virtually a commonplace observation today to describe inter-country adoption as a "market" or "traffic" in children, one that typically moves from south to north, east to west, or Third World to First. International documents – such as the United Nations *Convention on the Rights of the Child* (1989) and the *Hague Convention on Protection of Children and Cooperation in Respect of Inter-country Adoption* (Hague Conference 1993) – have sought to regulate this traffic by establishing "a system of cooperation amongst Contracting States" (Article 1, *Hague Convention*) that will secure, when necessary, the legitimate movement of children across family, national and cultural borders while preventing their abduction or sale.

In spite of these efforts to legitimize and regularize the transnational movement of children in adoption (a movement which for the past decade has involved approximately 20,000 children each year) the everyday representation of this flow is inevitably pulled back to market imagery, with the child as a highly valued commodity.[2] This pull "back to" the market blurs the distinction between illegal traffic and desirable transit, while hinting at complex issues of national identity, of inter-state power and of transnational politics. These issues provoke (and not only among adoptees) a re-examination of "belonging" and suggest the dependence of what we call "identity" on transgressions of the conventional borders (national, familial, cultural) which seem to constitute who we are, as individuals, as "a nation," and so forth, and thus of the ways "who we are" may be inextricable from the very mobility of circuits of capital, commodities, information and populations that seem to threaten identity.

That it is a traffic in **children** that provokes concern – a concern that is expressed as intensely in the so-called "giving" as in the "receiving" nations – is tied to the extension around the globe of what Viviana Zelizer (1985) has described as the "sacralized" child. This child emerged in nineteenth century Europe and America in tandem with the domestication of family and of motherhood, a process that accompanied the spread of wage labour and a capitalist market economy, and that involved the expulsion of children from the "cash nexus" (Zelizer 1985: 11). As Zelizer argues persuasively, this expulsion of children from the cash nexus was not simply a change in economic, occupational and family structures. It was part of "a cultural process of 'sacralization' of children's lives," in the sense that children became objects that were invested with sentimental meaning. The economic and sentimental values of children were declared to be "radically incompatible" (1985: 11). Yet Zelizer also argues that with the "exclusively emotional valuation" of children came paradoxically "an increasing monetization and commercialization of children's lives" (1985: 15). She demonstrates how this simultaneous monetization and sacralization of children played out in the arena of domestic adoption in the United States. Sentimental adoption created both an unprecedented demand for children (and specifically for infants) in the early decades of the twentieth century, and a baby market in which the priceless child became increasingly monetized and commercialized.

This chapter examines what might be called, but with considerable caution, the "globalization" of this historically and culturally specific concept in the policies and practices of inter-country adoption, and the accompanying effort to define the flow of children from south to north as "not" a market and "not" a traffic in children. When I say that I am cautious about calling the diffusion of the sentimentalized child as "globalization," I mean that as with most so-called globalizations, this one is not truly global. It affects only a tiny minority of children under the age of five living in absolute poverty in the developing countries.[3] In this sense, there are what Boaventura de Sousa Santos describes as "globalized inclusions" and "globalized exclusions" in the production of a sentimentalized adoptable child. Finally, the globalization of a sentimentalized western concept of childhood is also "localized" in terms of hierarchies of race and gender that affect how children are perceived and categorized in sending as well as in receiving countries. In this sense, as Santos notes, globalization entails localization . . . Once a given process of globalization is identified, its full meaning may not be obtained without considering adjacent processes of relocalization occurring in tandem and intertwined with it.

It is this "relocalization" of the sentimentalized child in inter-country adoption that is my particular focus. It happens as sending countries infuse their concepts of an adoptable child as a "cultural resource" with specific kinds of racialized and gendered value. And it happens in receiving countries, which reconstitute the globalized child with specific western interpretations of the "cultures" from which adopted children come and inscribe their bodies with the specific forms of western desire.

Two children's stories of abandonment and adoption begin my demonstration of these processes. "Abandonment" is a crucial term because it is by being "abandoned" or orphaned that children become "available" for adoption. One of my concerns in this chapter is with the connection of "orphan status" and of an official state of **legal** abandonment, to what one commentator on international conventions governing inter-country adoption describes as the "clean-break model of adoption" (Duncan 1993:52), which is privileged in these conventions.[4] The clean-break model involves an exclusivist, either/or approach to adoption in which the integration of a child into an adoptive family (and adoptive nation) is premised on the complete severance of ties with the biological family, and the reconstitution of its national identity – as "Swedish" or "American" rather than "South Korean," "Colombian," or "Chinese." While insistence by a sending or receiving nation on the child's "legally abandoned" status would thus seem to protect the child, securing its new identity, as well as protecting its biological kin from abduction in the interests of "marketing" the child illegally for adoption abroad, I suggest that legal abandonment and the implied "voluntary" withdrawal from the child by its biological family can also be seen as a way of constituting certain children as particular kinds of resources for the nations in which they are born.

Suh Yeo

Astrid Trotzig, now 27 and living in Stockholm, describes what is known of her coming into being:

> I was found by the police in Pusan, South Korea on the 31st of January, 1970. There is no information about my biological family. I was placed in an orphanage, I don't know where, perhaps in Pusan, more probably in Seoul. On the 10th of February I came to a foster family in Seoul and there I spent my first five months (Trotzig 1996: 12; freely translated).

Trotzig has three pictures from this period, two showing her in the arms of a foster mother ("She is Korean. She smiles a little, an unsure smile"), a third in which "they have cut away (*skurit bort*) the foster mother" and only her own face can be seen. This picture is in her passport, her permit to enter "The Kingdom of Sweden" (1996: 23).

Officials at the Pusan City Temporary Home for Abandoned Children, where the baby was taken, listed her "presumptive" birth date as January 12, 1970 and provided her with a name – Park, Suh Yeo. In the social study compiled by the authorities in Seoul, she is described as "a little cute girl who can be grown healthy a proper environment is to be provided [sic]. She can be beloved by anyone. It is therefore, recommended that she will be adopted by a suitable family for her healthy growth and development. She is a lovely small and cute girl" (1996: 11). The social study was sent to Suh Yeo's prospective adoptive parents in Sweden on March 27, 1970, accompanied by the following letter from South Korea's Child Placement Service:

Dear Mr. and Mrs. Trotzig,
It is my pleasure to recommend a child to your home, hoping you will accept the child after closely checking the child's materials such as social study, medical statement and pictures, and then write to the Socialstyrelsen or to us on your decision.
If you accept the child, please pay us the adoption processing cost at $270 at your earliest convenience. Please keep in mind that when you speed up the child's visa and travel arrangement, you can have the child sooner. The child is kept well in our foster home.
Hoping your adoption plan will go ahead smoothly.

Trotzig arrived in Sweden on June 22nd, 1970. She was five months old and had with her a white silk bag embroidered in bright colours. As she says, "all adoptive children from South Korea brought that bag with them to their new homeland. As a memory of the land where they were born." But "my background, my history constitutes a nothing and no Social Study can make it into a something. The information there disappears into a large question mark."

I recount this story to illustrate the salience of three points related to the commodification of the adoptable child. This is **not** a story of the so-called illegal "traffic" in children. It is one of state-regulated adoption procedures, which in effect require a kind of generalized, disembedded, child in order for adoptions to "work."[5] The first point is the description of Suh Yeo in the social study as "a little cute girl who can be grown healthy [if] a proper environment is to be provided. She can be beloved by anyone. It is therefore recommended that she will be adopted by a suitable family for her healthy growth and development. She is a lovely small and cute girl." This is the sentimentalized child *par excellence*, but described in the most vacuous terms, as Trotzig herself points out: "In my siblings' Social Studies there was more or less the same thing. That one is pretty and has good prospects for being a happy and gifted person, as long as one lands in the right family." The concept of inter-country adoption required the child to be represented as a kind of open cultural space (little, cute, girl) which simply needed to be filled with love. This same kind of imagery is found in the Preamble to the 1993 *Hague Convention*, where the emphasis is on placing a child "in a family environment, in an atmosphere of happiness, love and understanding." At the same time, as I will suggest in more detail later, both the practices and policies of inter-country adoption are shot through with the contradictory assumption that the child placed is deeply rooted in a national soil, tied to its "biological" history, and that its transfer to another soil and another family will be disruptive and damaging to the child's "best interest." This competing assumption has become increasingly prominent in the past few years as domestic adoption programmes are developed in sending countries, as inter-country adoptees return to their birth countries seeking "roots" or birth parents, and as receiving countries develop elaborate schemes for training adoptees in their birth culture.[6]

A second point that emerges in Trotzig's story is the prominence of money and its rapid payment in order to speed up her arrival in Sweden. In this story, the sentimentalized child and the commercialized child are explicitly joined.

Finally, the story suggests the complexity for some adoptees of the legal and social "cutting away" of a child from its social surround, as in the image of the third picture in which Suh Yeo's foster mother has been cut away to enable the baby's entrance into The Kingdom of Sweden. As this image suggests, the physical abandonment of a child by its mother – in a park, in a hospital, at a police station, in the garbage – is inextricable from the policies and politics of nation states which determine who can belong and who cannot, who is expendable and who is not, and which enforce the terms (gendered, racialized) through which "belonging" is constituted. Suh Yeo was one of many thousands of South Korean babies who were physically abandoned by their unmarried mothers in the years following the Korean War, until a legal process for relinquishment was established by the Korean government in 1976. Adoption of Korean infants by western families began as a response to the plight of "war orphans," products of sexual relationships between Korean women and UN or American soldiers in the 1950s (Register 1991: 2). A decade later, however, Korea had signed adoption treaties with a number of western countries, and foreign adoption became a tacit practice for handling unwanted illegitimate children in a country where unmarried motherhood was considered "immoral" (Chun 1989: 256) and a child born out of wedlock "may as well not exist" (Register 1991: 11). Between 1954 and the mid-1990s, more than 130,000 Korean children were placed for adoption in western homes.[7]

For many inter-country adoptees, the reality of physical abandonment precludes the more complex history they seek, leaving them instead with a history that constitutes a "nothing" and that "disappears into a large question mark." But the intimate connection of physical abandonment to state reproductive policy (as in Korea, contemporary China, for example, or Ceaușescu's Romania) suggests, in turn, a more complex connection between the emergence of adoption as a global sociolegal practice involving the cooperation of nation-states and the accompanying social and legal "cutting away" of the adopted child from its social surround in the birth country. It is in this social and legal cutting away that the abandoned child becomes the adoptable child, just as the adopted child emerges in the reinscription of its body with a specific "ethnicity" and its accompanying "culture" in the receiving country to which it travels.

My second story makes this process even clearer. Unlike the story of Suh Yeo, which resembles thousands of other adoptions from South Korea to Sweden, the story of Carlos Alberto is unusual. I include it here because it underscores the complex role of the state in the "abandonment" of a child and highlights the connections of abandonment to the constitution of a particular child as an adoptable child by the state. It illuminates powerfully the violence of the amnesias that transform a specific child, with a specific history to which its identity as part of a family and nation is coupled, into a generalized "resource" in a global market in children. It also reveals the potential for grasping this lost history as it "flashes up at the instant when it can be recognized" (Benjamin 1968: 255) and the potential for intervention in identities (national, personal) that are based on forgetting.

Carlos Alberto

On the night of December 9, 1992, Nancy Apraez Coral was kidnapped with her 11-month old son, Carlos Alberto, from the home of her son's father in Popayan, a town in the district of Cauca in southern Colombia. The kidnappers were later identified as members of UNASE (*Unidad Antiextorcion y Secuestro*), an anti-kidnapping unit connected with Colombian state security forces in Popayan. They were apparently searching for the father of Nancy's child, who himself was suspected of involvement in a recent kidnapping. When they did not find him, they took Nancy and her infant son instead.

Nancy was killed some time in the next eight days. In the early morning of December 16, her baby boy was left, dressed warmly and with a bottle of milk, on a street in Pasto, a town about 300 miles south of Popayan, in the Andes near the Ecuadorian border. The child's cries were heard by Cecilia and Conrado España, who took him in and later that morning notified the Colombian child welfare department, *Instituto Colombiano de Bienestar Familiar* (ICBF). According to a subsequent Colombian newspaper story, "he was a precious child, swarthy [*trigueño*], robust, acceptably clothed and had a little white poncho" (Calvache 1995: 12A). The child was picked up that evening by welfare officials, and subsequently placed in a foster home pending location of his family or a legal declaration of abandonment. The local newspaper, *Diario del Sur*, published his picture on its front page the following day, along with an account of his discovery by local residents (Calvache 1992: 1).

Colombian law requires that efforts be made to locate a "lost" or "abandoned" child's family by placing a notice in the local or national mass media. If no family member appears to claim him, the child becomes available for domestic or international adoption. In this case, apart from the report in *Diario del Sur*, the effort to locate his family consisted of announcements on the local (Pasto) radio station on January 14, 15 and 18. When there was no response to these notices, he was declared legally abandoned on February 4, 1993, and was named Omar Conrado España, after the family who found him. Two months later, a Swedish couple was selected by ICBF as adoptive parents for the child, and on June 4, 1993 the adoption was completed in Colombia. The child left for Sweden with his new parents, and his adoption was officially recognized by the Swedish government on August 4, 1993. His new parents named him Omar Konrad Vernersson, retaining in his new legal identity the traces of the "intricate invasions" (Bhabha 1992: 141) and violent displacements that had shaped his brief life.

In September 1993, three months after the adoption of Omar Konrad and nine months after the kidnapping, the baby's maternal grandmother received an anonymous phone call telling her that her grandson had been abandoned at the town plaza in Pasto. When she arrived there and found no baby, she went from door to door with a picture of the child and eventually located the España family, who sent her to the ICBF. There she was told by the director of child welfare that her grandchild had been legally adopted, the adoption was final, and the record of the adoption was sealed, so that there was no possibility of locating the child (Calvache 1995: 12a,1b).[8]

The grandmother hired a lawyer who filed an appeal with the Pasto Superior Court to have the record opened, and the appeal was approved in February, 1994. On June 9, 1995, the adoption was overturned by a Colombian court, which ordered the Colombian authorities (ICBF) and the adoptive family to return the child to his maternal grandparents. Sweden, however (representing the position of Adoption Centre, which arranged for the adoption, and of NIA, the Swedish State Board for International Adoptions) did not recognize this action, arguing that since the child was now a Swedish citizen, a Colombian court decree could not affect his legal relationship to his Swedish adoptive parents. In Sweden, according to AC, "adoptions cannot be undone."

The child's grandmother visited Sweden in June 1995, with the assistance of Colombia's Association of the Family Members of the Disappeared (*ASFADDES*) and Norway's Council of Political Refugees. The Adoption Centre, under pressure due to widespread media publicity in both Colombia and Sweden, received the grandmother at their office in Stockholm, and facilitated a meeting between the grandmother, her grandson, and his adoptive parents. No agreement was reached, however, about the child's return and the Colombian government said that it lacked the resources to pursue the case in Sweden.

In 1996, Amnesty International intervened on the grandmother's behalf by providing a lawyer for her, and she made a second trip to Sweden, where she visited her grandson and his adoptive parents at their home. During this visit, an unofficial agreement regarding visitation and the child's education was drawn up and eventually (in 1997) signed by the adoptive parents and the grandmother. The agreement specifies that the child is to remain with his adoptive parents, that his grandmother has visitation rights once a year, that the child is to take Spanish classes, and that when it is "suitable," the adoptive family will visit Colombia. These terms satisfied Adoption Centre, which continued to affirm its position that it was in the best interest of the child (now six years old) to remain with his adoptive parents – "He has no other parents" – but conceded that "the biological maternal grandparents should continue to be the child's grandparents." This concession by adoption officials, together with the signed agreement between the parents and grandparents, blurs the concept of adoption as a "clean break" process, and tacitly contributes to the official endorsement of a model of "family" that is heterotopic (Foucault 1973), in that it suggests forms of belonging that disrupt the orders, divisions and groupings of "blood" kinship and of exclusive national identities.[9]

I return to Suh Yeo and Carlos Alberto later in this chapter. Here I simply want to note the ways their stories problematize the concept of parents' physical "abandonment" of a child, tying this event to the violence of state reproductive policies, to "internal" political struggles, and to international flows, forces, and interests. Physical abandonment and the legal erasures that follow (and may provoke) this abandonment are central to the commodification of the "adoptable" child. While the routinization in processing adoptive children described in these two stories has changed considerably over the years, and differs by country, by placement service or orphanage, and by agency, it is nonetheless revealing of the erasures of belonging – the effacement of whatever traces of embedding in a social, cultural, and political surround – that have accompanied the emergence of adoption as a practice for creating families among infertile couples of the north and for managing a political or economic "excess" of children in the south. These erasures – and the "identities" and histories they imply – have become a site of personal struggle for adoptees and their families, as well as an arena for ongoing policy negotiation between sending and receiving countries. These struggles and negotiations are one articulation of a more general pattern in the emergent spatial economy of late twentieth century globalizations in which there is at the same time an increasing internationalization of particular flows (of capital, commodities, populations, and so forth) and a reassertion of nationalisms, ethnicities, and of identities grounded in a particular national soil.

From this perspective, inter-country adoption is both the ultimate embodiment of the child-nurture priorities of the child saving movement that emerged in the late 19th and early 20th centuries and a radically transgressive act. Like domestic adoption procedures which took shape in Sweden and the U.S. in the last century as testimony "to a dawning concept by legal authorities of children as separate, if naturally dependent, individuals with their own needs and interests" (Grossberg 1985: 280), inter-country adoption extends to a global arena the "separateness" of children and the bourgeois family ideal to which this is linked (families brought together "by choice and affection, not nature" [1985:268]). In doing so, however, it both challenges (and entrenches ever more deeply) ideas of national and personal identity as deeply embedded in the "blood" connections of one generation to another "through" time. Astrid Trotzig's bitter comment about the "nothing" constituted by the standardized social study that accompanied Suh Yeo to Sweden, and the power of her image of the "information" in the study "disappear[ing] into a large question mark," suggest how closely entwined a "local root, a specific cultural embeddedness" is with a "successful globalization." The stubbornness of Carlos Alberto's grandmother in pursuing her "right" to a relationship with her grandchild, and her skill in mobilizing both national and international groups in support of this right, point to the complex connections of hegemonic and counter-hegemonic globalizations, and the ways both are deployed to secure a specific cultural embeddedness for a particular child, either as Carlos Alberto Apraez or as Omar Konrad Vernersson.[10] This case also suggests however the unexpected permutations these conjoined globalizations and localizations may effect.

In what follows I discuss the emergence of inter-country adoption as a particular form of globalization in the mid-twentieth century. My research involves archival and ethnographic research over the past three years with Stockholm's Adoption Centre, and focuses on the relations between agency staff and the private, local and state officals in India and Colombia through whom adoptive children are obtained. Drawing on this work, I examine how the "excess bodies" created by state policies and by global relations of difference and inequality that characterize the modern world system are transformed into "national resources" (commodified, adoptable children) during the period 1965 to the present. In the final part of the paper, I examine the challenge posed by inter-country adoptees to Sweden's politics of assimilation, and sketch the contours of counter-hegemonic processes that disrupt commodified racial identities as these emerge in the struggles of adoptees to "belong" in a country that is not their "homeland."

My research focuses on Sweden because, along with the United States, it is considered one of the pioneer countries where inter-country adoption was initiated on a large scale in the 1960s and 1970s. Today, Sweden has the highest number of inter-country adoptees per capita of any western nation (38,000 in a population of 8.8 million) and the country is widely known for its commitment to developing international guidelines for adoption and for its strong support of the 1993 *Hague Convention*. Sweden's advocacy of ethical adoption practices can be seen as a continuation of its efforts in support of internationally recognized children's rights since the early decades of the twentieth century.[11] At the same time, this advocacy was part of a politics of assimilation grounded in the assumption that race did not matter and that a child of "any colour" could become "fully Swedish." This assumption has been tested in complex ways in the past 30 years.

A Relationship of Exchange: the Child as Gift

The concept of a sentimentalized child as adoptable child emerged in the practices of the earliest Swedish adopters in the 1960s. My claim is that the emergence and globalization of a market in "adoptable" children, and the commodification of discrete "local" identities, ethnicities and racialized subjects that this has entailed, is as much the result of piecemeal fabrications, of discrete, disparate and often randomly connected events, of the desires, longings, and struggles of specific actors, of microprocesses, as it is the result of so-called "forces" that emerge from and seem to compel the practices of these actors.

With this in mind, I turn to what one of the founders of the Adoption Centre, Gunilla Andersson, described as her "crazy idea" that she wanted to adopt a child from India in 1964: "For most people here, it **sounds** crazy – you sit in a little corner here up in Sweden and say 'I'd like to make a family with an orphanage in India.' They'd never **heard** of the idea. So someone had to prove to them it could work" (Interview, 5/26/97). These people who "proved it could work" were what Andersson describes as "the pioneers, the naivists" (1991: 3) of inter-country adoption:

> We then in Sweden had a society where equality was THE word, the ideology par excellence. This political view was supported by the scientific trend of the "nature and nurture" debate where the stress was heavily on **nurture**. Moreover, Swedes are an homogeneous population with no colonial past, which means very little perceived racism or experience with majority/minority clashes. All this made Sweden a well prepared soil for the idea of inter-country adoption to grow. The Swedish adopters felt that it didn't matter that the child came from another country or that he had another genetic heritage; once he was adopted into his family and new society he would become fully "Andersson" and fully Swedish, integrated with the family as well as a citizen (Andersson 1991: 2).

The possibility of full integration was imaginable in part because of the development of transport and mass media, such that "suddenly we didn't only hear of the plight of children far away, we met them personally when travelling in their countries. We saw them on TV and met their faces in the newspapers" (1991: 2). At the same time, this familiarity was tinged with a certain strangeness, and many adopters "had their special favourite countries, to which they preferred to apply for a child."

The only sign of a doubt or an awareness of ethnical complications was that although adoptions took place from Asia, Africa, Latin America and a few European countries, many adopters felt that African children were too different, they didn't feel capable of raising a child with an African heritage. On the other hand, Ethiopia was early a favourite country for many adopters, because we had Swedish medical staff and missionaries there since many years, so Ethiopians were familiar to us (Andersson 1991:2).

This linkage of the familiar and the strange was crucial for Swedish inter-country adoption to take off. For the first generation of adopters, familiarity with "the strange" emerged from some of their earliest childhood experiences. When I asked Gunilla Andersson how she came to adopt her daughter in India, she explained:

It has to do with my mother going to Sunday school – and now we are somewhere between 1910 and 20 – and they had magazines already at that time with those kind of stories where you learnt morals. She collected those and had them made into books, heavy books, which I read as I grew up. And I started to read quite early, so I sat in a corner and read those stories, and two things remain within me from those two thick books. One is to do with gambling . . . because there were many stories about fathers who drank and gambled and left their children starving . . . And the other thing was a picture, and that picture was a picture of an angel holding the hand of a small child going over a small bridge over a cliff, and this picture of children needing someone helping them not to fall down on the cliffs – this I kept in my mind. When I grew up and read in the newspapers and when television came and showed pictures of children sitting in the orphanages in the world, I said to my husband-to-be that "When we marry, I'd like to adopt." So he said "Ja, ja" – he's used to my crazy ideas. So he said, "Ja, why not, if you want that, it's ok with me." We *knew* when we were married that this is what we were going to try. So we tried all over until we succeeded (Interview 5/26/97; emphasis added).

Margareta Blomqvist, another of this pioneer generation, adopted her first child, a daughter, in 1964 from Korea, then a sibling pair from Ethiopia in 1969. She describes her interest in adoption as "quite idiotic" (*hemskt fånigt*):

My husband is 15 years older than I. So when we married (in 1958) I was quite young, but we felt we should have children immediately if he wasn't to be too old to be a father. And then my best friend, whom I have known since we were 10, gave us a book. It was of a photo exhibition which was going around which was called *Family of Man.* It is wonderful. There is a picture of a little Chinese girl with small braids which stick straight out and who is trying to catch a soap bubble. I said, "That one there, that child is the one we want." That was what decided it for us, that of course one could adopt if one can't have children.

I became pregnant a year after we married, and then I gave birth to two boys with one year between them, and two years later we had a daughter . . .

And then we began actually to think about this business of "yet another child" and should we actually give birth to one more child. Just at that point, I remember, the whole family had influenza, and we were home, and an article appeared in a women's magazine about an agreement reached between Sweden and Korea about adoptions . . . So we said, "Look, here's something concrete. There must be some special significance in that." And that's how I got involved in it all. And then we actually did it and then we thought we should have one more child who was adopted so that she would have someone else in the family – so that there could be two who looked different (Interview 8/16/95).

The decision to adopt their second child from Ethiopia was "just chance," Margareta recounts. They got a call from the Child Welfare Office (which knew that they wanted another "different child") regarding a 3-year old girl in Ethiopia who already had an older sibling living in Sweden. They then found that the 3-year old had a younger brother, and they adopted both. While it was "chance" that the children were Ethiopian, Margareta mentioned the fact that the first overseas missionaries from Sweden went to Ethiopia in 1866, and she had heard talk about the country, so it "isn't a **foreign** country for many people in Sweden." "Besides," she added, "my father was good friends with a pediatrician who went to Ethiopia to open a children's hospital, the only one in the country."

As these conversations suggest, the involvement of their parents' generation in missionary and medical work that went hand-in-hand with European colonialism in Africa made this distant continent "familiar," just as in their own generation the plight of Korean war orphans was brought into their homes on television or met face-to-face in Sweden's *"Koreaambulansen,"* a project which provided medical personnel during the Korean War. In this way, Africa, Asia and eventually Latin America – the "Third World" that emerged in the 1950s and 60s and served as the source, until the breakup of the Soviet Union and the political transformation of Eastern Europe in the 1990s, of virtually all inter-country adoptions to the west – became "a geopolitical space, a series of imaginative geographies" (Escobar 1995: 9, Said 1979:55). Inter-country adoption and the interventions this implied on the part of "developed" nations, in the "underdeveloped" world, materialized this space.

These imaginative geographies were created by an international elite of professionals (lawyers, social workers), adoptive parents, and by activists involved in what Göran Therborn (1996: 33) describes as "international NGO politics." This geography is charted in documents such as the United Nations *Convention on the Rights of the Child* (1989), *The Hague Convention on Protection of Children and Cooperation in Respect of Inter-country Adoption* (1993), the *Guidelines on Procedures for Inter-country Adoption* (1992) prepared by the International Social Service in Geneva, and the *Guidelines for Practice on National and Inter-country Adoption and Foster Family Care* (Adoption Centre 1996) prepared by a working group of the International Committee on Social Welfare (ICSW) and subsidized by the Swedish International Development Agency (SIDA). It is reproduced (and occasionally transformed) in the strategies, plans, and everyday work of agencies such as Adoption Centre, in the demands of infertile western couples for specific kinds of children (light-skinned infants, black-skinned toddlers, "cute little" yellow-skinned girls), and in the "needs" and longings of the parents of these children. Like the colonial discourses to which it is linked, inter-country adoption "turns on the recognition and disavowal of racial/cultural/historical differences"; and it functions less through the imposition of guidelines and codes than through "the production of knowledge in terms of which surveillance is exercised and a complex form of pleasure/unpleasure is incited" (Bhabha 1990: 75). Guidelines, conventions, and codes synthesize these knowledges and give them official legitimacy; but they are themselves shaped, over time, in the desires and practices of people such as Gunilla Andersson or Margareta Blomqvist.

Central to the world view of these first adopters was a belief that they had a **responsibility** to adopt children from orphanages abroad – to be "an angel helping them not to fall down on the cliffs" in Gunilla Andersson's words – and a conviction that it was possible to do so because Sweden provided fertile ground – there was no colonial past, there was little perceived racism, there was an ideology of equality. Indeed, a key theme in my conversations with all of these adoptive parents today is their commitment to inter-country adoption as pivotal in realizing Sweden's potential as a model nation in an increasingly global world. Through inter-country adoption, Sweden's egalitarian ideology would materialize. Thus this group objected to the view of friends and relatives that their adoption projects were a form of charity or "foreign aid." Rather they saw it as a matter of ideology and politics, a commitment to the notion that a child from almost anywhere could become "fully Swedish."

These principles emerged most clearly as the first generation of inter-country adopters began to meet one another and in 1969 formed two fledgling organizations the Svensk-Indisk Förening (Swedish-Indian Society) and the Adoption Centre (AC). Ann-Charlotte Gudmundsson, the general secretary of AC today, recalled the first years of the Swedish-Indian Society:

> Both Gunilla and I, when we started in the Swedish-Indian Society, had small children and we didn't do anything 'til the children went to bed. I called up the [adoptive] families at 8pm or so. I got two or three letters per week from Rama [Ananth, in Bombay] – we were always after them in time, you know. And at 10 o'clock I started to write letters until 12 [midnight]. I had another job during the daytime (Interview 10/12/95).

Gunilla Andersson describes these first years as "Margareta Blomqvist in her bedroom and me in my kitchen having phone hours for people wanting to adopt and being in touch with families. And Ann-Charlotte was of course writing to India." All were volunteers.

The response to their calls, letters, talks, and articles was overwhelming. From the outset however it was clear that the callers were exclusively interested in acquiring children and had little interest in ideology or politics.[12] In the Nordic countries the politics of the welfare state had led to a steady decrease in the number of children available for domestic adoption, particularly after the mid-1960s, when changes in abortion practices, access to more effective contraceptives, and generous family allowances meant both that fewer unwanted children were born and that it was increasingly easy for parents, single or married, to care for their own children.[13] The number of out-of-wedlock childbirths increased dramatically between 1966 and 1989,[14] but the number of Swedish children placed for adoption in this period fell just as dramatically, from 1000 in 1965 to 20-30 per year in the early 1990s.[15] At the same time, the incidence of involuntary childlessness among couples of childbearing age in Sweden was reported to be 10-15 percent (Andersson 1988: 24).

These social and demographic patterns underpin AC's rapid growth in the 1970s. The rapid response by childless couples led to the merger of the Swedish-Indian Society and the AC in 1972, a consolidation that was closely linked to a shared ideological commitment that inter-country adoption should not dissolve into a competition for available babies – that is, it should not be about solving the infertility problems of adults, but should focus on finding homes for children. Nonetheless, constant compromises with the ideal have dominated Swedish inter-country adoption practice, especially since the mid-1980s. It is a constant source of tension in the work of AC.

The founding members of the association developed two complementary strategies for focusing on the needs of the child. One was to work through known, trusted people who shared (or, as the personal networks expanded, could be trained in) the principles of ethical adoption practice. The second (which evolved as increasing international competition made inroads on these trust networks) was to work to develop strong central regulatory bodies and powerful conventions recognized by *both* sending and receiving countries.

In the early 1970s the agency still operated, in Gunilla Andersson's words, "person-to-person." It was heavily dependent on one-on-one contacts in sending countries for its success in obtaining children. AC developed "a network of social workers, honorary secretaries of institutions, magistrates, doctors, lawyers in various countries and got a cooperation built very much on personal trust and a shared belief that children fared better in families than in institutions" (Andersson 1991: 7). In India, which was a key sending country in the 1970s and 1980s, and which has played a central role in shaping both Swedish and international inter-country adoption policy, the network was heavily comprised of "wealthy upper class women who were doing volunteer work and had 'discovered' the orphanages," together with "men who were lawyers and took the cases to court" (Andersson, interview 5/26/97). In addition, Swedish women, whose husbands worked for government, business, or development agencies such as SIDA, became "representatives" for AC.

For example, one of AC's earliest Indian contacts was Rama Ananth, now in her 60s, who visited Sweden in 1965 as group leader for an exchange programme. The family she stayed with included:

> a gentleman from FAO – Food and Agriculture Organization. He was also with SIDA and he'd been in India. His wife was a writer. A little intellectual family, you know, music in the house and all that kind of stuff. They were very much like our family in India. We kept writing to each other after I got back. We kept in touch. Then this gentleman wrote to me in 1969, to say that a friend of his, a couple very close to his house, wanted to adopt a baby from India. They needed a local guarantor for the whole procedure. That's how I started – in fact I didn't even know that there were, that it was possible for an adoption to take place. It was the first I'd ever heard of inter-country adoption (Interview 10/11/95).

After completing this first adoption, Rama Ananth received a letter from Ann-Charlotte Gudmondsson at AC asking her to continue to collaborate. Rama Ananth describes the first adoptions as "all very haphazard because we just gave them the names of the child and maybe the approximate date of birth, no child study, nothing at all. A little bit maybe about the medical . . . I still remember that at the homes we always selected the best looking and healthy babies for foreign adoption. Because there were no Indian adoptions in any case . . . Whereas, you know, the whole attitude has changed now."

The AC's network expanded quickly and adoptions from India to Sweden rose from 30 per year in the late 1960s, to 300 to 400 annually between 1979 and 1985.[16] A similar rapid growth in Indian adoptions to several western countries contributed to widespread crisis in the early 1980s, affecting both the giving and receiving nations.[17] In giving nations, established adoption organizations and national governments moved to develop policy regulating procedures and the pace of inter-country adoption, on the grounds that children had become an "export," degrading the national image and contrary to the children's "best interest." Equally significant, this regulatory activity involved a reformulation of what "the abandoned child" meant for countries that could "give" them away. At the beginning of the 1970s, the value of this gift child was only beginning to be appreciated. Thus, Rama Ananth, recalling her participation at an adoption conference organized by an Italian organization in Milan in 1971, described how:

> we had a lot of people approaching, you know, because we were the giving country, and all kinds of people came and left their cards and said, 'Will you work there?' And it felt very good at a number of the conferences to be such a person. We are an underdeveloped country, the only thing we can give away is children, you know? (Interview 10/11/95).

Regulation/Commodification

A decade later, the concept of the abandoned "gift child" had undergone a number of significant changes. At the core of these changes was an explicit conceptualization of orphaned and destitute children as national "resources." This idea informed, either explicitly or implicitly, the policy and practice of Indian social workers, child welfare officials, members of the legal profession and other elites involved with child welfare. It drew on a peculiarly western interpretation of childhood as a developmental phase to which children as individuals have a right and which it is incumbent on nation-states to protect.

This right to childhood is interpreted as the child's right to "a family," that is "to love and be loved and to grow up in an atmosphere of love and affection and of moral and material security" (*Lakshmi Kant Pandey v. Union of India*, 1985: 6). As Göran Therborn (1996: 30) notes, "modern childhood [is] . . . a creation by the nation-state, against the threatening encroachments of the market (for child labour) and against the sovereignty of *patria potestas*, of paternal power and the seclusion of the family." While this concept of childhood implicitly informed international movements for children from the early decades of the twentieth century forward, it acquired global hegemony in the 1970s, specifically through a number of UN conferences, "decades," and "years" devoted to women and children and through the emerging practice of international NGO politics, a form of politics that depended on the mobilization of organizations that operate across state boundaries. This activity culminated in the drafting of the UN *Convention on the Rights of the Child* in 1989.

In India and elsewhere inter-country adoption proved a catalyst for these emerging concepts of children (broadly interpreted) as having rights, and particularly for formulating these rights as a protection from a threatening market. For example, Andal Damodaran, Secretary of the Tamilnadu Council on Child Welfare, whose introduction to inter-country adoption began through a contact made with AC in 1978, describes a broadening of perspective regarding child poverty in India at this time, bringing in "issues of children's rights, human rights, which is not that earlier approach of a welfare organization" (Interview 11/6/95). If the "welfare" approach began with the concept of the abandoned child, a "child rights" approach had to begin with other questions:

> How do you prevent abandonment? How do you prevent destitution? It's not enough for Adoption Centre to pick up from the fact that a child is abandoned. It's not only Adoption Centre, I feel all agencies – both placement agencies in India and receiving agencies abroad – have a responsibility to stop abandonment if it's possible. I'm not saying it's possible in every case. It brings me to a very basic thing: You don't grab children just because you want children. And . . . I don't think placement agencies in India should keep finding children because they've got families and they can't run without doing a quota of inter-country adoptions . . . . Now these are, I think very wrong relationships to create. We're talking about children, not commodities. This is not an export market (Interview, Andal Damodaran 11/6/95).

This re-evaluation of the Indian orphan as a child with "rights" who is "not a commodity" was in part the *result* of the child's construction as an object of western desire. Thus, for example, Nina Nayak, an Indian social worker who is the mother of two adopted Indian children and is now a passionate advocate of in-country adoption, told me:

> It was probably my exposure to Adoption Centre that gave me the courage to adopt a child in 1980. It just gave me the courage to fight the system, to fight my family, my extended family . . . My in-laws couldnot accept that we would bring a child of unknown lineage into the family. Especially since my husband is the only son, with his inheritance and all that (Interview 11/13/95).

This slow shift in attitude against what was perceived to be a growing "traffic" in Indian children to the west and toward an interpretation of the children in Indian orphanages as having "rights" to an Indian family, emerged over more or less a decade in the exchanges of people such as Rama Ananth, Nina Nayak, Andal Damodaran, and others with counterparts in Sweden, the US, and other western countries. It was shaped as well in regional and international meetings of professional associations such as the International Council on Social Welfare (ICSW) in which Indian elite and professional women played a prominent role. One of the central documents of inter-country adoption, the "Bombay Guidelines," was formulated at a workshop on inter-country adoption held at a regional meeting of the ICSW in 1981. The workshop was funded by Sweden's Adoption Centre and organized by Tara Ali Baig, then president of the Indian Council for Child Welfare. These Guidelines, in turn, were incorporated into an Indian Supreme Court judgment issued in 1985 by the Honorable Justice P. N. Bhagwati, Chief Justice of India, in the case of *Lakshmi Kant Pandey v. Union of India.*

That judgment, which established a policy for in-country and inter-country adoptions and eventually led to a "quota" system that permitted no more than 50 percent of Indian adoptions to foreign parents, is perhaps the key legal moment for inter-country adoption, at a global level, in the past thirteen years. It emerged from a suit brought to the Indian Supreme Court in 1982, charging that Indian children sent abroad for adoption were becoming beggars or prostitutes in the west. It resulted in a detailed formulation of Indian adoption policy that subsequently shaped the terms for debate in international fora.

At the heart of Justice Bhagwati's ruling, which drew on affidavits and statements from the Indian Council on Child Welfare, the Indian Council on

Social Welfare, and a range of concerned domestic and foreign agencies, including AC, is a narrative about the meaning of the child to the nation which was beginning to shape the way children and their "rights" are imagined in India. Justice Bhagwati's (1985: 4-5) ruling makes this emerging ideology explicit:

> It is obvious that in a civilized society the importance of child welfare cannot be over-emphasized, because the welfare of the entire community, its growth and development, depend on the health and well-being of its children. Children are a 'supremely important national asset' and the future well-being of the nation depends on how its children grow and develop. The great poet Milton put it admirably when he said: 'Child shows the man as morning shows the day' and the Study Team on Social Welfare said much to the same effect when it observed that 'the physical and mental health of the nation is determined largely by the manner in which it is shaped in the early stages.' The child is a soul with a being, a nature and capacities of its own, who must be helped to find them, to grow into their maturity, into a fulness of physical and vital energy and the utmost breadth, depth and height of its emotional, intellectual and spiritual being: otherwise there cannot be a healthy growth of the nation. Now obviously children need special protection because of their tender age and physical and mental immaturity and incapacity to look after themselves. That is why there is a growing realisation in every part of the globe that children must be brought up in an atmosphere of love and affection and under the tender care and attention of parents so that they may be able to attain full emotional, intellectual and spiritual stability and maturity and acquire self-confidence and self-respect and a balanced view of life with full appreciation and realisation of the role which they have to play in the nation building process . . .

This articulation of an ideology of the child is elaborated by ranking different kinds of family environments in which the child might be cared for, beginning with the biological parents "or other near relative," then adoptive parents within the country, and finally, "foreign parents." The least acceptable environment for a child is institutional care. To ensure that in-country adoptions are given priority, the ruling states that "it is only if no Indian family comes forward to take a child in adoption within a maximum period of two months that the child may be regarded as available for inter-country adoption, subject only to one exception, namely that if the child is handicapped or is in a bad state of health needing urgent medical attention . . . the recognized social or child welfare agency need not wait for a period of two months and it can and must take immediate steps for the purpose of giving such a child in inter-country adoption" (1985:21). This is because:

by and large, Indian parents are not enthusiastic about taking a stranger child in adoption and even if they decide to take such child in adoption they prefer to adopt a boy rather than a girl and they are wholly averse to adopting a handicapped child, with the result that the majority of abandoned, destitute or orphan girls and handicapped children have very little possibility of finding adoptive parents within the country and their future lies only in adoption by foreign parents (1985: 15).

Justice Bhagwati's ruling lays out what were to become the key issues in inter-country adoption, all of which might be seen as a gloss on Rama Ananth's notion that, "We are an underdeveloped country, the only thing we can give away is children." This statement hints at the potential of abandoned children as a "resource" and at the importance of western desire in shaping how this potential was realized. On the one hand, the growing focus on children's rights at the international level in the 1970s shaped the way elite Indian women came to think about the children in these institutions (as bearers of rights rather than objects of charity); on the other hand, the interest of foreigners in these same children as potential family members began slowly to make inroads on deeply held views in India, where adoption of a child of "unknown lineage" was unthinkable.

Today, when approximately 50 percent of adoptions of healthy infants in India are said to be in-country adoptions, inter-country adoption involves the least desirable children in India's orphanages: older, seriously handicapped, or dark-skinned children. Thus, the abandoned Indian child as a national resource depends on the colour, age, health, and gender of the child. The youngest, lightest, and healthiest boys are channelled into domestic adoption programmes. It is said that significant inroads have been made on the domestic bias against adopting girl-children, and that increasing numbers of healthy infant girls, and of somewhat older children, are being adopted within India as well.[18] Seriously ill or handicapped children are channelled into foreign adoption programmes, where possible. The oldest, most seriously handicapped children remain in Indian institutions. Indeed, inter-country adoptions provide resources needed by orphanages, placement agencies, and other organizations to promote in-country adoption and foster care, to care for institutionalized children who are considered "unadoptable," and to develop prevention programmes to address problems of abandonment, infanticide and other practices that accompany absolute poverty in India.

While *Lakshmi Kant Pandey v. Union of India* was directed specifically to the regulation of inter-country adoption in India and raised some questions unique to the Indian situation, the problems and issues it outlined have been taken up in all international conferences on inter-country adoption since that time. The effect of the Indian Supreme Court ruling was that adoption was seen as a less good, but often necessary, solution to child abandonment or child "relinquishment," and that inter-country adoption was (in principle) only to be resorted to when efforts to place a child in his or her country of birth had failed. It also meant that adoption – like other actions involving the custody of children – was claimed as the legitimate territory of the state, just as children were claimed as a state resource.[19]

These principles are incorporated in the 1986 UN *Declaration on Adoption and Foster Care*, in the 1993 *Hague Convention on Protection of Children and Cooperation in Respect of Inter-country Adoption* and in the *Guidelines for Practice on National and Inter-country Adoption and Foster Family Care*, which were finalized at the 27th International Conference of the ICSW at Hong Kong in 1996. At the Hague Conference, for example, which took place between 1990 and 1993, and included more than 60 delegations representing all of the major sending and receiving nations involved in inter-country adoption, one of the key controversies was whether (and how) inter-country adoption could be reconciled with sending countries' views of the abandoned child as a "national resource." That is, **does** the child's "fundamental right to a family" (a position that was broadly shared by the professional elites who dominated the national delegations participating in the Hague Conference) supercede the child's "right" to "an identity" (ethnic, religious, cultural), a right which should be secured by protecting its chances to grow up in the land of its birth? The flip side of this right to a birth country for the child is "a nation's right to prevent the loss of its natural resources – children – to other nations" (Carlsson 1994: 256).

There were generally two camps at the Conference, with receiving countries such as the United States eager to facilitate inter-country adoption, and sending countries concerned about loss of resources, and specifically about the characterization of this loss in the media as an "export" of babies (1994: 256-57). At the same time, however, the public stand taken by sending countries against inter-country adoption as a **loss** of resources was in tension with their dependence on inter-country adoption to **supply** resources for maintenance of abandoned children in institutional or foster care, to support domestic adoption programmes, and to provide aid to develop prevention programmes, a dependence which gave them a stake in the continued desire by countries of the north for southern children, and an interest in shaping this desire in particular ways. The "resource" issue was finessed at the Hague Conference in a most creative way, by insisting, in effect, on the child's right to the **preservation** of its identity (Article 30), both by requiring that records of its family of origin (if known) be kept and by requiring attention in the child's "upbringing" to its "ethnic, religious and cultural background" (Article 16).[20]

The issue of how the adopted child's identity can be "preserved" is connected to a related question, that of the so-called (legal) "clean break" (Duncan 1993: 51): the termination of the legal relationship between adoptee and birth parents. The *Hague Convention* acknowledges the right of a sending country to preserve this relationship, although a clear preference is expressed for so-called "strong adoptions" which terminate any pre-existing legal tie between a child and his or her biological mother and father (Articles 26, 27). This preference for "strong" adoptions is a dimension of a culturally and legally specific view of what "identity" means, and of what is required to achieve an identity. Identity, as understood in the western legal framework that shaped discussions at The Hague, involves both likeness (those sharing an identity are assumed to be the same) and equality (those who share an identity are equal before the law). In the US and in Sweden, legislation to terminate the legal relationship between a child and its birth parents and (in the US or in Colombia, but not in Sweden) to "seal" adoption records so that the parentage and history of the adopted child is made legally inaccessible for decades, is premised on the idea that adopted parent and child need legal protection from the ways in which they are **not** "the same," so that they can develop "a lasting personal and psychological bond" (Hollinger 1993: 49; Agell and Saldeen 1991: 78ff). By creating a clean break from the past, a past which is assumed to mark them as having different "natures," adoptive parent and child are placed on an equal footing before the law (that is, as citizens in the receiving nation). The clean break obscures the assumption underlying it – that both child and parent are tied to "natures" (sexual, racial, ethnic, cultural, national) that they cannot escape.[21] It provides a legal space in which the child can develop these innate characteristics ("develop his or her personality"), as long as she or he can be placed "in a family environment, in an atmosphere of happiness, love and understanding" (*Hague Convention*, Preamble).

Conclusion

In my concluding section, I examine the implications of these assumptions for adoption policy and practice in the west, focusing on the Swedish experience. I argue that the clean break policy in inter-country adoption creates a potential space in which (paradoxically) the inseparability of the adoptee from his or her past is repeatedly proven. At the same time, I suggest that the experience of identity by Swedish adoptees reveals a more complex movement between "past" and "present," a movement that is provoked by roots tours, heritage camps, and culture days, but that is as likely to complicate the identities of adopted children as it is to stabilize or "complete" them, and that reveals the contingency and historicity of all narratives of identity.

Un Niño de Cualquier Color

> Because of my exterior, the foreigner, the unknown, is always with me (Trotzig 1996: 58).

In Sweden, as elsewhere, the adoptees of the 1960s and 70s are now adults who are increasingly outspoken about their experiences of growing up in the west. The publication of Astrid Trotzig's memoir (*Blod är tjockare än vatten* [Blood is thicker than water]) in Stockholm in 1996, and the flood of media attention which followed, focused the Swedish public on Trotzig's experience of repeatedly being identified as a foreigner in her own country, and of the impossibility for her of ever feeling that she is "100 percent Swedish." Trotzig's book was followed by a two-hour long television documentary about Meaza Kisanga, who was adopted from Ethiopia when she was six weeks old, and chose to return to Africa in her twenties rather than raise her 5-year old daughter in Sweden (Hagström 1996). Most recently, Anna von Melen, an adoptee from South Korea, published a collection of conversations with adult adoptees (von Melen, 1998). Here, a dominant theme is the unstable, often painful, border that emerges between self and other, Sweden and birth country, adoptee and adoptive family, black and white, over the course of a lifetime. But von Melen also demonstrates the diversity of adoptee experiences and the extent to which adoptees occupy, at various times, a space on both sides of this border. In this way, her book complicates the question of what it means to be 100 percent Swedish and of how "the identity" of an inter-country adoptee simultaneously defines and transgresses "Swedishness."

For staff at AC, the problem of simultaneously accepting and transgressing Swedishness has been at the core of their activities from the outset, and was expressed in their commitment to the idea that a person of any "genetic heritage" could become fully Swedish, even as they admitted the potential "ethnical complications" of adopting children from Africa. Inter-country adoption in Sweden has been described as "a genuine Swedish folk movement, a grass roots project" that emerged together with "egalitarianism, public schooling and *folkhemssträvan*" – a social movement that defined the Swedish nation as a "home" for its people and that emerged simultaneously with the welfare state (Von Melen 1998: 185). Arguably, inter-country adoption provided the ultimate challenge for this movement, by testing the limits of whom Sweden could accept as "its people," revealing what Judith Butler (1993: 8) would describe as the "constitutive outside" of Swedish identity.[22] The persistent efforts of AC staff to create a space in Sweden for children who many potential adoptive parents were unwilling to accept, worked the boundaries of this "constitutive outside."

These efforts were most apparent in the commitment of AC staff to broadening their pool of adoptable children from Colombia, and in the concept of the child of "any colour" that was developed in the context of this expansion. The concept was invented by a senior AC staff member working in Colombia in the early 1980s, as the agency sought to encourage an increasingly cautious adoptive parent pool to be open to the adoption of black children from Colombia's Pacific coast region, where there is a significant Afro-Colombian population (Grueso *et al.* 1998). In Colombia, these "black" children are described as "Negritos" and are locally perceived as the least desirable adoptees. At the same time, Sweden and other European countries, such as Holland, are viewed as ideal adoptive settings for these children, because of the perception that there is less racism in these countries than in the United States, the country that adopts the largest number of Colombian children annually.[23] The mutual interest of Colombian social workers in finding suitable homes for children described as "black," and of AC staff in expanding parent interest in these children, led to the development of an innovative system of "colour coding," so that the greatest range of "colours" would be entertained by parents. The categories still available to prospective Swedish adoptive parents of Colombian children (who must choose the colour and age of a child, but not the sex) are the following: *"Un niño de cualquier color"* [a child of any colour]; *"no negro"* [not black]; and *"moreno/mulato"* [brown/mixed race]. The concept of a child of "any colour," which is a trope for "black" child, represents the openness of AC to transracial adoptions while eliding the difficulties that "black child" adoptions pose for the agency. "Any colour" can be almost "any thing" – both "black" and "not black," different and "the same," Afro-Colombian and Swedish at the same time.

AC has achieved a modest, but from their perspective, important degree of success with black adoptions. One adoptive parent of three Afro-

Colombian children estimates that "of all who apply in Colombia, there aren't more than 5 percent" willing to take such children. But she and her husband realized that "it is a child we want and whatever colour it is, that's what it is" (*och den färg det är, det är det*) (Interview 8/30/96). Black child adoptions, she noted, "go really fast" because the demand for them is so low.

The difficulty posed by the black child in Sweden is indicated poignantly in a chapter of Anna von Melen's book discussing the experiences of Tedros, an adoptee from Ethiopia. Von Melen notes that both she and Tedros "stand out in our own homeland." But she points out that while for her "this has meant both positive and negative things," Tedros has had a less "nuanced" experience than hers. He maintains that "'it is worse to be nigger than to be chingchong in Sweden'," (1998: 67; freely translated).

"Black" is at one extreme of a range of shades and facial configurations that include "*tjingtjong*" and "*moreno/mulatto*," but that do not include "Swedish," the unmarked category. This is tacitly acknowledged in a brochure published by Sweden's National Board for Inter-country Adoptions (NIA) in a discussion about "attitudes to the [adopted] child's appearance." Noting that "our adopted children today typically have an appearance that differs from the prevalent Nordic appearance," the brochure goes on to say that "the child with its appearance will trumpet out [*basonera ut*]" to the society at large the fact that its parents cannot have biological children (NIA n.d.: 21; freely translated). This discussion is accompanied by the following illustration of an adoptive family.

Figure 1   *Reference* (NIA n.d.:23)

This picture of Swedish whiteness against the adopted child's blackness points to the ways in which the colour, black, (and its implied connection to any kind of "colour") is deeply entrenched as a marker of what "Swedish" is not.[24] Thus, for example, Sara Nordin, who is 27 and was adopted from Ethiopia when she was eighteen months old, recounts her experience of growing up black, in the journal *Svart Vitt* [Black White], a publication that often features stories about Swedish adoptees. Nordin says that the meaning of the word "black":

> has grown with each year that passes, until I have finally understood that I am black. It is something big, personal and hard. It is a fact for me . . . When I walk by a mirror I see something exotic that I barely recognize from TV, newspapers and books. Sometimes I am happy, sometimes sad and sometimes astonished. But most often the reflection in the mirror evokes questions that have no simple answers. I have tried to absorb [*ta till mig*] the "black" but then I have difficulty holding onto [*få med mig*] the Swedish. I have tried to absorb the "Swedish" but then I haven't understood what I see in the mirror (1996: 4-5).

Similarly, Meaza Kisanga, who was adopted when she was six weeks old from Ethiopia, is quoted in a newspaper article as "often treated like a tourist, a guest who doesn't belong" (Stahl 1996: B20). Named Katarina by her adoptive parents, Meaza says "they thought it would be easier for us in school if we had Swedish names":

> But I always felt different and excluded. People insisted that I tell them who I was and what my appearance meant and I didn't know. Finally I realized that the feeling of being foreign was in part dependent on the colour of my skin and took back my African name. It was better to have a name that matched my colour (Stahl 1996: B20).[25]

Astrid Trotzig, whose story of abandonment in Korea was the starting point of this chapter, describes the curiosity of strangers about her origins as persistent:

> I can see that they want to say something . . . Many of them come right to the point. Others begin by commenting on the weather. Their curiosity is not threatening. I need only answer their harmless questions and take note that they do not regard me as Swedish, but as 'almost.' They compliment my good Swedish and say that I have an 'un-Swedish' manner. As though, in spite of everything, I represent another country . . . What is annoying is to

always be met with questions about me and my origins. That it is not natural that I am here (1996: 62; freely translated).

Far more sensitive for Trotzig than the harmless questions of strangers was the gift of a Korean flag she received from her parents – "Yin and Yang. A symbol in red and blue, on a white background. Black border." She looked at it twice, then threw it away, "so that I didn't have to see it. So that I didn't have to be reminded of it and of the land on the other side of the world" (Trotzig 1996: 116; freely translated).

Experiences such as these reveal the impossibility of cutting away the adopted child's "past," even as they illuminate the historical and contingent nature of all myths of origin. For inter-country adoptees like Sara Nordin, Meaza Kisanga, or Astrid Trotzig, their names, skin colour, facial configuration and manner tie them to a forgotten past that infuses the present, connecting adoptive parent to child, The Kingdom of Sweden to its immigrant adoptees, and adoptees to the country of birth that made them "adoptable." This past will always haunt the present, dividing the identity of the adoptee and challenging the unstable boundaries of nations which seek to absorb them as citizens.

The challenge posed by the divided consciousness of the adoptee to national boundaries is tacitly implied by the fact that in Sweden, for example, the legal status of the adoptee as "immigrant" is permanent. Unlike her parents or their biological children, she will *never* be "fully Swedish," an official fact that is in tension with the ideology of complete absorption that inspired the work of the earliest Swedish adopters, but that is in keeping with the ideology of preservation that predominated at the Hague Conference. In this approach, it is incumbent on receiving nations to help the adoptee discover who she "really" is, even (or perhaps especially) when she, like the nations which call themselves home to her, has no clearly identifiable birth (Anderson, 1983:205) but emerges from "amnesias," "oblivions," and "estrangements." It is these estrangements that "engender . . . the need for a narrative of 'identity'" (1983: 204-205).

Today, the perceived "need" for a cultural narrative that will realize the inherent identity of the adopted child has profoundly shaped contemporary adoption practice in all western countries, where attention has been focused particularly on realizing the "ethnicity" and the "culture" of internationally adopted children. For example, at an international conference on adoption organized in Delhi by the Indian Council for Child Welfare in October, 1996, Susan Cox, an executive of the prestigious Holt agency in Eugene, Oregon, and herself a Korean adoptee, recounted her story of adoption from South

Korea in the 1950s, and concluded by saying that "no one can take your ethnicity from you." Cox's presentation was lauded by other participants at the conference as an important personal statement with significant implications for adoption policy. Building on her lead, a key refrain in most of the presentations by other western agencies at the conference was **how** preservation of the Indian cultural identity of children adopted by western families might best be guaranteed. A representative from one of the Scandinavian countries spoke with some frustration about the monitoring of families who had adopted Indian children, by officials from the Indian embassy in his country, and suggested that the goal of securing the Indian identity of adopted children might better be achieved if the embassy were to make cultural resources available to the families, rather than carrying out home visits.

While this kind of identity policing may be extreme, the belief that adopted children are **entitled** to a birth identity that they need in order to complete themselves – that while "love . . . [may be] thicker than blood" (Trotzig 1996: 287), love is not enough – is increasingly central to an understanding of the best interests of the adopted child, whether the child is adopted domestically or internationally. In domestic adoption policy, this understanding of best interest has resulted in intense political struggles (in countries such as the United States) over "opening" sealed records, "open" adoptions, and changing state adoption laws to permit disclosure to adoptive and birth families of identifying information about each other (Yngvesson 1997). In inter-country adoption, there has been more emphasis on culture, with "heritage" or "culture" camps organized by adoption agencies and other groups (Aronson 1997), Colombian, Indian, or Chilean "days" or festivals organized by agencies or families, attention to language training (in Korean, Chinese, and so forth) for adoptees (Scott 1997; Luo 1998), and the arrangement by adoption agencies of "roots trips" or tours to the birth country for adoptees and their families. Sweden's Adoption Centre has been active both in the organization of cultural days and in organizing roots trips: there has been a roots tour to Korea each year for the past 15 years; the agency has been supportive of individual families, or groups of parents, who have travelled to their children's birth countries; and AC organized an extremely successful first return trip to Chile in April, 1998, for thirteen families of adoptees who came to Sweden during the Pinochet years.

This emphasis on recovering or realizing a cultural or ethnic identity is arguably a continuation of the experiences described above by Astrid Trotzig and others, and could be viewed as yet one more form of policing the identities of adopted children. But I want to argue here that, as

Radhakrishnan (1996: 166) suggests, "the politics of the 'return' [to indigenous identities] . . . are full of possibilities," as long as these identities are understood to be historically produced rather than "primordial."[26] These historically produced identities are generated in acts of cutting away, like the separation of Suh Yeo from the arms of her foster mother so that she could enter The Kingdom of Sweden in 1970, and the kidnapping of Carlos Alberto, and his subsequent placement for adoption in Sweden in 1993. They are constructed in the definition of adoptable children as national resources by their birth countries, as cultural "ambassadors" by western agencies, or as in need of "study" by academics interested in the "meaning of biological and ethnic origins" (Irhammer 1997). These constructions, like the everyday acts of curiosity by well-meaning strangers and the gifts of well-meaning parents, constitute adoptees as always already foreigners in their own countries and leave the idea of "Swedish" ("American," Dutch," "Colombian," "Indian," and so forth) and the territorializations of these imagined identities intact. But the material reality of adoptees, who are Swedish "inside" but whose "outside" bears the imprint of the foreigner, challenges this concept of identity. Identity is neither about a cut-off nor about an unbroken narrative of embedding, but about an ongoing and painful movement between a racialized birth culture, an unknown land that is inscribed upon their bodies, and a known land that is impossible to hold on to because of the way their bodies set them apart. This movement reiterates the imagery of belonging as fixed – by race, by gender, by native soil – while at the same time evoking the transgressions adoptees represent, their simultaneous affirmation and disruption of what identity and personhood is supposed to be about.

The experiences of the adoptees demand a different concept of what the conventions of inter-country adoption should be: not the clean break from a past which inevitably leaves its marks on the bodies of the adopted children we raise, and not a glorification of a child who was placed in adoption to foreign parents because she was the only resource her country could give away. Rather it requires attending to the problematic practice of inter-country adoption in which adoptees "be liberated from themselves (stripped of their identity)" (Dirlik 1996: 35) so that their identities can be reconstructed in a global market of cultural resources in which children are key icons, representing what is most natural about the nations and cultures from which they "come" (Stephens 1995: 10).

The inadequacy of such reconstructions becomes apparent as the private struggles of individual adoptees move into a more public arena in the 1990s, in published memoirs, internet discussion groups, and in various forms of political activism. Particularly impressive was the recently organized "Forum

97," a meeting of over one hundred inter-country adoptees from 23 countries, held in Sweden in May, 1997, under the auspices of AC. This forum served as a starting point for shaping collective understandings about racism, identity and roots, and about the roles adoptees might play in shaping inter-country policy and practice. Exchanges such as these are contributing to a cosmopolitan (counter-hegemonic) consciousness among adoptees, a consciousness that pressures us to reconfigure ourselves in relation to the worlds they represent, to see the interconnections of our histories, to decentre our world. Inter-country adoptees are potent signs in a global economy where they are, at the same time, markers of our power as consumers in a world that seems tantalizingly within our reach and increasingly within our power to remake, and a constant reminder of our inadequacy in the face of their difference, their unassimilability, their insistence on being **both** this and that, and on defying our efforts to regulate them.

Notes

1. Research upon which this chapter is based was supported by the National Science Foundation (grant #SBR-9511937). Earlier versions of the chapter have been presented to a Sociology colloquium at the University of Michigan in Ann Arbor in February, 1998, and at the Law and Society Association Annual Meeting in Aspen, Colorado in May, 1998. I am appreciative of comments on earlier drafts from Margaret Cerullo, Kay Johnson, Nina Payne, and Sigfrid Yngvesson. I thank Jane Jenson for her careful editorial work.
2. See, for example, Chira (1988), Glaser (1992), Swenarski (1993), Schemo (1996), Hegstrom (1997).
3. UNICEF's (1991) *State of the World's Children* lists 155 million children under the age of five living in absolute poverty in developing countries. In 1998, UNICEF no longer attempts to estimate absolute poverty for children under the age of five, but provides an under-five mortality rate (the probability of dying between birth and exactly five years of age expressed per 1,000 live births) as the principal indicator of child well-being. In the developing countries, the under-five mortality rate in 1996 was 97 (compared to 7 in industrialized countries) (UNICEF 1998: 127).
4. For a discussion of problems connected to the requirement that a child be legally abandoned, and of problems with the definition of "orphan status" in inter-country adoptions where the United States is the receiving country, see Bogard (1991) and Goldsmith (1995: 181-193). INS regulations published in 1994, for example, included a requirement that in order for a foreign-born child with two surviving parents to qualify for "orphan" status (required for adoption by US citizens), she or he must be "abandoned" by both parents, which includes "not only the intention to surrender all parental rights, obligations, and claims ... but also the actual act of surrendering such rights, obligations, claims, control, and possession. A relinquishment or release by the parents to the prospective adoptive parents or for a specific adoption does not constitute abandonment" (Goldsmith 1995: 186).

5. See also Sharon Stephens' (1995) discussion of how the generalization of childhood as an ideal in Western society shaped the emergence of conceptions of children's rights encoded in the 1989 United Nations *Convention on the Rights of the Child.*
6. In a recent study of identity among inter-country adoptees in Sweden, for example, Cederblad *et al.* (1994: 72) note that "inter-country adoptees have their roots in another country at the same time as they have grown up in a Swedish family in Sweden." They suggest that "a low integration of the 'foreign' part of the personality can increase vulnerability for discriminatory experiences" (74).
7. This flow was diminished only in the late 1980s, following the broadcast of a feature story on Korea's adoption policy to a worldwide audience during the Seoul Olympics.
8. Colombian law requires that adoption documents be sealed (*reservados,* hidden or shut away) for 30 years (*Codigo del Menor* 1990: article 114).
9. As Foucault argues, "*Heterotopias* are disturbing . . . because they make it impossible to name this **and** that, because they shatter or tangle common names, because they destroy 'syntax' in advance, and not only the syntax with which we construct sentences, but also the less apparent syntax which causes words and things to 'hold together'" (1973: xviii).
10. The success of Carlos Alberto's grandmother in mobilizing international support for her right to a relationship with her daughter's son is surely connected, in part, to the publicity surrounding the efforts of the Mothers of the Plaza de Mayo in Argentina to establish their right to a relationship with grandchildren who had been "adopted" by agents of the state, following the murder of their parents. See Bouvard (1994) for a study of the Mothers.
11. The Swedish international child welfare organization, *Rädda Barnen,* was organized in conjunction with and only a few months after Save the Children was established in Great Britain in 1919. Sweden became a central player in the subsequent movement to place children's rights on the international political agenda. For a discussion of Sweden's role in international child welfare, see Hammarberg (1992).
12. A recent study of 152 adoptive families in Skåne, Sweden, who adopted between 1970-1977 (Cederblad *et al.* 1994: 60) notes that 80 percent of the parents adopt due to infertility.
13. See Grönwall *et al.* (1991: 31ff) for a discussion of the emergence of a welfare state in Sweden after 1932.
14. From 15 percent in 1966, to 25 percent in 1972, 36 percent in 1978, 50 percent in 1987, and 52 percent in 1989 (Agell and Saldeen 1991: 15).
15. The Swedish Adoption Act of 1917 (and an accompanying law affecting the rights of illegitimate children) made adoption of Swedish children possible and began a long-needed reform process to improve the care of children left in orphanages, placed in foster care, or living on the streets. After passage of the Adoption Act, adoptions increased steadily until the late 1940s (900 in 1928, 1000 in 1935, 3600 in 1947), and then began to drop. See Bohman (1991) for a discussion of conditions that led up to passage of the 1917 Adoption Act in Sweden.
16. NIA (1996). Not all of these were through AC. A number of smaller Swedish organizations and "private" adoptions continued throughout this period.
17. There were 231 adoptions of Indian children to the United States in 1979. In the 1980s, the United States quickly outstripped the Scandinavian countries in all areas of foreign adoption. In 1987, the peak year for US adoptions from India, 807 Indian children were adopted by American families (US Immigration and Naturalization Service, 1990, as reported in Pilotti 1993).

18. Andal Damodaran of the Tamilnadu Child Welfare Council reported in 1995 that "about five years ago we could only place children under eighteen months. Today they are willing to take up to two and a half, three years. I think we have also matured. Our counsellors have matured. Now they know how to counsel older couples to take older children. You know, to show them examples of other couples who have taken slightly older children and are happy with it. And five years ago, more boys were demanded. Today our waiting list for girls is longer than our waiting list for boys." (Interview, 11/6/95).
19. Ironically, but not unexpectedly, it was precisely the increasing bureaucratization of inter-country adoption in India, and specifically the establishment of agencies and functionaries as check points and oversight mechanisms for compliance with the law, that increased the potential for corruption in the adoption process. Today Indian adoption is viewed by some observers as laced with corruption and burdened with inefficiency, as a few unethical officials delay licenses or clearances and regularly request payments to secure their favorable action on even the most standard adoption applications.
20. For a discussion of this issue in a related area (1989 *UN Convention on the Rights of the Child*), see Stephens (1995: 37-38).
21. Collier *et al.* (1995: 3) suggest that "for people living in the twentieth century, one's position as a worker or capitalist in the class hierarchy seems open to change in a way that one's race, sex, parentage, or place of birth does not – at least, not without intervention against a seemingly natural order of things."
22. Butler (1993:8) defines the constitutive outside as that which "can only be thought – when it can – in relation to [the boundaries of discourse] . . . at and as its most tenuous borders."
23. Between 1979 and 1991, a total of 8,127 Colombian children were sent to the US in adoption. The annual figures ranged from a high of 735 in 1989 to a low of 527 in 1991 (Pilotti 1993: 176). Only in the period 1992-1995 did annual adoptions fall below the 500-level (National Adoption Reports, January/February 1996, as reported by National Committee for Adoption, 1996). In Sweden, by contrast, 2,995 Colombian children were adopted between 1979 and 1991. Annual figures ranged from a high of 320 in 1985, to a low of 175 in 1989 (Pilotti 1993: 176; NIA 1996).
24. It might be argued that the centrality of race to Swedish identity is in inverse relation to official silence about race in that country. A recent article notes that in Sweden "it is not fitting to describe immigrants in terms of race or ethnic minority groups. Even if there is a terminology for race (e.g. black or white skin colour) and ethnic minority groups (e.g., Gypsies, Jews, Sami, etc.) in everyday language, no official concepts have been developed to register persons in such terms. It would be widely considered as discriminatory to ask a person about his or her "race" in a survey or official questionnaire. The basic concepts used when officials classify immigrants' ethnic background are citizenship and country of birth" (Martens 1997: 183).
25. Cederblad *et al.* (1994: 69) note that in a study of 181 Swedish adoptees, 35 percent of adoptees 13-17 years of age, and 43 percent of those 18-27 years of age, said they had been taunted because of their appearance. This included a range of actions "from sometimes, for example, being called Chinese to regular and protracted harassment [*mobbning*]." They note that these figures appear to be higher than in groups of not-adopted Swedish children (70).
26. As Benjamin (1968: 255) argues, "to articulate the past historically does not mean to recognize it 'the way it really was' . . . It means to seize hold of a memory as it flashes up at a moment of danger. Historical materialism wishes to retain that image of the past which unexpectedly appears to man singled out by history at a moment of danger. The

danger affects both the content of the tradition and its receivers . . . In every era the attempt must be made anew to wrest tradition away from a conformism that is about to overpower it."

References

Adoption Centre 1997, *The Child's Right to Grow Up in a Family: Guidelines for Practice on National and Inter-country Adoption and Foster Family Care*, Bangalore: Adoption Centre.

Agell, Anders and Salden, Åke 1991, *Faderskap, vårdnad, adoption*, Uppsala: Iustus Förlag.

Anderson, Benedict 1983, *Imagined Communities*, London: Verso.

Andersson, Gunilla 1988, *The Adopting and Adopted Swedes and their Contemporary Society*, Sundbyberg: Adoption Centre.

---------- 1991, *Inter-country Adoptions in Sweden: The Experience of 25 Years and 32,000 Placements*, Sundbyberg: Adoption Centre.

Aronson, Jaclyn C. 1997, *Not My Homeland: A Critique of the Current Culture of Korean International Adoption*, Unpublished senior thesis, Hampshire College, Amherst, MA.

Benjamin, Walter 1968, *Illuminations*, New York: Schocken Books.

Bhabha, Homi 1990, 'The Other Question: Difference, Discrimination, and the Discourse of Colonialism', in Ferguson *et al.* (eds.), *Out There: Marginalization and Contemporary Cultures*, New York: The New Museum of Contemporary Art/Cambridge: MIT Press, pp.71-89.

--------- 1992, 'The World and the Home', *Social Text* 31/32: 141-153.

Bogard, Howard E. 1991, 'Who Are the Orphans?: Defining Orphan Status and the Need for an International Convention on Inter-country Adoption', *Emory International Law Review* 5: 571-616.

Bohman, Michael 1991, 'The Swedish Adopted Child: Social Heredity from an Historical Perspective', Umeå: Unpublished manuscript.

Bouvard, Marguerite Guzman 1994, *Revolutionizing Motherhood: The Mothers of the Plaza de Mayo*, Wilmington: Scholarly Resources.

Butler, Judith 1993, *Bodies That Matter: On the Discursive Limits of 'Sex'*, New York: Routledge.

Calvache, Jaime E. 1992, 'Caso de un nino conmueve a habitantes del Javeriano', *Diario del Sur*, (Pasto, Colombia) 17/12/92:1.

--------- 1995, 'Abandonado en Pasto y hallado en Suecia', *Diario del Sur* (Pasto, Colombia) 01/09/95: 12a.

Carlsson, Richard R. 1994, 'The Emerging Law of Inter-country Adoptions: An Analysis of the Hague Conference on Inter-country Adoption', *Tulsa Law Journal* 30: 243-304.

Cederblad, Marianne *et al.* 1994, *Forskning om barn och familj*, Skriftserie från Institutionen för barn: och ungdomspsykiatri, Lunds Universitet.

Chira, Susan 1988, 'Babies for Export: And Now the Painful Questions,' *New York Times* 5/21/88.

Chun, Byung Hoon 1989, 'Adoption and Korea,' *Child Welfare* 68: 255-260.

Codigo del Menor, Decreto 1310 del 1990 (junio 20), Republica de Colombia, Santafe de Bogota: ecoe ediciones.

Collier, Jane F., Maurer, Bill and Suarez-Navaz, Liliana 1995, 'Sanctioned Identities: Legal Constructions of Modern Personhood,' in Collier *et al.* (eds.), *Sanctioned Identities*, Special Issue of *Identities: Global Studies in Culture and Power* 2: 1-2.

Duncan, William 1993, 'Regulating Inter-country Adoption: An International Perspective,' in Bainham and Pearl (eds.), *Frontiers of Family Law*, London: John Wiley and Sons Ltd.

Escobar, Arturo 1995, *Encountering Development: The Making and Unmaking of the Third World*, Princeton University Press.

Foucault, Michel 1973, *The Order of Things*, New York: Vintage Books.

Glaser, Gabrielle 1992, 'Booming Polish Market: Blond, Blue-Eyed Babies,' *New York Times* 4/19/92: 8.

Goldsmith, Sara 1995, 'Recent Development: A Critique of the Immigration and Naturalization Service's New Rule Governing Transnational Adoptions,' *Washington University Law Quarterly* 73: 1773-1793.

Grönwall, Lars *et al.* 1991, *Socialtjänstens mål och medel*, Stockholm: Gothia.

Grossberg, Michael 1985, *Governing the Hearth: Law and the Family in Nineteenth Century America*, Chapel Hill: University of North Carolina Press.

Grueso, Libia, Rosero, Carlos and Escobar, Arturo 1998, 'The Process of Black Community Organizing in the Southern Pacific Coast Region of Colombia,' in Alvarez, Dagnino and Escobar (eds.), *Cultures of Politics and Politics of Cultures: Revisioning Latin American Social Movements*, Boulder: Westview Press.

Hagström, Annika 1996, 'Den Långa Vägen Hem' and 'Från Hökarängen till Kilimanjaro' Documentary aired on Swedish television December 4 and 11.

Hague Conference on Private International Law, Final Act of the 17th Session, May 29, 1993, 32 I.L.M. 1134.

Hammarberg, Thomas 1992, 'Alla barns rättigheter', in Rembe (ed.), *Barnets rättigheter . . . och samhällets skyldigheter: lagar och regler*, Stockholm: Wahlström och Widstrand.

Hegstrom, Edward 1997, 'Black market in adoptions described in Guatemala', *The Boston Sunday Globe* 9/14/97: A17.

Hollinger, Joan H. 1993, 'Adoption Law', *The Future of Children* 3: 43-61.

International Social Service 1992, *Guidelines on Procedures for Inter-country Adoption*, Geneva: ISS

Irhammar, Malin 1997, *Att utforska sitt ursprung: Identitetsformande under adolescensen hos utlandsfödda adopterade; Betydelsen av biologiskt och etniskt ursprung*, Lunds Universitet.

Lakshmi Kant Pandey versus Union of India (Writ Petition Crl. No. 1171 of 1982. Decided on 27/09/85).

Luo, NiLi 1998, 'Let Us Build a Special Bridge', *Families with Children from China Newsletter*, January.

Martens, Peter 1997, 'Immigrants, Crime, and Criminal Justice in Sweden,' in Tonry (ed.), *Ethnicity, Crime, and Immigration: Comparative and Cross-National Perspectives*, University of Chicago Press.

National Committee for Adoptions 1996, *Statistics Collected from National Adoption Reports*, Washington DC, January/February.

NIA 1996, *Barn som 1969-1995 invandrat till Sverige och adopterats senare, fördelade på år, världsdelar och länder*, Stockholm: Statens nämnd för internationella adoptionsfrågor.

---------- n.d *Gruppsamtal om adoption*. Stockholm: Statens nämnd för internationella adoptionsfrågor.

Nordin, Sara 1996, 'Mer eller mindre svart,' *Svartvitt* 1: 4-6.

Pilotti, F. 1993, 'Inter-country Adoption: Trends, Issues and Policy Implications for the 1990s,' *Childhood* 1: 165-177.

Register, Cheri 1991, *Are Those Kids Yours? American Families with Children Adopted from Other Countries*, New York: Free Press.

Schemo, Diana J. 1996, 'Adoptions in Paraguay: Mothers Cry Theft,' *New York Times* 3/19/96: A1.

Scott, Janny 1997, 'Orphan Girls of China Find Eager US Parents,' *New York Times* 8/19/97: A1, A22.

Stahl, Anna-Britta 1996, 'Hon återvände till sina rötter', *Dagens Nyheter* (Stockholm, Sweden), 12/4/96: B20.

Stephens, Sharon 1995, 'Children and the Politics of Culture in 'Late Capitalism,' in Stephens (ed.), *Children and the Politics of Culture*, Princeton University Press.

Swenarski, Lisa 1993, 'In Honduras, a Black Market for Babies,' *The Christian Science Monitor* 5/13/93: 12.

Therborn, Göran 1996, 'Child Politics: Dimensions and Perspectives,' *Childhood* 3: 29-44.

Trotzig, Astrid 1996, *Blod är tjockare än vatten*, Stockholm: Bonniers Förlag.

United Nations 1986, *Declaration on Social and Legal Principles Relating to the Protection and Welfare of Children, with Special Reference to Foster Placement and Adoption Nationally and Internationally*, G.A. Res. 41/85, U.N. GAOR, 41st Session, Annex at art.5 (1986).

--------- 1989, *Convention on the Rights of the Child*, G.A. Res. 44/25, U.N. GAOR, 61st plen. mtg., Annex at art. 21 (1989).

UNICEF 1991, *State of the World's Children*, New York: Oxford University Press.

---------- 1998, *State of the World's Children,* New York: Oxford University Press.

Von Melen, Anna 1998, *Samtal med vuxna adopterade*, Stockholm: Raben Prisma.

Yngvesson, Barbara 1997, 'Negotiating Motherhood: Identity and Difference in 'Open' Adoptions' *Law and Society Review* 31: 31-80.

Zelizer, Viviana A. 1985, *Pricing the Priceless Child: The Changing Social Value of Children*, Princeton University Press

PART III
DEMOCRACY, DEMOCRATIC INSTITUTIONS AND GLOBALIZATIONS

8 Globalization, Civil Society and Islam: The Question of Democracy in Turkey

E. FUAT KEYMAN

It is a truism nowadays to propose that the world as we know it is in turmoil and that "all that is solid melts into the air." The historical conjuncture in which we live is in fact displaying significant transformations on a number of fronts and disturbing our sense of certainty in relation to our pursuit of the promises and ambitions of modernity. While the foundational grounds on which the project of modernity has been able to produce its hegemony are breaking down and/or melting, ambivalence appears to be the key notion for understanding the nature of the present. Antonio Gramsci's famous statement that "the old is dying and the new cannot be born: in this interregnum a great variety of morbid symptoms appear," although penned as early as the 1930s, captures and expresses eloquently the ambivalence that renders it difficult to pinpoint the direction of movement in our inter-societal and inter-national relations.

One of the sites at which the sense of ambivalence does, and continues to, occur is that of "the political" where "the crisis of essentialist universalism as a self-asserted ground" of political identity (Laclau 1996: 2) has meant the emergence of a discursive void in which particularistic conflicts have begun to increasingly dictate the mode of articulation of political practices and ideological/discursive forms in national and global relations. Inasmuch as the crisis of universalism does not rule out its existence, the sense of ambivalence in the present generates the *mutual effort of sameness and difference to cannibalize one another* and thus to proclaim their successful hijacking of the twin Enlightenment ideas of the triumphantly universal and the resiliently particular (Appadurai 1990: 17).

This politics has a name: the politics of identity. Debates over multiculturalism and citizenship in Western Europe and North America, ethnic conflict in the Balkans, the rise of Islamic fundamentalism in the Muslim world, and the increasingly apparent crisis of national identity, to name a few, while being different manifestations of the politics of identity, are also all indicators of the ambivalent nature of the present.

It would certainly be a mistake, however, to celebrate such ambivalence or by defining it as positive thereby to establish an essential link between the politics of identity and the democratic rearticulation of the political. Instead, we must recognize the ambivalent nature of the present. While constituting grounds for what William Connolly (1996) calls "the ethos of pluralization," it can easily give rise to communitarian attempts at renouncing a democratic vision of society, as in the cases of ethno-nationalism, meta-racism and religious fundamentalism, all of which are examples of the politics of identity. It is in this sense that a critical analysis of the present is of utmost importance. It will help to mediate the relation between the universal and the particular in a way that makes the democratic rearticulation of the political possible.

This chapter provides a critical analysis of the ambivalent nature of the present by focusing on one specific case where it has taken the form of "the dilemma of cultural identity on the margin of Europe," namely the Turkish social formation (Keyder, 1993a).

The present political landscape in Turkey exemplifies very clearly the tension between the universal and the particular. At stake is the clash between a secular national identity as the bearer of cultural homogenization and the revitalization of the language of difference through the rise of Islam, the re-emergence of Kurdish nationalism in organized form, and the feminist movement that has been effective in putting the "women question" at the center of the process of "rewriting Turkish historiography."[1] Despite significant differences among them, especially as to their political agenda,[2] all these movements directly challenge the unifying conception of cultural identity which is the basis on which secularist Turkish nationalism reproduces itself.

Given the limited scope of this chapter, I will take as the organizing reference point of my analysis the rise of Islamic identity and the concomitant construction of a polarity in Turkish political life, that of 'secular modernism versus Islamic traditionalism.' This polarity reveals the paradox of the post-1980 coup period of Turkish modernization: a paradox which was marked by two seemingly-contradictory processes. The first is a neo-liberal structuration of the state/economy interactions. The second is the emergence of Islam as an increasingly strong political force, resulting in the success of the Welfare Party that won the general election of 1995 and then formed the coalition government, thereby becoming the ruling party of what is defined as a strictly secular society.

This paradox was crystallized when the Supreme Court decided in 1997 to close down the Welfare Party and ban for five years its power bloc, including the party's leader (Necmettin Erbakan), from politics. The decision was justified on the ground that the party's activities were clearly intended to denounce the modern, secular, and democratic regime of the Turkish Republic. Thus a party that had come to power through democratic elections was shut down in the name of democracy and modernity.

The Supreme Court's decision was based on the belief that secularism constitutes the crucial link between democracy and modernity, and therefore any anti-secular attempt, which should be seen as anti-modern and anti-democratic by definition, poses a threat to the regime, even if its condition of existence is embedded in multi-party parliamentary life. Although the decision was "legal" in the sense that it was grounded on the Constitution, its "legitimacy" has been subject to intense debate, because it gave priority to the secular regime over the principle of democratic pluralism, and even more importantly because it did not alter the sociological fact that the Islamic identity still constitutes a strong political and symbolic force in Turkish socio-political life.[3]

These two paradoxical developments – the neo-liberal restructuring of politico-economic life and the resurgence of Islam – cannot be understood unless we locate them in a broader world-historical context. Following Santos' analysis of globalization(s) (Chapter 10 in this book), I will argue that because the multiple processes of globalization have the potential of undermining the "national/territorial" constitution of social action, they function as the world-historical context in which state-society relations of post-1980 Turkish modernization is embedded.

With this perspective, it is possible not only to recognize the importance of the global-historical context, but also to analyze Turkish modernization without falling into a sort of reversed-Orientalist trap that would treat Turkey as a "unique experience." More specifically, I will show that post-1980 Turkish modernization exemplifies, in a specific way, what Santos calls "the weak state consensus." In particular, the weakening of the state, derived from the logic of the neo-liberal restructuring of the economy, produces a "discursive space" for the emergence of Islamic resurgence as a powerful political and symbolic force, rather than its democratization.

However, to embed Turkish modernization in a global-historical context as a unit of analysis is not to ignore its particularity, its unique historical features. To understand the seemingly paradoxical connection between neo-liberalism and Islamic resurgence, as well as its manifestation in "the weak state consensus," it is necessary to analyze historically, *as a derivative discourse of Western modernity,* what I call the dilemma of Kemalist nationalism. I will argue, in this context, that the rise of Islamic identity is intrinsically bound to the crisis of Kemalist nationalism and that Kemalism in this sense should be regarded as *integral* rather than external to the increasing politicization of Islam. It is in this context that we can understand the linkage between the universal (the post-1980 acceptance of the triumph of liberalism) and the revitalization of the language of difference as a resistance to the secular national identity.

It is, therefore, necessary, as a first step, to delineate the way in which the dilemma of Kemalist nationalism comes into existence. To do so, I will provide a critical reading of the dominant paradigms of Turkish modernization, which will allow me to suggest that Kemalism should be seen as a project of modernity. Secondly, I will analyze the way in which as a project of modernity Kemalism becomes the hegemonic mode of governing society. I will demonstrate how Kemalism reproduces its hegemony by articulating itself in its alternatives, especially as far as their totalistic and organic visions of society are concerned. Thirdly and finally, I will explore the possibilities of democratic rearticulation of state/society relations in Turkey.

Kemalism and Modernity

As Feroz Ahmad (1993) correctly observes, "Turkey did not rise phoenix-like out of the ashes of the Ottoman Empire. It was 'made' in the image of the Kemalist elite which won the national struggle against foreign invaders and the old regime." The making of modern Turkey raises an interesting question for students of social change, since neither the class-based understanding of revolution nor post-colonial state-oriented development theory can be used as an explanatory model. This is precisely because Turkey had never experienced "colonialism" in the real sense of the term. Nor had its national independence been produced by a social class. However, just as in post-colonial states, the history of the making of modern Turkey has been that of Westernization, conditioned by what de Ferro calls "the will to (Western) civilization" (de Ferro 1995).

In the process of this "making" of modern Turkey, the Kemalist elite sought to "reach the contemporary level of civilization" by establishing its political, economic, and ideological prerequisites, such as the creation of an independent nation-state, and fostering industrialization and the construction of a secular and modern national identity. The Kemalist elite thus accepted the universal validity of Western modernity as *the way* of building modern Turkey. In this sense, the making of Turkey was based both on gaining independence from Western imperialism and on accepting its epistemic and moral dominance.

Two Paradigms of Turkish Modernization

Seeing that the Kemalist will to civilization is embedded in Western modernity requires a new theoretical framework that goes beyond existing paradigms of Turkish modernization. Such a view provides us with a significant clue for understanding the increasing strength and importance of the "Islamic turn" in politics.

Generalizing only a little, one can discern in the available literature on Turkish modernization the dominance of two paradigmatic readings of Kemalism – those of *modernization* and *identity*. It should be pointed out from the outset that these paradigms are not unique to the Turkish experience, but can be found elsewhere, such as in the modernization experiences of Japan, Egypt and Peru. My intention here is only to point out that there is a need to understand the Turkish experience as "a project of modernity," in order to see both the hegemony of Kemalism and its constitutive role in the process of the resurgence of Islamic identity.

The modernization paradigm situates the Kemalist will to civilization in a transition from *Gemeinschaft* ('community') to *Gesellschaft* ('society'). However thinking of it as such a transition has different consequences, depending on the version of the modernization paradigm employed. Political modernization sees this transition as a process of nation-building, in which the nation-state is taken to be the unfolding essence of modernization. The making of modern Turkey then becomes a process of political modernization which, through nation-state building, creates a modern nation while the Ottoman past is represented as a backward, traditional society. Whereas political modernization sees this transition as a positive break from the past and a move forward, economic modernization in line with dependency theory considers it to be a new form of "peripheralization" and dependent capitalist development which started with the integration of the Ottoman economy into the world capitalist system in the 19th century.

However useful these visions are for accounting for the making of modern Turkey, the modernization paradigm is limited in its scope and reductionist in its methodological procedures. It is limited as it attempts to analyze its subject-matter by privileging a certain type of social interaction as "the prime mover" of social change. Thus, either nation-state building or economic development is considered to be a process that produces a *system-transforming effect* in the formation of social interactions, which results in a lack of attention paid to the role of other processes, thereby neglecting their transformative capacity. The modernization paradigm is also reductionist insofar as it attributes (in a Hegelian fashion) to society the quality of an expressive, constituting totality in which the conditions of existence of various social interactions are regarded as necessarily linked to and determined by the unfolding essence.

In contrast to the modernization paradigm, the paradigm of identity seeks the essence of the manner in which Kemalism approaches the question of national identity. Two alternative accounts of the essence are produced in this paradigm, which are derived from two different interpretations of the meaning that the notion of "Turk" connotes in cultural practices in the process of the making of modern Turkey. On the one hand, there is a tendency to interpret Kemalism as a nationalist discourse whose understanding of national identity was "cultural" in its essence. In this sense, the notion of Turk is referred to as a "meta-identity" that is situated above and beyond "the difference principle," and thus operates as a point of sameness at which the claim to the impartiality and the universality of the state is constructed. On the other hand, there is an interpretation of Kemalism on the basis of the difference principle, claiming that the notion of Turk is framed to a large extent by and within an ethnic-based understanding of national identity. In this sense, Kemalism is regarded as an ethno-nationalist discourse whose aim was to impose a secular and ethnically-essentialist vision of modern Turkey on what Kevin Robbins (1996) terms "the other but real Turkey."

Despite the fundamental difference between them, these two modes of interpretation share two highly problematical epistemological and methodological gestures. The first concerns the *historicist* nature of the paradigm of identity, insofar as its search for discovering the true essence of the Kemalist vision of national identity rests upon an attempt to *read the past in terms of the present* (Dean 1994: 9). This is so, because this paradigm is not attempting to analyze Kemalist nationalism in its own right or in its own context, but rather to find a legitimizing ground for the competing political discourses of the present political landscape over such issues as political Islam, the Kurdish question, laicism, ethno-nationalism or the crisis of representation in state/society relations.

The second problem concerns the *essentialist* nature of the paradigm. The notion of identity employed assumes that each individual or collectivity possesses a fixed, coherent, and totalizing self. This means that each identity involves an unfolding essence which makes it a self-contained, self-referential and self-propelling presence, and therefore that the variations that occur historically in terms of the identity formation of individuals or collectivities do not alter the essence of their identities. The paradigm of identity thus acts as an essentializing gesture that ignores the relationality, multiplicity and historically constructed nature of identity formation. As such the Kemalist understanding of national identity becomes a universalizing discourse with a fixed, unchanging and original identity.

Kemalism as a Project of Modernity

There is, then, a need to "go beyond" these paradigms so as to recognize the crucial fact that *the Kemalist will to civilization is intrinsically linked to and operates within the discursive horizon of global modernity.* The Kemalist elite's will to civilization was not simply an economic or a political modernization. Nor was it based upon an attempt to create a national identity. As will be apparent later, it was much more complex and at the same time ambiguous than presented by these paradigms. To understand this however requires regarding the Kemalist will to civilization as *a project of modernity* which was premised on the equation of modernity with progress, that is, on the making of a modern nation through the introduction and the dissemination of Western Reason and rationality into what were regarded as traditional and backward social relations. It is in this sense that the connection between Kemalism and modernity, ignored by these paradigms, needs to be explored, in order to provide an adequate account of the dilemma of Turkish nationalism.

In his analysis of the making of modern Turkey, Mardin (1994a) argues that the meaning of Kemalism lies in "the conceptualization of the Turkish Republic as *a nation-state in its fullest form*," and finds its expression in its constant effort to create a modern nation. Mardin's seemingly straightforward and commonsensical argument in fact carries with it a number of crucial insights for a more adequate understanding of Kemalism. Firstly, to think of Kemalism as "an act of conceptualization" is to present it as a "project" of creating a nation on the basis of a set of epistemological and normative procedures. Secondly, to argue that Kemalism means the conceptualization of the Turkish Republic as a nation-state in its fullest form is to recognize that it constitutes a project of modernity; a project of creating a *modern* nation that "accepts the claim to universality of the 'modern' framework of knowledge" (Chatterjee, 1986:11). Thirdly, to think of Kemalism as a project of modernity is to recognize its *modus operandi* as a social engineering project that aims at creating a modern nation in a social formation where the material and institutional availability of the conception of a modern nation as a nation-state in its fullest form was absent.

These three points also indicate that Kemalism is a nationalist discourse that operates as a "will to civilization" by producing at the conceptual level a boundary between what is civilized and what is uncivilized. Thus, by accepting rational thinking and rational morality as the way of becoming modern, Kemalist nationalism is directed to reaching the level of civilization, that is, the making of modern Turkey as nation-state in its fullest form.

Kemalism and the Will to Civilization

According to Mardin (1994b), the conceptualization of the Turkish Republic as nation-state manifests itself in: (i) the transition in the political system of authority from personal rule to impersonal rules and regulations; (ii) the shift in understanding the order of the universe from divine law to positivist and rational thinking; (iii) the shift from a community founded upon the elite-people cleavage to a populist-based community; and (iv) the transition from a religious-community to a nation-state. These transitions are regarded by Mustafa Kemal as the pre-condition for the possibility that "Turkey would live as an advanced and civilized nation in the midst of contemporary civilization" (Ahmad 1993: 53). It is in this context that the Kemalist elite attempted to remove from political discourse the notion of an Islamic state, the existence of which was regarded as the main cause of the perpetuation of the backwardness of Turkey. Thus, the foundation of a modern nation-state was seen as the key element of the will to civilization.

For the Kemalist elite, modern Turkey could thus possess secularity and rationality, employ Reason to initiate progress, and establish a modern industrial economy, thereby fostering the processes of industrialization and modernization. In a Weberian fashion, the purpose of political power was considered to be to "carry out a social and economic revolution without which the political revolution would dissipate" (Ahmad, 1993:72). This means that for the Kemalist elite, political power was not reducible but interrelated to the economic.

The rationalization of the political and the rationalization of the economic were seen to be relational processes whose reproduction could be made possible through the construction of a national identity. In this respect, the Kemalist will to civilization was based upon an articulation of modernity (Reason) and capitalism (Capital) into Turkish society through the construction of a modern nation-state.

As Metin Heper (1985) points out, the idea of the state employed by the Kemalist elite was by no means abstract: rather it was derived from a reaction to two fundamental problems which they saw as key to the decline of the Ottoman empire. First, the Ottoman state was identified with the personal rule of the sultan, which eventually led to its inability to compete with the

European nation-state system (Heper 1985: 49). Second, the Islamic basis of the Ottoman state was regarded as the primary obstacle to progress in Ottoman society. For the Kemalist elite, there was therefore a need to create a nation-state distinct from the person of the sultan and secular enough to reduce Islam to the realm of individual faith. This meant a reconstruction of the idea of sovereignty as national rather than popular sovereignty. Underlying this, as Heper argues, is the association of the Kemalist elite with the Durkheimian conception of the state as the agent of rationality. The state is thus viewed not as an arbitrary institution nor as an expression of class interest but as an active agent that, while taking its inspiration from the genuine feelings and desires of the nation, shapes and reshapes it to "elevate the people to the level of contemporary (Western) civilization" (Heper 1985: 50). Therefore, the Kemalist idea of the state was embedded in the question of how to activate the people towards the goal of civilization, that is, how to construct a national identity compatible with the will to civilization.

Ernest Gellner considers the Kemalist idea of the state to be a commitment to political modernity, which sees the modernization of the polity and society as linked to the state. This commitment "constitutes its legitimation and is itself in turn justified by the strength which it bestows on the state" (1994: 83). However, it would be wrong to view the Kemalist idea of the state as institutional. As Bobby Said has correctly pointed out, the Kemalist elite:

> took seriously the Weberian answer to the riddle of the 'European miracle'; that is, that the reasons behind Western advancement could be located precisely in Western cultural practices. Kemalism understood modernization not just as a question of acquiring technology, but as something that could not be absorbed without a dense network of cultural practices which made instrumental thought possible (1994: 269).

This means that the commitment to political modernity has to be supplemented with a set of cultural practices in order to ground the articulation of reason and capital via the nation-state, that is, via the institutional and discursive construction of national identity. It is for this reason that the Kemalist elite initiated a set of reforms needed to be *imposed from above* to "enlighten the people and help them make progress" (Heper 1985: 51).[4] These reforms were designed to equate the general will with the national will, thereby creating a vision of society not as an aggregation of different interests, but almost in a Platonic vision as an organic totality organized around the principles of division of labour and the reciprocity of needs.

Republicanism, nationalism, etatism, secularism, populism, and revolutionism-reformism (from above) were the six principles of the act of governmantality. Republicanism defined the nation-state as "impersonal rule," which was contextualized as national sovereignty through nationalism. Thus, these two principles constituted the political image of the Kemalist elite. Etatism was designated to foster capitalist industrialization through import-substitution policies carried out by the state, and gave expression to the politico-economic logic of the Kemalist elite. These three principles indicate the acceptance of the dominance of the West. They also indicate the significance of nation-state building for nationalist discourse. What gave specificity to Kemalist nationalism, however, was its populist character, its rejection of the West as a class-based social formation. Populism meant, in the Turkish context, the affirmation of the non-class character of Turkish society. As Toprak put it:

> Kemalist populism defined 'people' as an organic unit composed of professional groups rather than classes. As opposed to class solidarity, populism emphasized the solidarity of the whole nation. There were no classes, hence no privileges based on class differences, and hence no class conflict (Toprak 1987: 218).

In this sense, Kemalist nationalism was an attempt to base its will to civilization on populism rather than liberalism, whose reflection on the economic level was the replacement of *laisser-faire* with etatism. The last two principles, secularism and reformism, served to construct a national identity compatible with republicanism, nationalism, and etatism, and at the same time to concretize populism and its appeal to organic unity into the identity of the individual subject. They were also central to the determination of who is included in and who is excluded from the organic unity.[5] It is through secularism that Kemalist nationalism initiated its boundary-producing performance between the Self and the Other, thereby giving a concrete form to its populist-based creation of the national identity. Hence, the national identity was meant to be an organic unity of the secular non-class based identity which necessarily involved the subjugation of its Other, that is the Muslim identity.

Kemalism and the Specificity of the Political

It is striking that the basis of Kemalist nationalism was identification of popular sovereignty with national sovereignty within the context of the organic conception of society, derived not from "to whom sovereignty belonged" but from "to whom it did not belong" (Heper 1985: 45). In other words, embedded in the making of modern Turkey was, to use Foucauldian terminology, the governmentality of nationalist discourse that practiced inclusion and exclusion by creating identity in relation to difference, and by freezing the Other, the Islamic identity, into history.[6]

By assuming a self-identity as the primary agent of progress, the Kemalist elite thus came to locate secularism within binary dichotomies such as progressive versus conservative, modern versus traditional, and progress versus backwardness.[7] It is in this sense that, as Toprak has observed, up until the 1961 constitution which liberalized political discourse according to the multi-party system, Kemalist nationalism was able to manage, especially with the aid of its non-class based populist ideology, to define the political landscape on the basis of the secularist-anti-secularist axis, as well as to categorize political forces in accordance with their stand on secularism (Toprak 1987: 219). Secularism, in this context, served not only to reinforce the image of the Kemalist elite in the making of modern Turkey but also to create a secular national identity by excluding and marginalizing the Islamic identity.

It should be pointed out that the Kemalist preoccupation with secularism and the marginalization of Islam was not without basis. At least three factors are worth emphasizing.[8] First, insofar as Islam is characterized by the incorporation of the political into the religious realm, it constitutes a radical alternative to both secularism and secular political authority. Second, Islam is conducive to the creation of an alternative political community and identity on the basis of divine revelation, and in this respect is able to have a unifying appeal to the masses as a source of common identity. Third, "the Islamic impact on Ottoman social and political life serves as a reminder that Islam can indeed be a base of resistance to modernization efforts that follow the Western pattern" (Toprak, 1987: 220). These three factors constitute the very basis of the sensitivity of the Kemalist elites on the issue of Islam and their attempt to impose a strict version of secularism on Turkish society.

However, such strict secularism did not prevent Islam from remaining a significant agent in the formation of social and political life in modern Turkey. While being excluded as the Other of the national identity, Islam has been a significant "symbolic system" providing meaning to human existence and thereby forming the bases of both individual and community identity. In other words, while Kemalist nationalism was successful in transforming Islam into "the position of a purely individualist faith," "the transformation of the Ottoman subject into a citizen of the Turkish republic proved much more complicated than *de jure* acceptance of equal treatment before the law" (Toprak 1987: 221). It was Islam that caused the complication by providing religious group norms and values by which the individual subject can be integrated into a political community that presents itself as able to supersede an abstraction like nation and national identity.

Thus, strict secularism was only a solution to keep Islam in its place as an individual faith. Its attempt to construct a national identity did not lead to excluding Islam from the symbolic construction of identity. In fact, from the beginning of the making of modern Turkey, the process of identity construction was determined by the discursive struggle between the will to civilization through secularism and the will to tradition, a will to traditional political community based on Islam. As a symbolic system, while Islam did not function as a political force able to mobilize the masses against the Kemalist elite, it did allow interpellation of the individual subject as a Muslim.

By functioning as a boundary-producing practice, nationalist discourse with its six operative mechanisms – republicanism, national sovereignty, etatism, populism, secularism, and reformism – enabled the state to successfully exclude the Islamic Other from the political landscape, to subjugate it to secular political discourse, and to prevent it from becoming a political actor. It can be argued in this respect that the Turkish nation-state did not have an ontological status apart from the above-mentioned acts that constituted its reality and therefore that its identity was *performatively* constructed.[9]

This theoretical extrapolation provides a crucial insight for an adequate understanding not only of the relegation of Islam to the position of an individual faith, but also, and more importantly, of the rise of the Islamic identity in the post-1980 coup period in Turkey. If Kemalist nationalist discourse helped reproduce the will to civilization as a whole as a way of keeping Islam in its place, the very crisis of such discourse is also central to the rise of the Islamic identity in Turkey. My goal is not to establish a causal linkage between the two phenomena, but to emphasize that the crisis of the former provides "a context," or "a discursive space" for the possibility of the transformation of Islam into a political factor and of Islamic identity into a radical alternative to the secular national identity. Implied here is also the suggestion that the 1980 military coup brought about a radical transformation of the Turkish political landscape, one as fundamental as the post-1923 nation-building period.

Before focusing on the post-1980 coup period, however, it is important to explain briefly how Kemalist nationalist discourse remained hegemonic despite the emergence of the alternative visions of the Turkish political landscape after World War II.

The Continuance of Hegemony in the Changing Political Landscape

Although, especially since the transition to the multi-party system (1945) and the rise of the New Left (1960s), it was no longer possible to define the Turkish political landscape on the basis of the secularist versus anti-secularist axis, Kemalist nationalism can be said to have maintained its hegemony over Turkish political and social life. With the multiparty system, the emergence of the liberal vision of Westernization and modernization presented a serious alternative to the Kemalist principle of etatism and populism. At the same time, with the rise of the New Left, the emergence of the socialist vision challenged the non-class based populist image which had been used to define Turkish society as an organic totality. However, these challenges did not lead to a significant transformation in the construction of state identity. Nor did they give rise to a radical rupture in the performativity of Kemalist nationalism in giving meaning to the making of modern Turkey. In fact, both liberal and New Left political discourses functioned in relation to Kemalist nationalism and, to a significant extent, took as given its will to civilization, thus employing its principal *modus operandi*, that is, creating the general will "in the name of the people."

Several reasons explain the continuing hegemony of Kemalist nationalism. First, neither liberal nor New Left discourses constituted an alternative to the essentialist posture of Kemalist nationalism towards secular national identity. Instead, they affirmed and reaffirmed such essentialism and its practice of inclusion and exclusion. For this reason, to the extent that they pursued "in the name of the people" and "revolution/reform from above," they were unable to construct an alternative subjectivity to the secular national identity.[10] The liberal critique of Kemalism and its monopartism, which was put forward by the Democratic Party, was intended to reconstruct the political landscape as a multi-party democracy. However, this critique was meant only to secure the representation of the private sector which the Democratic Party saw as the precondition for the modernization of Turkish society (Ahmad 1993: 103-120). In this sense, liberal discourse, while presenting itself as an alternative to Kemalist nationalism, functioned by accepting its two fundamental characteristics, namely those of the equation of modernity with progress and the need to construct a rational self as the agent of modernization. Likewise, leftist formulas such as national democratic revolution, which were espoused by the Workers' Party of Turkey and its counterpoint the Yön (Direction) movement during the 1960s, were derived from what Ahmet Samim called "a left-Kemalist substitutionalism" whose aim was to resist imperialism and to lead Turkey democratically "on behalf of the workers and peasants - for the people, in spite of the people" (Samim 1981: 155).

Secondly, both liberal and New Left discourses were intrinsically bound with modernity, and in this respect they were by no means a challenge to the Kemalist will to civilization. Both accepted the validity of the Kemalist notion of the state as the privileged agent of rationality the existence of which was central to the process of modernization. Both provided a reading of Turkish society through the lenses of the state by assuming that it is the state that shapes and reshapes social relations. The liberal critique of Kemalism was therefore only partial: it was directed exclusively to the strict etatist and populist policies by which the state coped with the problems of capitalist industrialization. On the other hand, the New Left critique of Westernization as imperialism and its characterization of Kemalist nationalism as an agent of the subordination of Turkey to Western imperialism was derived solely from the rejection of capitalism. In other words, while capitalism was being rejected as a mode of production generating inequalities and uneven development, the modernity aspect of the will to civilization, that is, its epistemic dominance and its Reason, was accepted as given. However, as noted, it is not capitalism but Western modernity upon which the Kemalist will to civilization was based.

Thirdly, although etatism was subjected to serious criticism, import-substituting industrialization remained as the motor of industrialization after the transition to the multi-party system. Whereas its counterparts in Latin America faced military coups due to the deepening crisis of import-substituting industrialization (such as Brazil, Argentina, and Chile), the Turkish economy during the 1960s, experienced an economic boom. For this reason, liberal discourse, though critical of etatism, was linked with import-substituting industrialization. According to Keyder, an explanation for this long-lasting dominance of import-substituting industrialization as a form of economic nationalism can be found in the fact that nationalism was a site of global capitalism, a way of reproducing it, and therefore did not present a contradictory tendency. This made it possible for Kemalist nationalism to foster industrialization not against but in concord with global capitalism

(Keyder 1987 and 1993b). For Keyder, it was only when global capitalism was formed by the liberal market logic that nationalism became a contradictory discourse to the systemic logic. The point here is that the transition to a multi-party system did not involve the replacement of the economic logic. Hence, Kemalist nationalism was menaced by industrialization policy. [11]

The Crisis of National Identity and the Politics of Difference

The 1980 coup brought a radical rupture, the impact of which was deeply felt at every level of Turkish society. At the economic level, the goal of industrialization was decisively shifted from import-substitution to export-promotion, and much more emphasis was placed on market forces. It should be noted, however, that the primary agent of this shift was the state and that it was primarily a political act, or an outcome of political decisionism, which had no specific class belonging. As Eralp has observed:

> those who were supposed to be the main actors in the different development policies [that is, export-oriented development] were *the same industrialists* who, with substantial support from the state, had been transformed from merchants into industrialists in the 1950s. Again, it was through state support that import substituting industrialists were transformed into exporters in the years following 1980. Thus, contrary to belief, export promotion did not lessen state intervention, *it merely changed its direction* (Eralp 1990: 221).

State intervention was directed toward the privatization and neo-liberalization of the economy, the creation of a new trade regime, and the employment of new modes of foreign policy in search of markets for export. It was also directed, similar to the new right policies of Reaganism and Thatcherism, at the managerial and technocratic reconstruction of political discourse to shape state-society relations on the basis of technical-instrumental rationality that was to operate by privileging efficiency over social welfare.[12] The crucial point to be emphasized here is that since export-promotion was the form of adaptation to the international division of labour, the shift in industrialization was in fact the transformation of the Kemalist will to civilization to civilization via *laisser-faire*, which was fundamentally contradictory with the Kemalist image of the organic state. That is to say, while serving to create a secure ground for the liberal restructuring of economic life, the 1980 coup ironically created a ground for a new idea of the state which was to replace the Kemalist republican populist state, the existence of which it was supposed to protect. Indeed, the 1980 coup resulted in the transformation of state identity from radical secularist to what Birtek and Toprak term neo-republicanism. An appeal to national and ideological uniformity was no longer dictated by the basic principles of Kemalist nationalism. Instead, by incorporating "Islamic discourse and implicitly [taking] *umma* [a community of believers who are united by the same (Islamic) faith] as its model of social organization," and also by abandoning "the radical secularism of the early republic" to secure its popular support and to open up the domestic market to Islamic capital, the post-1980 military regime weakened the very conditions of existence of Kemalist nationalism and the republican state (Birtek and Toprak 1993: 197).[13]

This was the specific nature of the "weak state consensus," first established by the military regime and then consolidated by the neo-liberal Mother Land Party government. Its particularity derived from the fact that although it was embedded in the logic of global capital and global modernity, it also opened itself to Islamic discourse and made use of it to the extent that it contributed to the resurgence of Islamic identity as a strong political force.

The use of Islamic discourse and its notion of *umma* was considered by the military regime to be a temporary and short-term pragmatic strategy to restructure the political and to restore the performative power of the Kemalist republican state.[14] However, such a contradictory move led to unintended consequences. The first was that in the 1983 national election, which was the beginning of civilian rule, the neo-liberal Mother Land Party came to power despite the resistance of the post-1980 coup military regime and its publicly announced support for the Nationalist Democracy Party which was formed as the "state party" of the post-1980 coup regime. This result indicated, on the one hand, the crisis in the performance of the state to carry out the Kemalist will to civilization. On the other hand, it gave rise to the construction of a new state identity whose performative acts are no longer bound with radical secularism and the populist conception of the people but are embedded in *laisser-faire* market ideology, the managerial and technocratic understanding of the state, and the dissemination of the discourse of economic rationality within Turkish society. Hence, the post-1980 coup period characterized not only the export-oriented integration of Turkish economy into global capitalism but also the deepening of the crisis of Kemalist nationalism to reproduce its hegemony.

Secondly, the regime's temporary and pragmatic appeal to Islamic discourse to create ideological unity has become one of the enabling factors for the emergence and re-emergence of Islamic organizations within both state and civil society as a political party or as *tarikats* (the religious brotherhoods) and also for their increasing strength within the Turkish political landscape.

In other words, the primary aim of the 1980 coup to depoliticize the society and to restructure political activity contained in itself a fundamental contradiction. Notwithstanding its overtly Kemalist orientation, the coup opened a discursive space for the revitalization of the language of difference, a discursive space which created a possibility for the marginalized and silenced identity to surface and express its resistance to the national secular identity as the privileged modern self. More concretely, and even ironically, while the military coup targeted the left, actually unthreatening to the Kemalist identity, it was fostering discourses aimed primarily at dismantling that identity. Thus, depolitization brought into existence once again the secularist versus anti-secularist axis.[15]

Consequently, it can be argued that the rise of the Islamic identity in Turkey is one outcome of the "weak state consensus," in which neo-liberalism went hand in hand with Islamic discourse. It is for this reason that besides its relation to "the newly emergent upwardly mobile middle classes which were organized within the newly laid avenues that the anti-left politics of the 1980s created" (Birtek and Toprak 1993: 193), it emerged, in a discursive fashion, in a context in which Kemalist nationalist discourse was facing a serious identity crisis and its will to civilization was no longer capable of limiting the imagination of political community within the horizon of modernity. More importantly, it emerged at a time when the total exposure (through the increasing modernization of economy based on the export-oriented development) of Turkish society to global modernity was radically transforming identity-conceptions and social configurations into ambivalence and uncertainty. Islamic discourse acted successfully as an articulating principle of resistance to such uncertainty by identifying ambivalence with global modernity and certainty with community, that is, with a turn to religion.

The simultaneous rise of neo-liberalism and Islam, in this sense, should be understood as a product of the historical dilemma of nationalism as a derivative discourse and its increasing inability to demarcate the boundary between identity and difference. This means that the rise of Islamic identity is not simply a "revival" of an essential and coherent identity which, although being marginalized by Kemalist nationalism, was always and already operative in civil society. Rather, Islam appeared to be one of the (indeed, significant) articulating elements of difference by which to construct an alternative subjectivity to the unifying vision of national identity, in an historical context where the depolitization of social relations and the reorganization of political life in a non-participatory mode *unintentionally* created the possibility of thinking of political community outside the terrain of Kemalist nationalism. For this reason, an adequate analysis of the rise of Islamic identity should be situated in the historical context in which it occurred and in relation to the deepening of the crisis of the Kemalist will to civilization.

The Impasse of the Political and the Possibility of "Democratic Opening"

The search for a political community continues to be one of the significant sites that has formed and still gives meaning to Turkish politics in the 1990s. The present conjuncture of the Turkish political landscape is based upon a clash between the discourses of progress, secularism, and Reason and the discourses of traditionalism and anti-secularism. More precisely, the intersection between the decline of the hegemony of Kemalist nationalism and its definition of national identity and the rise of Islamic discourse as an effective articulating principle is one crucial site where the politics of identity is taking place in Turkish political life. Kemalism can no longer be considered an exclusive source of modernity. Instead there are alternative modernities, different articulations of globalization by different discourses, among which Islamism is primary.

Such an occurrence might be considered a positive, insofar as the emergence of alternative visions of modernity might be an indicator of multi-culturalism and pluralism. However, as has been pointed out, the Islamic resurgence was mainly the outcome of "the weak state consensus." To the extent that the weak state consensus aims at minimizing state power rather than democratizing it, it does not contain any possibility of the democratic regulation of the state/society relations in which Islamic identity acts not as the essence of an alternative vision of society, but as an identity among others in a multi-cultural, plural setting.

For this reason, when analyzing the language of difference within the context of Islamic discourse, it is necessary to point to two crucial points of demarcation in order to avoid the trap of falling into the position of reversed-essentialism that the discourse of political Islam, as in the case of the Welfare Party, employs. The first is that the crisis of national identity and the revitalization of the language of difference, while creating "the relative autonomization of economic activities, political groups, and cultural identities," and giving rise to "an autonomous societal sphere" which "has increasingly shifted (the focus of political practice) from the state to society"

(Göle, 1994: 221-222), has also created essentialist identity claims as the primary reference-points of political discourse. In other words, the shift in focus towards civil society and the changing patterns of political discourse reproduced the same essentialist binary logic between secular versus anti-secular, modern versus anti-modern, West versus anti-West, which the discourse of difference aims to repudiate. As we have witnessed in the recent debates over the question of Turkey's entry into the European Union, the issue of multi-culturalism and ethnicity, and the problem of democratization, the language of political Islam tends to be essentialist by promoting a fixed and coherent Islamic community. It does so by speaking the language of difference against what it regards as the totalizing secular national identity. In this way, the political Islamic discourse of the Welfare Party employs a nationalistic standpoint (the Muslim brotherhood) as it articulates its idea of "the just order and the just society" and employs communitarian political strategies. In this sense and in a paradoxical mode, the language of difference turns out to be as nationalistic and totalizing as the national identity to which it is radically opposed.

Ali Yaþar Sarýbay in his important book, *Postmodernity, Civil Society and Islam*, captures and accounts for the paradoxical nature of the discourse of political Islam (Sarýbay 1994). For Sarýbay, the development of an autonomous societal sphere, which he calls "civil society," brings about a pluralist mode of organization of the state/society interactions that creates a space for the presence of Islamic discourse. In this way, civil society with its pluralistic institutional quality can be said to be a pre-condition for Islamic discourse to act as a discourse among others. Viewed in this way, it is internal to civil society and to the projects of democratizing the state/society interactions. However, with its operation based on the principle of *tevhid*, Islamic discourse necessarily aims at rendering plurality into singularity, that is, at reorganizing civil society as a homogeneous space. This paradox that characterizes the double-gesture of Islamic discourse as acting both for and against pluralism indicates that it would be mistaken to take for granted the shift towards civil society as a given and an unproblematic space that provides the foundational ground for democratization. That is to say, while employing the language of difference, the discourse of political Islam also operates as a totalizing discourse, attempts to reinscribe national identity on the basis of a return to Islamic principles, and employs a communitarian notion of political community as a organizing principle of state/society interactions. The result of this paradox is the promotion of the binary logic that situates the secular versus anti-secular polarization at the center of the political, which elevates the essentialist and communitarian claims to identity to the fore of the political agenda.[16]

The second point of demarcation is that the changing terms of political discourse from grand strategies of modernization to identity politics, while characterizing the crisis of Kemalist nationalism, did not mean the end of nationalism. On the contrary, nationalism has become the dominant ideology of the reorganization of civil society in the 1990s. As Tanýl Bora describes, the 1990s have exhibited "the dark spring of nationalism," especially of ethnic nationalism, which provided the ideological dressing of essentialist and communitarian claims to identity (Bora 1995). In other words, the emergence of the language of difference in the post-1980 coup period that had brought with it the shift to civil society resulted in "cultural struggles" in which each and every position put into service nationalist ideology to articulate its identity politics.[17] A quick glance at these positions in cultural struggles, which have been organized around a binary logic, first between secular identity and Islamic identity, second between Turkish identity and Kurdish identity, and third between European identity and Turkish national identity, illustrates the resurgence of nationalist ideology in the form of (ethnic) identity politics in the 1990s. In these positions, it is nationalist ideology that made it possible for each to speak of its identity as if it is coherent, fixed, and constituted by an eternal essence, to redescribe the political through the practice of inclusion/exclusion and based upon the us/them distinction, and to pose itself as the foundational ground of political community. It is also nationalist ideology that enabled each to present itself as a unifying element of civil society. Thus, the discourse of political Islam attempted to unify different identities under the notion of Muslim brotherhood, Kemalist nationalism under the notion of secular identity, ethnic nationalist discourse under the notion of Turkish identity. As a result, essentialist claims to identity with a nationalist dressing marked and dictated the boundaries of the political in the 1990s.

What these two points of demarcation indicate is that Turkish politics in the 1990s has been and continues to be characterized both by the end of certainty, established by the Kemalist will to civilization through its economic, political, and cultural meta-narratives of modernization, and the presence of ambivalence in the way in which the state/society interactions are regulated and managed. On the one hand, we have the emergence of civil society as a site of political practice and the revitalization of political identities as discourses of difference that have created a new ground outside the terrain of Kemalist nationalism for thinking about the question of democracy. Thus, the democratization of the state/civil society interactions within the context of the recognition of differences as a challenge to the mono-culturalism of a republican search for national identity has become a significant term of political discourse of the 1990s. On the other hand, we have nationalist attempts to render the discourse of difference into an essentialist claim to identity, that have resulted in the organization of civil society through communitarian lines which prevents rather than enables the project of democracy to be consolidated. In using Ayþe Kadýoðlu's terminology, what marks the nature of Turkish politics in the 1990s is the ambivalent relationship between "the state in search of its nation" and the nation in search of its description (Kadýoðlu 1995).

The main conclusion, which can be extrapolated from the recognition of the presence of ambivalence as the marker of Turkish politics in the 1990s, is the following. If it is true that the possibility of the project of democracy has been impeded by the essentialist and communitarian claims to identity, then it is necessary to think of identity in relation to difference, to problematize any unifying and totalizing notion of identity, to put identity under an historical investigation to discover how it is constituted in relation to difference, that is, to recognize that the very unity of an identity is always achieved through the practice of the exclusion of other identities. To do so requires an epistemic shift to the problematic of identity/difference that sees identity in relational terms and resists its essentialist and communitarian articulation. It can be argued in this sense that the possibility of strengthening the project of democracy is present only when we recognize that each and every identity is constructed in relational terms and that the historical and discursive construction of every identity, whether it be national, ethnic or religious, gains unity and coherence not internally by an eternal essence but in relation to other identities. It is precisely because of this fact that the very possibility of the project of democracy is dependent upon the recognition of "the limit of an identity" as a way of resisting the essentialist and unifying notions of political community.[18] The problematic of identity/difference therefore helps us not only to see how democratic possibilities can turn out to be possibilities for the articulation of essentialist claims to identity (as in the case of Turkey in the 1990s) but also, and more importantly, to develop effective strategies against essentialism, nationalism and communitarianism in the attempt to consolidate the project of democracy. Such strategies, I believe, are our only chance to break the weak state consensus, generating a suitable climate for the nationalist and communitarian visions of society, and to build a "democratic consensus" between state and civil society, identity and difference, and the self and the other.

Notes

1. The difference that rewriting Turkish history based on "the woman question" makes has been very convincingly elaborated by N. Göle (1991). See also D. Kandiyoti (1991).
2. Whereas the rise of Islam and the re-emergence of Kurdish nationalism appear to be reactionary in terms of their essentialist appeal to political identity, feminist discourse aims at democratic reconstruction of civil society on the basis of the recognition of difference.
3. After the Supreme Court's decision to close the Welfare Party, a new party with the name of Virtue Party, was created and all the members of the Welfare Party were transferred to this new party. There is now a new case at the Supreme Court to shut down the Virtue Party, based on the claim that it is not a new party but just a replica of the Welfare Party. In this sense, the debate on the legitimacy of the Supreme Court decision still continues in Turkey.
4. These reforms include "the hat revolution," the reform of attire, the adaption of a civil code, "the alphabet reform," and religious reforms. For detail, see S. Yerasimos (1987).
5. For a different explanation of this practice of inclusion/exclusion, see L. Köker (1990). However, Köker's aim to challenge the claimed relationship between Kemalism and democracy seems to me to be problematic due to his reliance on the institutional conception of democracy as well as his complete neglect of the self/other question which I believe constitutes the basis of Kemalist nationalism.
6. Foucault defines governmentality as a way of subjugating differences to the domain of subjectivity. As he puts it, "In this sense, 'to be subject' is therefore 'to belong to,' in other words to behave as both an element of and an actor in a global process whose development defines the current field of possible experiences, inside of which the fact of being subject can only be situated." For detail, see M. Foucault (1979).
7. By locating secularism in a binary dichotomy between modernity and tradition, "the woman question" occupied an important space for Kemalist nationalism. The symbolic representation of women as the bearer of modernization was the strategy used against the anti-secular Islamic identity. The recognition of the place and the role of women in the public life of the republic as "educated social women," the adoption of the Swiss civil code in 1926 with which Turkish women gained new rights (the abolition of polygamy and repudiation), and the enfranchisement of women in 1934 were the policies by which the secular identity and its essential role for progress was justified against the anti-secular Islamic identity. It should be noted however that the rights and the reforms provided by the Kemalist elite, although they were based upon the recognition of the equality of Turkish men and women, were also obstacles to the emergence of an independent women's movement. In other words, the state-proclaimed gender equality rested on the symbolic representation of women as "symbolic pawns" rather than "political actors". For a detailed reading of the process of modernization from the angle of "the woman question," see N. Sirman (1989) and D. Kandiyoti (1989).
8. Here I am relying on Toprak's interpretation of Islam as a political force. See B. Toprak, (1987: 219).
9. For this theoretical extrapolation, I am drawing on David Campbell (1992). Campbell demonstrates such performative construction with reference to security discourse and foreign policy practice in the United States.
10. For a detailed analysis of the New Left and its relation to Kemalism, see A. Samim (1981).

11. Similarly, the New Left discourse had no alternative vision of economic development. In fact, the vision of the economy it proposed was based also on import substitution industrialization with the state as the primary agent by which inequalities and uneven development were to be coped with in the name of dominated classes.
12. For the connection between the state and new right discourse, see M. Tünay (1993).
13. For an account of the changing nature of Turkish foreign policy toward the Middle East and especially with respect to Islamic capital, see B. A. Yeþilada (1993).
14. Interestingly enough, the use of Islamic identity by the military regime in the form of the Turkish-Islam synthesis, in order to depoliticize society and eliminate the Left-discourse from the political sphere, which contributed to the resurgence of Islamic identity as a political force, ended in 1997, as the National Security Council declared that Islamic fundamentalism constitutes a fundamental threat to the secular regime. In this sense, the post-1980 Turkish modernization indicates the ambigious and the pragramatic role of Turkish military with respect to Islam.
15. For a very good account of this contradiction, see F. Birtek and B. Toprak (1993: 193-201).
16. For an elaboration of the communitarian claim to identity and its ambivalent relation to the process of democratization, see E. F. Keyman (1995).
17. I borrowed the term "cultural struggle" from Sarýbay (1994).
18. I discussed in a detailed fashion the importance of the recognition of the limit of identity for the project of democracy in Keyman (1995 and 1996).

References

Abdel-Malek A. 1981, *Social Dialectics*, Albany: State University of New York Press.
Ahmad F. 1993, *The Making of Modern Turkey*, London: Routledge.
Anderson B. 1983, *Imagined Communities*, London: Verso.
Appadurai A. 1990, "Disjuncture and Difference in the Global Cultural Economy," in Featherstone, M, *Global Culture*, London: Sage.
Berberoglu B. 1982, *Turkey in Crisis*, London: Zed Books.
Birtek F. and Toprak B. 1993, "The Conflictual Agendas of Neo-Liberal Reconstruction and the Rise of Islamic Politics in Turkey: The Hazards of Rewriting Turkish Modernity," *Praxis International*, 13, pp.192-211.
Bora T. 1995 *Milliyetciligin Kara Bahari*, Istanbul: Birikim.
Campbell D. 1992, *Writing Security*, Minneapolis: University of Minnesota Press.
Carrier J. G. 1992, "Occidentalism: the World Turned Upside-down," *American Ethnologist*, 19, pp. 43-57.
Chatterjee P. 1986, *Nationalist Thought and The Colonial World; A Derivative Discourse*, The United Nations University: Zed Books.
Connolly W. 1996, *The Ethos of Pluralization*, Minneapolis: University of Minnesota Press.
de Ferro C. 1995, "The Will to Civilization and its encounter with Laisser-Faire," *Alternatives*, 27, pp.89-103.
Eralp A. 1990, "The Politics of Turkish Development Strategies," in Finkel, A. and Sirman, N. (eds), *Turkish State, Turkish Society*, London: Routledge.

Foucault M. 1979, "Governmentality," *Ideology and Consciousness*, 6, pp.5-21.

Göle N. 1991, *Modern Mahrem*, Istanbul: Metis.

Göle N. 1994, "Toward an Autonomization of Politics and Civil Society in Turkey," in Heper, M. and Evin, A. (eds) *Politics in the Third Turkish Republic*, Boulder: Westview.

Gülalp H. 1983, *Gelişme Stratejileri Gelişme Ýdeolojileri*, Ankara: Yurt Yayýnlarý.

Hall S. Held D. and McGrew T. (eds), 1992, *Modernity and its Futures*, Cambridge:Polity.

Heper M. 1985, *The State Tradition in Turkey*, North Humberside: The Eothen Press.

Kadýoðlu A. 1995, "Milletini Arýyan Devlet: Türk Milliyetçiliðinin Açmazlarý," *Türkiye Günlüðü*, 33, pp.91-100.

Kandiyot, D. 1989, "Women and the Turkish State: Political Actors or Symbolic Pawns," in Yuval-Davis, A. and Anthias, F. (eds), *Woman-Nation-State*, London: Macmillan.

Kandiyoti D. 1991, *Women, Islam, and the State*, London: Macmillan.

Keyder C. 1987, *State and Class in Turkey*, London: Verso.

Keyder C. 1993a, "The Dilemma of Cultural Identity on the Margin of Europe," *Review*, 16, pp.19-33.

Keyder C. 1993b, "Türk Milliyetçiliðine Bakmaya Başlarken," *Toplum ve Bilim*, 62, pp.7-18.

Keyman, E.F. 1995, "Demokrasi. Toplululk, Fark," *Toplum ve Bilim*, 66, pp.140-167.

Keyman, E.F. 1997, Globalization, State, Identity/Difference, New Jersey: Humanities Press.

Köker L. 1990, *Modernleşme, Kemalism, and Demokrasi*, Ýstanbul: Ýletişim Yayýnlarý.

Laclau E. 1996, *Emancipation(s)*, London: Verso.

Landau J.M. (ed.), 1984. *Ataturk and the Modernization of Turkey*, Boulder: Westview Press.

Lewis B. 1968, *Emergence of Modern Turkey*, London: Oxford University Press.

Onis Z. 1997, "The political economy of Islamic resurgence in Turkey," *Third World Quarterly*, 4, pp. 743-766.

Robertson R. 1992, *Globalization*, London: Sage.

Robins K. 1996, "Interrupting Identities: Turkey/Europe," Hall, S. (ed.), *Questions of Cultural Identity*, London, Sage.

Said E. 1979, *Orientalism*, New York: Vintage Books.

Said E. 1993, *Culture and Imperialism*, London: Chatto and Vindus.

Samim A. 1981, "The Left", in Schick I.C. and Tonak, A.E. (eds) *Turkey in Transition*, New York: Oxford University Press.

Sarýbay A. Y. 1994, *Postmodernite, Sivil Toplum ve Ýslam*, Ýstanbul, Ýletişim.

Sirman N. 1989, "Feminism in Turkey: A Short History," *New Perspectives on Turkey*, 3, pp.1-34.

Spivak G. C. 1987, *In Other Worlds*, New York: Methuen.

Steinbach U. 1984, "The Impact of Ataturk on Turkey's Political Culture since World War II," in Landau, J.M (ed), *Ataturk and the Modernization of Turkey*, Boulder: Westview Press.

Toprak B. 1987, "The Religious Right," in Schick, I.C and Tonak, A.E. (eds), *Turkey in Transition*, New York: Oxford University Press.

Tünay M. 1993, "The Turkish New Right's Attempt at Hegemony," in Eralp, A.,Tunay, M., and Yeşilada, B.A. (eds), *The Political and Socioeconomic Transformation of Turkey*, Westport: Praeger.

Yerasimos S. 1987, "The Monoparty Period" in Schick I.C. and Tonak E. A. (eds) *Turkey in Transition*.

Yeşilada B. A. 1993, "Turkish Foreign Policy toward the Middle East," in Eralp, A., Tünay, M., and Yeşilada, B.A. (eds), *The Political and Socioeconomic Transformation of Turkey*, Westport: Praeger.

9 Restructuring Citizenship Regimes: The French and Canadian Women's Movements in the 1990s

JANE JENSON

Restructuring under the effects of globalization is a complicated phenomenon. Social policies are being restructured, if not dismantled. Patterns and institutions of political participation are changing. New civil rights and recognition are being won. All of these are happening, in part, as the result of struggles by social movements to confront the many faces of globalization or to make sense of the many globalizations they confront. In all of this, citizenship regimes are being changed.

This chapter begins from the observation that women's movements and their organizations were sometimes active participants in the design of the post-1945 citizenship regimes, and that they were certainly major actors in the extension of programmes crucial to that regime in the 1960s and 1970s. It therefore focuses on the actions of these movements and organizations in the face of retrenchment and redesign of citizenship since the mid-1980s. It uses two cases – Canada and France – to show that women's participation and influence can differ widely across movements.

In brief, the chapter demonstrates that a central wing of the French movement has made a major shift in strategy, focusing on changing the rules of the political game, and more specifically the electoral law.[1] In so doing, it downplays any social agenda, participating actively in the entrenchment of a political discourse which limits republican citizenship to political equality and allowing issues of social and economic equality to be left to market forces.

By the 1990s, French women were leaders in a European movement for gender parity in elected assemblies, and they had some significant successes. In the 1997 legislative elections (as in the Europarliamentary elections before them), the long-standing minuscule representation of women in the *Assemblée Nationale* leapt forward, almost doubling from one election to the next, to reach 10.9 percent. This shift, which was concentrated in parties of the Left, and especially the Socialist Party, was an explicit response to the parity movement, in this case by "reserving" 30 percent of constituencies for women. Then, after several years of active mobilization for reform, the French parliament voted in 1999 to reform the Constitution of the Fifth

Republic. Section 3 now provides that "the law supports women and men's equal access to office," while the next Section instructs political parties to achieve this equality.

The Canadian movement, in contrast, was one of the central defenders of the post-war citizenship regime. It made progress on its legislative agenda, despite the rhetoric of neo-conservatism which dominated the government of the day (Bashevkin 1994). It was deeply involved in the constitutional politics around both the Meech Lake Accord (1988-90) and the Charlottetown Agreement (1991-92) as well as in the campaigns against the Free Trade Agreement (FTA) with the US (1985-88) and the North American Free Trade Agreement (NAFTA). Its positions were always presented as the defence of equality of social programmes. Despite this, the women's movement is now reduced to virtual invisibility, its institutional supports have been wiped out within the state (Jenson and Phillips 1996), and its organizational base weakened by funding cuts.

These two case studies of women's and their organizations' participation in the restructuring of citizenship regimes are useful for what they can tell us about women's participation in regime shifts. More specifically, the paper argues that strategic choices about policy and alliances have determining effects on the capacity of women's movements to participate in and influence regime redesign. Neither inclusion nor exclusion is automatic. It depends upon past practice, the alliance situation, and the strategic assessment of how to respond to other actors' efforts to alter citizenship regimes.

Citizenship Regime: A Brief Presentation [2]

Citizenship is a social construction. As such, it varies across both space and time.[3] We define a citizenship regime as the institutional arrangements, rules and understandings that guide and shape concurrent policy decisions and expenditures of states, problem definitions by states and citizens, and claims-making by citizens. A citizenship regime encodes within it a paradigmatic representation of identities, of the "national" as well as the "model citizen," the "second-class citizen," and the non-citizen. It also encodes representations of the proper and legitimate social relations among and within these categories, as well as the borders of "public" and "private." It makes, in other words, a major contribution to the definition of politics which organizes the boundaries of political debate and problem recognition in each jurisdiction.

These representations of identities and social relations are the foundation for claims-making. It is only by representing their identity that groups and individuals can make sense of their interests to themselves and others. In other words, representation of self is an integral aspect of representation of interests. The state has a role, too, in that it has the power to recognize citizens, both in general and as particular categories of citizens. The state uses such recognition to make sense of the claims addressed to it.

Being regimes, they are relatively stable. Indeed, we might characterize a stable regime as one in which the status proffered and the status anticipated match, so that the representation of citizens by the state accommodates citizens' representations of themselves. Being a regime, citizenship does not alter quickly or even easily. Nonetheless, we can expect to find change at moments of economic and political turbulence. In such moments of fundamental restructuring of the role of the state, the division of labour between state and market, and between public and "private," definitions of the "national" as well as of the "model citizen" may alter. The same general cast of characters is involved in the redesign of the citizenship regime, that is the state and its institutions, and the political forces of civil society, including social movements.[4]

The Canadian Women's Movement After 1985: The Last Gasp of Progressive Forces?

By the mid-1970s, the postwar citizenship regime included country-wide institutions which addressed citizens as individual "Canadians," thereby and for a few short decades, mapping the whole country as a single political space with which its citizens might identify. Simultaneously, however, there was symbolic and programmatic acknowledgement of particular **categories** of citizens, thereby granting legitimacy to the intermediary associations of civil society representing those particular interests (Jenson 1991). Initially, intermediary associations had been recognized as vital aspects of the citizenship regime because, by organizing marginalized groups, they reinforced a fledgling national identity and built loyalty to it. By the 1970s, they were accepted as important representatives of citizens' identities and advocates for social rights, contributing to the fairness of the democratic process by giving a voice to the socially and economically disadvantaged. Canadian identity had come to include a social component.

Construction of the regime was a long-term project. It began in the war years, and the 1946 Citizenship Act which created Canadian citizens from

British subjects was an important moment for defining national identity. It reached its most elaborated form in the Charter of Rights and Freedoms which was embedded in the Constitution in 1982.[5] A discourse of equity and social development supplemented the liberal grounding of social rights. Through the postwar years, progressive forces assumed that the principal institution for achieving national development was the federal government.[6] The result was a legacy in left-wing, progressive politics of a strong preference for federal action and a mistrust of "decentralization" and too much provincial responsibility.[7]

The discourse of equity and social justice was pervasive, shaping proposals for everything, from reforming party financing to health care, and concretized by a boom in state support for intermediary organizations to assure representation of citizens to, and in, the state.[8] In this discourse, realization of the political rights of citizenship required both regulation and state support for these basic institutions guaranteeing access to citizens. As Bernard Ostry, a former Assistant Under Secretary in the Citizenship Branch of the Secretary of State said, the goal of the branch was to "develop and strengthen a sense of Canadian citizenship, chiefly through programmes that would aid participation and assuage feelings of social injustice" (quoted in Pal 1993: 109).

The women's movement was a priority for government funding because gender inequality had become an acknowledged – and unacceptable – form of social injustice. The second-class citizenship which the Royal Commission on the Status of Women had documented and recommended against, was to be altered by supporting (and indeed creating) a range of organizations which would function as advocates for women. The National Action Committee (NAC) resulted from such a recommendation, and its founding meeting in 1972 received $15,000 from the federal government (Burt 1995: 87). Subsequently, funding continued to NAC (in the early 1980s, 90 percent of its funding came from the federal government [Bashevkin 1996: 220]) and to a wide range of other women's groups (in SecState alone the budget for women's groups went from $223,000 in 1973, to $12.5 million in 1985 [Burt, 1995: p.87]).

The agenda of the women's movement reflected its place in the citizenship regime. In 1984, Sandra Burt surveyed women's groups about their priorities, and found "they concentrated primarily on the reform of the abortion law, sexual equality in the workplace, an end to violence against women and national child-care strategy" (Burt 1995: 88). For the subset of national-level groups, "their goals were woman-centered and focused on breaking down the barriers to the fair and equal treatment of women in the home or workplace" (Burt 1995: 89). These were all policy domains in which the federal government had either exclusive responsibility or, in the days of "interventionary federalism," played a major role. Thus, Bashevkin's description of NAC in its first decade applies not only to it, but to a wide range of women's groups: "Overall, NAC's outlook reflected a centralist vision that saw the federal government as the primary vehicle of policy change, as well as a liberal vision that emphasized legal rights, equal employment opportunities and other types of institutional reform" (Bashevkin 1996: 221).[9]

In these years, then, the women's movement's work and struggles fit into the citizenship regime. It spoke for a group which did not yet have full citizenship and which was fighting to achieve it. To say it "fit" does not mean that gains were handed on a platter. Obviously this was not the case. Even in the most "citizenship-like" struggle, that for the protection of equality rights in the Constitution in the early 1980s, Section 28 was won only through massive mobilization and political action. However, in these years, when the movement mobilized against gender injustice, it found allies not only among progressive forces but also within the federal government, where femocrats played important policy roles among political parties, including the major opposition party, and provincial governments. Its claims "made sense" within the terms of political discourse at the time and it had allies among elites as well as other political forces.

The movement's claims made sense because they were located in a widespread political discourse about equity and equality. Pay equity as it emerged in Canada provides an example of the way the women's movement used the language of social justice and helped to define what social justice was. The Canadian way to say "comparable worth" – that is, the struggle for pay equity – was a struggle organized by women with links to the trade union movement, who sought legislative remedies maintaining a role for collective actors, including unions, in the process. Thus, it was struggle which depended less on individual action, through the courts, than did comparable worth in the US. It was more a struggle of women and unions than women against unions; there was a shared notion that intermediary associations were crucial to a well-functioning civil society. It sought to use the political process rather than the courts. Indeed, the very decision to call the struggle that of "equity" reflects the extent to which the citizenship regime was centred on the concept of "fairness."

In her second survey of national groups in 1993 Sandra Burt found basic continuity. The intervening years had been difficult for the internal life of the movement which had been challenged to be more inclusive in its definition of women's needs. This was reflected in the emphasis placed on the rights of minority and immigrant women, but when asked to define feminism the groups continued to use the language of equality. "For them, feminism meant the full equality of women, equal opportunity for women, or the attainment of women's legal equality" (Burt 1995: 90-91). Moreover, the route to equality for the groups was quite specific. "This call by feminist advocacy groups for equal rights is primarily a call for government action, in the form of either social programmes or of funding of women's groups" (Burt 1995: 92).

Unfortunately this definition of how to achieve equality – and even the language of equality – was falling on deaf ears. In 1985 the Tories led by Brian Mulroney had begun to cut funding for advocacy groups, including women's groups. When the Liberals returned to office in 1993, they continued the cuts, joining the right-wing populist Reform Party and the Tories in tagging almost any kind of advocacy group a "special interest," and therefore not really representative of any one (Phillips 1991). It was the Liberal government which also dared simply to close down the machinery of the "women's state." That other body recommended by the Royal Commission, the Advisory Council on the Status of Women, disappeared (Jenson and Phillips 1996). Moreover, the Liberals, as the Tories before them, were engaged in redesigning the Canadian state. Responsibility for social services was being off-loaded in three directions: to the provinces, to the "third sector" and to the market.

These changes were not directed particularly against women. They marked, rather, the collapse of the postwar citizenship regime and the rise of a political discourse of neo-liberalism. The federal government is busily divesting itself of its roles. With its participation in the FTA and NAFTA it has handed over a portion of state sovereignty to the rules of "free trade." It is attempting to convince "third sector partners" to become providers of services which were previously public. Moreover, it has willingly abandoned its commitment to its own role as the "central government," advocating greater "decentralization" to the provinces. In general, in English-speaking Canada, the direction of movement has been from equity toward marketization.[10] Not only has the growing support for a neo-liberal definition of the relations among markets, states and communities been central to this transformation, but the analogy of the market has been superimposed directly on the concept and practices of citizenship. According to this analogy, representation of interests is a competitive market – ideally a free market – whose most appropriate participants are individuals. For neo-liberals, individuals should look out for their own and their family's interests, being responsible for their economic, social and political successes and failures. Political parties may compete for citizens' support but intermediary associations have no role to play. The value placed on competition also implies minimal interference by the state in supporting equality of access to the rights of citizenship, either in ensuring that a wide range of citizens are actually being represented, or in assisting disadvantaged categories of citizens to develop the capacity to participate at all. Any gap between formal rights of citizenship, and actual access to them, is the result of individual differences or differential engagement.

This proposed replacement for the older citizenship regime did not immediately gain popular support. Indeed, beginning with the free trade negotiations of the mid-1980s, progressive forces – self-named the popular sector – fought each element of the federal government's strategy. They did so in the name of their commitment to a strong central government capable of resisting the pull of US liberalism and protecting Canadian identity, symbolized by social programmes, and especially public health care. The popular sector was fighting to protect its definition (which had previously been hegemonic) of what it meant to be a Canadian citizen. The groups making up the popular sector certainly considered themselves to be fighting for what it meant to be Canadian.[11]

In all these struggles, NAC and many of the other parts of the women's movement were front and centre.[12] First there was free trade, and the argument that job losses would hit women in particular, and that the Agreement threatened Canada's social policy regimes (Cohen 1992). Opposition to the Meech Lake and Charlottetown Accords was framed as jeopardizing Charter equality rights by giving too much discretion to Quebec (Meech), or to the institutions of Aboriginal self-government (Charlottetown), opposition which is credited with the defeat of both agreements (see for example Rebick (1993); she was President of NAC through these years). In between, there was opposition to the government's child care strategy, opposition which contributed to the death of the Bill (Phillips 1989), and the struggle against the Goods and Service Tax (Cohen 1992).

These were all the big battles of the late 1980s and 1990s, pitting the defenders of Canadian social traditions against neo-liberalism. These defenders were becoming fewer and fewer, however. After the Meech Lake debacle, groups from Quebec (even those leaning toward federalist positions) were out, which meant a loss of voices for an active state. When the Liberals were elected in 1993 they immediately disabused any who might have believed that the agenda had been simply a "neo-Conservative" one; the Liberals began to implement the Mulroney programme with enthusiasm.

Indeed they pushed it further. As much as the Conservative party, the Liberals had to "protect" themselves on the right from the populism and market individualism of the Reform Party. Key provinces (first Alberta and then Ontario) fell into the hands of even more committed right-wing governments.

By the mid-1990s, in other words, the women's movement's defence of the old citizenship regime and its place within it was becoming harder and harder. As Bashevkin says of the years after the mid-1980s, "NAC functioned less and less as a moderate but critical interest group, and became increasingly identified as an oppositional protest group" (1996: 223). The question is: why? We have seen that the political opportunity structure fundamentally altered. The movement's allies among elites and within the state disappeared, or were disappeared.[13] But more than that, the very project which the movement defended and which defined its identity had lost resonance.

The women's movement had been defending a set of programmes and practices which expressed a vision of citizenship that went beyond gender issues. Women's equality had been folded into a set of broader claims for social justice, its movement and organization had been one of the important intermediaries between individuals and the state, upon which it claimed democracy and justice both depended, and all of this had been seen as an expression of Canadian identity. This project that has been "reconfigured" out of existence, and the second-wave of the women's movement which was both a central expression of it and a core carrier of its values, found that it made sense to fewer and fewer people. The previously powerful movement, which had been able to make change in the 1980s **despite** the difficulties of its struggles, had been pushed aside, gone from the state, gone from the media, and facing mounting internal dissension.

France's *Mouvement pour la parité*: The Wave of the Future?

Readers have noted, I hope, that in the various lists of claims and descriptions of the women's movement in Canada, the politics of gender presence was not a major item on the agenda. In the conferences leading up to the Charlottetown Accord, there was some discussion of reforming the Senate, not only to make it an elected body, but also one guaranteeing gender parity. However, the idea was pushed off the table when the New Democratic government of British Columbia changed its position and withdrew its support. In the final analysis, as a feminist lawyer deeply involved with the negotiations wrote afterwards:

> NAC has been concerned from the beginning that institutions of government be inclusive of women in all our diversity, as well as men of colour, men with disabilities, gay men and poor men. We would prefer to see an inclusive institution with 40 percent women than a perfectly gender-balanced institution that is still dominated by those who are white, able-bodied, heterosexual and professional (Day 1993: 62).

This is not the position of the movement for parity in France and the rest of the European Union.

In France, the movement began to gain supporters with the publication, in 1992 by Françoise Gaspard, Claude Servan-Schreiber, and Anne Le Gall, of *Au pouvoir citoyennes: Liberté, Egalité, Parité*. In 1993 a Manifesto of 577 (289 women and 288 men) was published in support of parity-based democracy. In June 1996, ten female ex-Ministers from governments of the Right and the Left published a Manifesto for Parity in *L'Express*.[14] Private members' bills were tabled in the National Assembly, proposing methods for achieving parity, ranging from a constitutional amendment, to quotas and changes in public funding of political parties. The political parties and candidates have also responded. After a glance at public opinion polls in 1994, Michel Rocard, head of the Socialist list for the Europarliamentary elections, announced he would run a parity list.[15] Indeed, fully six lists looked quite *paritaire*.[16] In the 1995 presidential elections, all of the candidates (except Jean-Marie Le Pen) declared their support for "parity".[17] After Jacques Chirac won the election, he honored only one of his promises: to create an *Observatoire de la parité*. That body commissioned a report by Gisèle Halimi, one of the "historic feminists" of the second wave. This report was submitted in December 1996 and recommended a constitutional amendment. After the surprise legislative elections of June 1997 that returned a Left majority, Prime Minister Lionel Jospin declared that a constitutional amendment was part of his government's programme. The amendment of 1999 resulted.

Where does this movement come from? It clearly reflects a long-standing frustration with the virtual exclusion of women from elected bodies. In 1968, the National Assembly was 98.4 percent male. After two decades of second-wave feminism, the number had decreased to 93.9 percent in 1993. Indeed, the 6 percent of women in the National Assembly, if the highest score since 1945, still meant France's rate of representation of women was half that of the European Union in general and the lowest except for Greece in the EU in 1993.

The idea of enshrining gender parity in the Constitution of the Fifth Republic follows directly from the failure of a previous strategy. In 1982, the Socialist government, with the unanimous support of the National Assembly, had proposed a quota of 25 percent for lists in municipal elections. In effect, the law would have limited all lists to a maximum of 75 percent of candidates of the same sex. This timid effort to impose a quota was immediately found unconstitutional by the *Conseil constitutionnel,* which declared, on November 18, 1982, that the law contravened both Section 3 of the Constitution of the Fifth Republic, and Article 6 of the Declaration of the Rights of Man and the Citizen. In essence, the argument was that a 25 percent quota, in the name of affirmative action, interfered with the equality of all citizens before the law. In order to get around the judgement against quotas and affirmative action, some activists recommend altering the Constitution.

Despite the differences in the propositions and modalities proposed, it is important for our purposes to understand three things about the *mouvement pour la parité:* its composition, its focus on electoral institutions, and its discourse. They move away from the basic premises of the postwar French citizenship regime and propose a replacement stressing only the political rights of citizenship in a republican framework.

The movement crosses traditional political boundaries, as the Manifesto of politicians clearly showed; elected women of the Right stood alongside those of the Left (Besnier 1997: 2). More than that, with the exception of the far left, particularly the Trotskyists, there is widespread support for some kind of institutional adjustment to achieve gender parity.[18] In organizational terms this is not a grassroots movement. For example, a major coordinating body is *Demain la Parité*, which describes itself as going beyond religious, political or ethnic cleavages. The eight affiliated associations or federations are: *Action Catholique Générale Féminine* (ACGF); *Association Française des Femmes Diplômées des Universités* (AFFDU); *Coordination Française pour le Lobby Européen des Femmes* (CLEF); *Elles Aussi; Organisation Internationale des Femmes Sionistes* (WIZO); *Parité-Infos; Union Féminine Civique et Sociale* (UFCS); and *Union Professionnelle Féminine* (UPF) (Massé 1996: 4).[19] The *Verts* have also been active supporters of the movement, designating Alain Lipietz to speak frequently at public meetings. Indeed, the ecologists can be said to be one of the few really broad-based organizations within the movement. The rest are either traditional women's associations, or small elite groups of dedicated activists.

The focus on electoral institutions is clear. Indeed, the movement says nothing about – indeed refuses to raise the issue of – policy content to be expected from achieving parity. The goal is to change the functioning of institutions; the movement refuses to start down the slippery road followed by some first-wave and second-wave feminists, who claimed that electing women would have particular and positive policy outcomes. Of course, activists must defend themselves against those, usually from the left of the political spectrum, who would prefer a solidly left-wing man to a right-wing women.

The fundamental political philosophy of the movement reveals the links to alterations in citizenship regimes. We can identify this philosophy in two steps. The principle presented first here is really tributary to that presented secondly. It is the **how**. There must be no quotas. Absolute equality – 50/50 – is not a quota, and therefore not "special treatment." Rather, it is a way of translating formal equality into reality. As Gisèle Halimi claims, this is a way of guaranteeing the *"passage de la liberté formelle au droit réel"* [the move from formal freedom to real rights] (Sineau, 1996: 9).[20] In this way, activists claim they can avoid being dismissed by the Court as contravening the Declaration of Rights of Man and the Constitution which says that *"la loi garantit à la femme, dans tous les domaines, les droits égaux à ceux de l'homme"* [the law guarantees to the woman, in all realms, equal rights to those of the man].

The central principle, the one upon which the whole structure stands, is the **why**. In the founding document of the movement, we find a denunciation of "the pernicious idea that women can be treated as class, as a category . . . Women are neither a corporate body nor a lobby. They constitute one half of a sovereign people, one half of humankind." (Gaspard *et al.* 1992: 164-66; freely translated). This is the foundational idea of the movement. It is repeated constantly, and it challenges in a basic way the construction of France's post-1945 citizenship regime, while fitting well with the elements proposed to replace it.

France's post-war citizenship promoted republicanism, to be sure.[21] The Constitutions of the Fourth and Fifth Republic both retained elements of the revolutionary tradition, and the Declaration of the Rights of Man and the Citizen. Thus, the state, as the expression of the Republic, would be used to achieve social justice. Republicanism defined a set of "universal" rights in which liberty and equality would be guaranteed to all citizens, at the same time as society assumed responsibility for the well-being of all its members in the name of solidarity. The state was a privileged agent guaranteeing these rights and the privileged actors were the organizations of the people, whether parties or associations, which would be recognized as representatives of corporate bodies.[22]

Moreover, just as we saw that Canada's fundamental liberalism was modified by a discourse of social justice and a definition of representation which depended on intermediary institutions assuring the link between the individual and the state, France's postwar republicanism was modified by other discourses. Of particular importance was that of class. In institutional terms, this meant numerous institutions, based on the principle of parity, were set up or reinforced in the post-war decades. The definition of parity was not what it is now, however. Then it meant the **equal representation of employers and workers** in various bodies governing relations in the work place and elsewhere. The movement for gender parity cites this historical precedent, making the following claim: if the political institutions could accommodate one kind of parity, why object so vehemently to another?

Any uncertainty that the distinction between social classes and between left and right were the core social and political difference in France's citizenship regime had disappeared by the mid-1960s. Electoral politics of the Fifth Republic at this point clearly divided into two, with the Communists being readmitted to the status of a legitimate party, and centrist Christian Democracy folding its tent. All other politics turned on this same distinction between right and left. For example, throughout the postwar period, associations representing any "category" of the population were aligned, at least with a political family, and often with a political party. The latter was the case of the *Union des Femmes Françaises*, a flanking organization of the Communist Party. But there were also parent-teacher associations divided by political family, teachers and professors unions, hunting and fishing associations, and so on. The result was that French citizens' political identity simply depended on their position on the left-right spectrum.

In many cases, as for the unions, for example, the line of division was less between the left and right (although for a long time it was between Catholic or not) as **within** the Left. Therefore, when the second-wave women's movement appeared after 1968, its organizations faced a choice. Either they were aligned with someone on the left-right spectrum or they were "autonomous." While the autonomous groups, such as *Psych et Po* or *Femmes en mouvement*, may have been the most visible, fostering both the "famous French feminism" and huge battles within the movement, the majority of feminists – whether revolutionary, egalitarian or syndicalist – had a political allegiance which went beyond the movement (Duchen 1986). Many of these allegiances produced stormy relations, to be sure, but there is no denying their importance.

There were two concrete consequences of a citizenship regime which forced a choice. The first was that French feminism was never non-partisan. For all the talk of "women" as unified whole, groups continued to act separately, usually under the banner of their party or formation. The second was that, despite all their efforts to unite Marxism and feminism into a unified whole, or to make gender equality as important as economic equality, second-wave feminists never succeeded in altering left-wing discourse. Women remained a category, one of the "and the" added on the list of all those who would benefit from the victories of class forces. On the right, of course, women were never other than a category, if they achieved any visibility at all.

This citizenship regime became shaky and started to lose its underpinnings in the mid-1980s. One important moment came when President Mitterrand and Prime Minister Fabius led the Socialist government to the historic decision not to fight the European Union's economic policy. With this historic choice, Mitterrand moved the economic policy of the Socialist governments toward a broad centre republican tradition, and away from the more left-wing vision of republicanism which placed the goal of reducing inequalities – both social and sexual – front and center. The goal according to the President and his supporters within the Socialist Party and elsewhere was to "modernize" France by reconfiguring the role of the state and its relationship with civil society.

The nature and extent of the *tournant* is captured by the following assessment after two years of Fabius' residence at Matignon. In this assessment we find that all the elements of the postwar citizenship regime have altered:

> When Laurent Fabius lists the differences between Left and Right, he does not speak about reducing social inequalities but more modestly about 'equality of opportunity.' And Lionel Jospin emphasizes the need to 'better harmonize the collective interest with the interest of the individual.' Steadily we are moving from the condemnation of inequalities to the **recognition of differences**. Overall, the constraints of economic modernization, flexibility and efficiency take the place of pressures to be solidaristic, promote social justice and reduce inequalities. . . . Thus, everything happens as if what was seen, in the past, as an unjust inequality had become, today, a legitimate difference. "The pursuit of equality . . . seems to have given way to the right to be different." [23]

But what differences? Here, in the quotation, the accent is on economic inequalities, and in effect the "right" to be rich or to be poor. France had succumbed to the same enthusiasm for competitive individualism as we have seen elsewhere.

But the late 1980s were also marked by the appearance of conflicts over the right to social and religious difference; the issue of whether Muslim girls could wear veils in republican schools was only one sign that universalism was at risk. The fear was that "communtarianism" was on the rise everywhere.

Secondly, we must remember that this shift was provoked by "Europe." The choice made to submit to the economic discipline of the Commission meant that from 1983 on, France would join Germany in constructing Europe. The very definition of what it meant to be "French" would change. The national identity became pluralist. The French were called upon to be good French citizens by being good Europeans.

The third factor which fundamentally shook the citizenship regime was the decline of legitimacy of the most basic institutions of the Republic, its elected assemblies. The *Front National* was on the rise. With its racism it could not be swallowed by, or accommodated by, the rest of the Right. Its electoral success challenged the workings of political institutions. Legitimacy also suffered from a huge number of banal scandals about election financing and party profiteering. The health of electoral democracy was not what it might be.

Of course, there was no unanimity among the French, any more than in Canada, that these changes to the citizenship regime are appropriate or desirable. There were deep divisions about the commitment to Europe (the referendum on Maastricht won by the barest of margins . . .), about republican assimilationism versus multiculturalism, about the *Front National* (voters were choosing Le Pen after all . . .), and about economic policy. In the latter case, governments of the right and the left were confronted by mounting opposition, organized by what is termed *le mouvement social*, a collection of associations, groups, individuals and others who refuse to be fitted into existing categories of left and right and to accept institutional discipline.

It is precisely at this point that the *mouvement pour la parité* arrived on the scene, effectively aligned with the forces for change . . . to the citizenship regime. It was not defending the old but promoting the new; it is in the camp of republican political elites. Moreover, it helped with some arguments against the threats to republicanism and its institutions. The movement argued that political institutions were absolutely crucial; indeed they were so important that women must be fairly admitted to them. There is no attack on the institutions *per se* involved in the discourse on parity; the argument is always about how they had been misappropriated by men and their parties for their own advantage.

The movement also reinforced the theme of equality of opportunity. Women were asking for no special treatment, no more than a level playing field. Who would win elections, in any terms (such as socio-economic or ethnic) other than gender, was left up to the functioning of the existing institutions. Finally, by insisting, as we have seen above, that parity neither implies nor depends upon any particular policy content – it is about presence not ideas, in Anne Phillips' (1995) terms – the issue of what governments were doing to, and for, women with their economic and social policies is kept out of sight.

It is with respect to the other themes, however, and primarily the question of Europe and the definition of republican citizenship, that the movement's goals match the aims of those political forces restructuring the postwar citizenship regime. By its very origins, the movement is thoroughly European. The European Network of Women in Decision-making, organized by the Commission, has been active since the early 1990s. One of its first products was the Athens Declaration of 1992 that declared, "a democratic system must assure equal participation by its citizens in public and political life. . . . Women represent half the population. Equality requires parity in the representation and administration of countries." The Third Action Plan of the Equality Opportunities Unit (1990-1995) had made such equality a fundamental principle and focus of action, while the preparations for the Treaty of Amsterdam included the Charter of Rome.[24] Thus the call for parity does not challenge in any way France's commitment to the regional body; indeed, it reinforces it by casting French activists in the role of the "cutting edge" campaigners for eliminating the democratic deficit.

It is with respect to the definition of republicanism that the fit between the proposals for the new citizenship regime and the parity movement are clearest. Despite being cast by some as enemies of republicanism, they are hardly this. As Joan Scott points out, the movement is universalist (1997: 5; Schor 1995). The discourse of parity remains profoundly individualist, as any good republican discourse should be. The movement simply insists that rather than the "abstract" and de-sexed individual so often imagined by "male-stream" texts, **the** individual is always either male or female. Therefore, equality demands that no one suffer from this inevitable difference.

With its anti-categorial stance, the movement bars the door to any notion that the universalism of republicanism should attempt to accommodate the myriad of differences which many ethnic, and other, groups in France seek to have recognized – or which the "politics of diversity" in North America treat as normal. The movement provides protection against the "slippery slope" arguments that might lead to claims for better representation for other groups. It does so by insisting that sex is a case apart, not at all comparable to ethnicity, race, class, or language.

Both the individualism and the clear distinction between sex and other "differences" means that the movement for parity has begun to find a welcoming political opportunity structure. In particular, it can find allies among elites who seek to distance themselves from the post-war citizenship regime and build a new one in which the state would guarantee political, but not social, rights and in which each individual would be responsible for her success, once the rules have been changed to guarantee she has access and the gender playing field is level.

We can begin to understand the reasons why, despite all the *sturm und drang* of its criticisms, the parity movement actually makes headway within French politics. It has institutional space and it has allies. One of the striking characteristics of the parity movement, exemplified both by the Declarations of Athens and Rome, and the July Manifesto of French ex-Ministers, is that it is multi-partisan. Any European-level declaration will by definition involve women coming from a wide variety of political traditions, as a function of the electoral results of member states. But the French case represents a greater test of partisanship. Why might women of a variety of political horizons have accepted to speak in a single voice? Here the explanation has to be found in the weakening of party ties, as the party system itself dissolves in the face of institutional reinforcement of presidentialism, and the notion that little separates the politics of the right from those of the left in this era of neo-liberalism. In such a context the deep cleavage between right and left disappears somewhat, or at least sufficiently to allow common action on institutional change. Therefore, the debate about parity can be conducted in terms of universalism and political republicanism, with little attention to social rights or social policy. Opponents, as much as proponents, claim to speak in the name of the universal values of the Declaration of the Rights of Man. This commitment to universalism has not traditionally divided left from right in France. Both sides of the ideological divide claim to be the heirs of the Revolution. Therefore, it is possible for women and men of the traditional right and left to make a common cause in promoting a definition of "real equality" achieved via parity as a manifestation of republicanism, just as it is possible for others coming from the traditional right and left to reject it in the name of that same republicanism.

Conclusion

I want to end this chapter on both an epistemological note and a speculative note as we think about globalizations and restructuring citizenship regimes.

First, it is worth noting yet again, as these two case studies remind us, that we can never read the role of actors, including social movements, off the fact that adjustments to citizenship regimes are being made in this era of globalization. There are commonalities which have merged in state action. We have seen strong commitment to structural adjustment, and to controlling state deficits by limiting state spending. We have seen moves by states in both Europe and North America to impose formal limitations on their own sovereignty, by entering into regional agreements that set strict rules about forms of action. Both structural adjustment and limitations on sovereignty have been accompanied by major realignments of state-society relations and change in ideological representations of state and civil society. The "universal" rights of citizenship and the principle of equality has been displaced by notions of "differentiated citizenship," often to be realized via the activation of the principle of subsidiarity, in which the lowest possible level of government **and** other social institutions such as families and community associations are assigned responsibility for delivering and designing social services.

These are evidently the "heavy tendencies" of citizenship regime redesign. With slightly different mixes in policies, and slightly larger differences in the political discourses justifying these realignments, the direction of change is the same. If one adopts an "objective" and structural standpoint, one can even identify common threats to gender equality and women's achievement of full citizenship coming from these reconfigurations. Nonetheless, women's movements are never simply "victims" of these reconfigurations of state action and citizenship. They may participate in reinforcing and even, in some ways, designing them.

Just as women's movements made significant contributions to the specifics of social policies which eventually became post-1945 welfare states (Koven and Michel 1993), so too are women's movements making their own contributions to replacements for these welfare states – or being excluded from participation. We also know that we now consider some of those early movements to have been less "progressive" than others, in terms of their capacity to advance women's agenda. The lesson, in other words, is that there are always strategic choices, and that women's movements may not always make the "right" choice, either for their own future or for the long-term success of the agenda of equality.

Second: the speculation. Is the French movement a manifestation of a "third wave" of women's movements? If second-wave women's movements struggled inside the state and outside it so as to make women full citizens via economic and social reforms as well as cultural change, do we now see a third wave participating – albeit not necessarily with complete awareness – in a redefinition of citizenship and a reconstruction of citizenship regimes which erases social and economic equality from the agenda? In places like New Zealand, Europe and Canada, which were profoundly influenced by certain social democratic themes in post-1945 welfare states, citizenship is now being limited, confined to political rights, without social rights. There is also a clear emphasis on the individual, and on private, rather than collective, action. This is founded, in almost all cases on reasoning about what Anne Phillips calls a "politics of presence":

> Many of the current demands for democracy revolve around what we might call demands for political presence: demands for the equal representation of women with men; demands for a more even-handed balance between the different ethnic groups that make up each society; demands for the political inclusion of groups that have come to see themselves as marginalized or silenced or excluded. In this major reframing of the problems of democratic equality, the separation between 'who' and 'what' is to be represented, and the subordination of the first to the second, is very much up for question. The politics of ideas is being challenged by an alternative politics of presence (1995: 5).

Movements to change electoral law are a better match to the politics of reconfigured states than was the politics of the Canadian movement through the early 1990s, which remained a struggle to defend and advance the social agenda of second-wave feminism and progressive forces more generally.

New notions of individualized citizenship, as well as the reduction of the agenda of citizenship from a social project involving a measure of social equality, to a focus on electoral democracy fits with claims for "presence." In the current conjuncture, states are granted – and claim - less responsibility for resolving conflicts over social development and collective choices. A conflict of "ideas" about societal projects and social justice is less important when the decisions are made elsewhere, whether by markets or supra-national bodies. When choices are made by private, rather than by collective choice mechanisms, politics can safely be reduced to a matter of Who rather than What or Why.

Notes

1. The dominant tendencies in the French women's movement of the 1960s and 1970s shunned involvement with state institutions and particularly elections. Elections, let alone electoral law, were never a preoccupation. Until 1981 the group which was the major exponent of "revolutionary feminism" called for abstention in elections, while most of the rest organized their actions to minimize any risk of co-optation.
2. The concept of citizenship regime is developed in Jenson and Phillips (1996). Its description comes from the same source.
3. In his path-breaking work of historical sociology, T.H. Marshall told the story of British men's progress from civil to political to social rights. Cross-national differences were inevitable because other countries and other social groups were destined to live their own histories. A second legacy which we have from Marshall is the idea of change through time. His story is one of new rights won, of new groups gaining access to citizenship, of definitions of community altering through time.
4. The theoretical stance adopted here is that of the regulation approach to political economy and of historical sociology. Both teach us that the outcome of struggles for new rights, identities and access are never given in advance. While one would obviously expect historically created repertoires, as well as institutionalized policy legacies, to have some weight in the strategic choices of movements and states, there is no guarantee that they will maintain the same trajectory.
5. The regime was institutionalized in a variety of places. Most obviously was the Constitution and attendant documents, such as the Citizenship Act. But the state bureaucracy, parapublic advisory bodies, federalism and other institutions of representation, especially the federal party system, all made important discursive and practical contributions to it.
6. The exception here was obviously progressive forces in Quebec, which, after 1960, considered a strong provincial government the best guarantee of social justice.
7. Another reason for the lack of faith in provincial action was that many of the actors involved in creating this citizenship regime came either from Quebec (like Prime Minister Trudeau, who moved to Ottawa explicitly to counter the Quebec-based projects of nationalists), or from Ontario (a province which until very recently simply assumed its interests were those of the country as a whole).
8. For example, reform of the electoral system and party financing was prompted by the goals of assuring equitable treatment of parties by the media, and by the recognition that resources were not evenly distributed among social groups. Therefore, the electoral regime established in 1974 recognized political parties for the first time, then proceeded to regulate their access to the media, limited their campaign expenditures so the richest parties and candidates would not overwhelm the less well-endowed, and provided public funding for their campaigns, all in the name of equity (Paltiel 1970).
9. Again, Quebec-based groups were something of an exception here, but in the first years even they were willing to accept that the federal government had a role to play. The split from NAC and the rest of the women's movement in the rest of Canada came in the 1980s.
10. For some differences between the citizenship regimes of Quebec and the rest of Canada, see Jenson (1997).
11. In Canadian political discourse "popular sector" means an array of issue-oriented groups, ranging from anti-poverty organizations to the churches, feminists, environmentalists, farmers' unions, students, the unemployed, the disabled, nationalists, and so on. The

sector took organized form in 1987 when the Pro-Canada Network – renamed Action Canada in 1991 – was formed to fight the FTA, financed to a significant degree by the labour movement (Robinson 1993).

12. Feminist activists interviewed by Bashevkin in these years identified the point of rupture, starting their exclusion from political institutions, as NAC's decision to oppose free trade, which they linked to the neo-conservative agenda of the Mulroney Tories which was ". . . a direct challenge to the interventionist, social welfareist themes of modern Canadian feminism" (Bashevkin 1996: 235).

13. When it decimated the "women's state," the government did more than signal to femocrats that new times were at hand; it also dismantled policy networks which had been the carriers of state feminism. Its "decentralization" via "mainstreaming" can not substitute for those policy networks. In effect, mainstreaming declares that there is no need for a policy network at all. For the importance of such networks in the creation of the women's state see the testimony of one of the most active femocrats, Freda Paltiel (1997).

14. This strategy was similar in many ways to the one used to extract legalized abortion in the early 1970s – the use of manifestos by women, both well-known and not, as a sort of testimony that the system was not working. In the 1970s, the women testified to having had abortions and having escaped the costs imposed on so many ordinary women. This time they were testifying that, despite their personal success as Ministers, etc., the situation was unacceptable for the vast majority of women.

15. It was not strictly so. At the crucial "cut off" point for winning seats, the alternation was broken for a few places.

16. One of these was the *Verts*, who had always presented "alternating" lists.

17. While such declarations are politically significant, it is important to note that all candidates did not have the same ideas about how to achieve parity, or even what it is. For example, Edouard Balladur, a candidate of the Right, tends to define it as a quota, a definition which the *Mouvement pour la parité* rejects out of hand.

18. For an early debate, pitting proponents against opponents, see *Nouvelles Questions Féministes*, 15:4, 1994 and 16:1, 1995.

19. While a large women's organization like the *Union des Femmes Françaises* is not part of the co-ordination, the Communists, too, have expressed their support for parity.

20. Or as Eliane Vogel-Polsky, a leading Belgian lawyer and expert on European law writes, *"On exige la parité au nom de l'égalité de statut, et non pas au nom de la représentation d'une minorité,"* ["We claim parity in the name of equal status, not in the name of a minority"] (Sineau 1996: 9).

21. The descriptions of republicanism and the *tournant* after 1983 are drawn directly from Jenson and Sineau (1995).

22. Such visions shaped, among other things, the post-1945 social institutions, which are not universalist, but based on a series of different regimes, depending on employment in particular sectors, and granting representation to various associations for the management of the regimes.

23. *"Quand Laurent Fabius recense ce qui distingue la gauche de la droite, il ne parle plus de la réduction des inégalités sociales mais plus modestement de 'l'égalité des chances'. Et Lionel Jospin met en avant la nécessité de 'mieux harmoniser l'intérêt collectif et intérêt individuel'. Progressivement, on passe de la dénonciation des inégalités à **la reconnaissance des différences**. Globalement, les impéritifs de la modernisation économique, de la souplesse et de l'efficacité peuvent se substituent aux exigences de solidarité, de justice sociale et de réduction des inégalités. . . . Or, tout se passe comme si ce qui était perçu, auparavent, comme une inégalité injuste est devenu, aujourd'hui,*

une différence légitime. La revendication d'égalité . . . semble avoir faire place au droit à la différence." (Gélédan, 1993: 72-73). Emphasis added.

24. This document was signed on 18 May 1996 by 13 women Ministers from the 15 member states of the European Union (EC: 1997). The Charter identifies the principal responsibility of the IGC to be the reinforcement of democracy. In that context, these ministers claimed that democracy requires giving priority to actions with the potential to generate equal participation and a partnership between women and men. Moreover, only with such equal participation will citizens have confidence in their political institutions. In other words, for those who signed the Charter, the next step in the building of European institutions – via the elimination of the democratic deficit – required a radically increased presence of women in all decision-making institutions.

References

Bashevkin, Sylvia 1994, 'Confronting Neo-Conservatism: Anglo-American Women's Movements under Thatcher, Reagan and Mulroney,' *International Political Science Review* 15: 275-96.

--------- 1996, 'Losing Ground: Feminists, Conservatives and Public Policy in Canada during the Mulroney Years,' *Canadian Journal of Political Science* XXIX: 211-42.

Besnier, Frédéric 1997, 'Le mouvement pour la parité à la croisée des chemins,' *Parité-Infos* 17.

Burt, Sandra 1995, 'Gender and Public Policy: Making Some Difference in Ottawa,' in François-P Gingras (ed.), *Gender and Politics in Contemporary Canada*, Toronto: Oxford University Press.

Cohen, Majorie 1992, 'The Canadian Women's Movement and its Efforts to Influence the Canadian Economy,' in Constance Backhouse and Flaherty (eds.), *Challenging Times: The Women's Movement in Canada and the United States*, Montreal: McGill Queen's University Press.

Day, Shelagh 1993, 'Speaking for Ourselves,' in McRoberts and Monahan (eds.), *The Charlottetown Accord, the Referendum and the Future of Canada*, Toronto: University of Toronto Press.

Duchen, Claire 1986, *Feminism in France: From May '68 to Mitterrand*, London: Routledge and Kegan Paul.

European Commision 1997, *How to Create a Gender Balance in Political Decision-making*, Luxembourg: European Commission/DG V.

Gaspard, Françoise, Servan-Schreiber Claude and Le Gall Anne 1992, *Au pouvoir citoyennes: Liberté, Egalité, Parité*, Paris: Le Seuil.

Gélédan, Alain 1993, *Le Bilan économique des années Mitterrand, 1981-1993*, Paris: Le Monde.

Jenson, Jane 1991, 'Citizenship and Equity: Variations Across Time and In Space,' in Janet Hiebert (ed.), *Political Ethics: A Canadian Perspective*, vol. 12 of the Research Studies of the Royal Commission on Electoral Reform and Party Financing, Toronto: Dundurn Press.

--------- 1997, 'Fated to Live in Interesting Times: Canada's Changing Citizenship Regimes,' *Canadian Journal of Political Science* XXX: 4, pp. 476-93.

Jenson, Jane and Phillips, Susan 1996, 'Regime Shift: New Citizenship Practices in Canada,' *International Journal of Canadian Studies* 14: 111-36.

Jenson, Jane and Sineau, Mariette 1995, *Mitterrand et les Françaises. Un rendez-vous manqué*, Paris: Presses de Sciences Po.

Koven, Seth and Michel, Sonya (eds.) 1993, *Mothers of a New World: Maternalist Politics and the Origins of the Welfare State*, London: Routledge.

Massé, Véronique 1996, 'Les grandes associations féminines convergent sur la parité,' *Parité-Infos* 16.

Pal, Leslie A. 1993, *Interests of State: The Politics of Language, Multiculturalism, and Feminism in Canada*, Montreal: McGill-Queen's University Press.

Paltiel, Freda 1997, 'State Initiatives: Impetus and Effects,' in Andrew and Rodgers (eds.), *Women and the Canadian State: Femmes et l'État canadien*, Montreal: McGill-Queens.

Paltiel, K.Z. 1970, *Political Party Financing in Canada*, Toronto: McGraw-Hill.

Phillips, Anne 1995, *The Politics of Presence*, Oxford: Clarendon Press.

Phillips, Susan D. 1989, 'Rock-a-Bye Brian: The National Strategy on Child Care,' in Katherine Graham (ed.), *How Ottawa Spends 1989-90*, Ottawa: Carleton University Press.

--------- 1991, 'How Ottawa Blends: Shifting Government Relationships with Interest Groups,' in Frances Abele (ed.), *How Ottawa Spends, 1991-92*, Ottawa: Carleton University Press.

Rebick, Judy 1993, 'The Charlottetown Accord: A Faulty Framework and a Wrong-Headed Compromise,' in Kenneth McRoberts and Patrick Monahan (eds.), *The Charlottetown Accord, the Referendum and the Future of Canada*, Toronto: University of Toronto Press.

Robinson, Randy 1993, 'Democracy from Below: Action Canada. The Story of a Movement,' *Canadian Forum*.

Schor, Naomi 1995, 'French Feminism is a Universalism,' *Différences* 7: 15-47.

Scott, Joan W. 1997, 'La querelle des femmes' à la fin du vingtième siècle,' *Parité Infos*, 19.

Sineau, Mariette 1996, 'La parité à la française: un contre-modèle de l'égalité républicaine? Enjeux et débats récents,' paper prepared for the Conference, *Les femmes et la politique*, UFR de Saint-Quentin en Yvelines, 17 October.

10 Law and Democracy: (Mis)trusting the Global Reform of Courts

BOAVENTURA DE SOUSA SANTOS *

To say that we are entering a period of globalization – of markets and institutions as of culture – is today commonsensical. Globalization of democracy and law are also talked about in this context. As with all commonsensical notions, the phenomenon we call globalization is usually asserted rather than critically analyzed. In this chapter I shall analyze in some detail the globalization of democracy and law by discussing one of the most puzzling phenomena of sociology and political theory in the 1990s, namely, the greater social and political visibility and protagonism of courts in several countries, and the global call for the rule of law and the reform of the judicial system. This phenomenon is puzzling because in the modern state, with the possible exception of the USA, the courts have had a fairly uneventful existence. Marginalized by the executive and legislative powers, and far more impotent than them, courts have been a mere accessory of the other branches of government, or have paid for their institutional independence with insulation and irrelevancy *vis-à-vis* society. It is, therefore, hard to understand why, since the late 1980s, courts have become so prominent in the daily newspapers of many countries of Europe, Latin America, Africa and Asia; why so many projects for judicial reform have been started in different countries of the various continents; and why multilateral agencies and foundations for international aid have been giving priority to judicial reform programmes and rule of law programmes in such diverse countries as Russia, Guatemala, Colombia, Sri Lanka, the Philippines, South Africa, Mozambique, Nigeria, Uruguay, China, Argentina, Cambodia and so on.

Does the fact that this phenomenon is occurring in different countries make it a global phenomenon? Can it be explained in all cases by the same causes? Does it have a univocal political meaning? Is this new global interest in courts part and parcel of hegemonic globalization, or rather of counter-hegemonic globalization? I shall try to answer these questions focusing on two issues: the extent to which the role played by the courts in the modern state is linked to the transformations undergone by the state; and the prospects for democracy deriving from the world-wide focus on the rule of law and court reform.

The Rule of Law/Judicial Consensus

The rule of law/judicial consensus is the fourth pillar that grounds the hegemonic consensus on the alleged erosion of deep political cleavages in our time, referred to in the Introduction to this volume. This consensus derives from the other three consensuses: the neo-liberal economic consensus; the weak state consensus; and the liberal democratic consensus. The neo-liberal development model, with its greater reliance on markets and the private sector, has changed the ground rules of both private and public institutions, calling for a new legal framework for development conducive to trade, financing, and investment. The provision of such a legal framework and the responsibility for its enforcement is the new central role of the state, which is allegedly best fulfilled in a democratic polity. The rule of law is thus quintessential in development: "the development potential of law lies in that law is not only a reflection of the prevailing forces in society; it can also be a proactive instrument to promote change" (Shihata 1995: 13).   This, however, will only be possible if the rule of law is widely accepted and effectively enforced. Only then are certainty and predictability guaranteed, transaction costs lowered, property rights clarified and protected, contractual obligations enforced, and regulations applied. To achieve all this is the crucial role of the judicial system: "a well-functioning judiciary in which judges apply the law in a fair, even, and predictable manner, without undue delays or unaffordable costs, is part and parcel of the rule of law" (Shihata 1995: 14). The judiciary is responsible for delivering equitable, expeditious and transparent judicial services to citizens, economic agents, and the state.

But inasmuch as the role of the state has been reformed to serve the new global consensus, the judicial system must be reformed as well. Judicial reform is an essential component of the new model of development and the basis of good governance, the provision for which is the priority of the non-interventionist state. As the World Bank officials confess (and "confess" sounds right, since they seem to be atoning for old sins), "it has taken failures of government in Africa, the collapse of dictatorships in Latin America and profound transformations in Central and Eastern Europe to manifest that, without a sound legal framework, without an independent and honest judiciary, economic and social development risk collapse" (Rowat *et al.* 1995: 2).

Of all the liberal global consensuses, the rule of law/judicial consensus is by far the most complex and ambiguous. If for no other reason than because its focus is on the institution (courts) which, better than any other, represents the national character of modern institution-building and which, on this account, one might expect to resist globalizing pressures most effectively. Notwithstanding some high profile international courts in the past, and the European Court of Justice and the European Court of Human Rights today, the judicial system remains the quintessential national institution, and it has been far more difficult to internationalize it than the police or the armed forces.[1]

One of the most striking features of the focus on the judicial system is that the attention given to courts lies sometimes in the recognition of their function as the ultimate guarantors of the rule of law, sometimes in the denunciation of their incapacity to fulfill such function. In other words, the judicial system gains social and political visibility for being simultaneously part of the solution and part of the problem of the enforcement of the rule of law. When it is viewed as part of the solution, the focus is on judicial power and judicial activism; when seen as part of the problem, the focus is on judicial crisis and the need for judicial reform. However, in the latter case, the features or conditions that are now the object of criticism and reform were previously tolerated or ignored. The critical attention they now get is a product of the new role attributed to courts as a key instrument of good governance and law-based development.

The Globalization of the Rule of Law and Judicial Reform

The last decade witnessed the increasing social and political visibility of the judicial systems across the globe, the rising protagonism of courts, judges, and prosecutors in public life and the mass media, and the transformation of the once esoteric judicial affairs and proceedings into frequent topics of conversation among lay citizens. All this has been seen as evidence that we are entering a period of global expansion of judicial power. Is that so? And if so, what is its sociological and political explanation and meaning? Before trying to answer these questions, let us scrutinize the empirical evidence at hand. For analytical purposes, I shall distinguish among core, semi-peripheral, and peripheral countries, according to their position in the world system, even though my analysis will concentrate on core and semi-peripheral countries.[2] This criterion will be combined with two others: the different legal cultures and institutional traditions; and the different trajectories through which the various countries entered modernity and thus legal modernity.[3]

Concerning the core countries of Europe and North America, the most striking fact of the last decade is the large-scale battle of the Italian courts against the political corruption which devastated the political class that had dominated Italian politics since World War II, and indeed shattered the basic foundations of the Italian political regime. This battle, known as *Mani Pulite* (Clean Hands) started in Milan in April 1992. The whole process of corruption cases in the city came to be known as *Tangentopoli* (Kickback-City) and spread to other cities later on. Charges, arrests, and measures of preventive custody were issued against ministers, party leaders, members of parliament (at one time as many as one third of them were under investigation), civil servants, businessmen, financial journalists and members of the secret services. They were accused of bribery, corruption, abuse of public office, fraud, criminal bankruptcy, false accounting and illicit political funding. Two years later, 633 arrests had been ordered in Naples; 623 in Milan; 444 in Rome.[4]

The political turmoil was so vast and deep that many saw emerging in its aftermath a new political regime, the Second Republic, a product of an extreme form of judicial activism and of judicialization of politics, derogatorily called by some the "Republic of Judges." However unique in its radicalism, the Italian judicial protagonism does not stand alone in Europe. High-profile abuse of power charges, charges against members of the government, as well as corruption charges against politicians and businessmen have been brought to court in France, Belgium, Holland, Germany, Greece, Spain and Portugal.

But the expansion of judicial protagonism in Continental Europe is not limited to criminal justice. Besides the new activism of the constitutional courts and an emerging assertiveness of regular and administrative courts against the abuse of administrative power by state institutions in each of the European countries, it is particularly noteworthy that the high-profile role played by the European Court of Justice, a key institution in the creation of the European legal system, often forces member states to change their policies in line with its rulings. At a different level, and on a much smaller scale, the same has also been the case of the European Court of Human Rights.

But the social visibility of the courts in Europe resides as much in their accomplishments as in their failures. Indeed, the interventions of courts in high-profile and political cases – what I shall call dramatic justice – has contributed to sharpening the contrast with the everyday functioning of courts – routine justice – the judicial activity that is most likely to affect ordinary citizens. Particularly in Italy, France, Portugal and Spain, the courts have been harshly criticized for their inefficiency, inaccessibility, unreasonable delays, high expenses, lack of transparency and accountability, corporatistic privileges, large numbers of prisoners awaiting trial, investigatory incompetence and so on. In the study I recently conducted regarding the uses of courts in Portugal, a clear picture emerges of the citizens' great distance and diffidence *vis-à-vis* the judicial system, and their relatively low degree of satisfaction whenever they have been involved in court proceedings (Santos *et al.* 1996).

If we turn to the North American countries, the USA has been the motherland of legal and judicial activism (Galanter 1992), to such an extent that Shapiro (1993) refers to the recent judicial trends in Europe as "Americanization." Curiously enough, for the last decade, such a distinctive feature of American society has been under attack: the so-called litigation explosion, the public and political denunciation of excessive litigiousness and of the costs of litigation, the call for less active court intervention in policy-making, the changes in the Supreme Court etc. Moreover, while the call for the new centrality of the judicial system in social and political development across the globe seems to echo the American experience, in the USA the role of courts in bringing about progressive social change has been highly questioned in recent times (Rosenberg 1991). These developments have led some to believe that the USA "may have passed the peak of judicial policy-making in both constitutional and administrative judicial review" (Shapiro 1993: 64). In Canada judicial power seems to be on the rise, particularly after the adoption of the Charter of Rights of 1982, which granted the Supreme Court a major influence.

The global picture of courts in the core countries is thus one of expansion of judicial power, with a probable counterbalance in the country traditionally with the highest level of judicial power. The growing distrust of government and elected politicians is believed to have led to the judicialization of politics. Before engaging in a detailed analysis of this phenomenon, let me briefly mention the recent judicial trends in the semi-peripheral countries. Semi-peripheral countries tend to be highly unstable polities. Their intermediate position in the world system, their class structure, the conflictual coexistence of an active civil society, however fragmented and poorly organized, with a strong state, often a developmentalist state varying widely in legitimacy, coercive capacity and efficiency – all these features make social conflicts particularly complex in these societies, and social compromises more difficult to achieve. That is why these countries have tended to undergo more or less long periods of authoritarian rule alternating with periods of more or less consolidated democratic rule.

Concerning the semi-peripheral countries of Europe, Portugal and Spain lived under an authoritarian regime for four decades and, during that period, the judicial system was either reduced to an appendage of the government – in politically sensitive areas such as political crimes and labour disputes – or kept a low-profile independence and remained utterly isolated from society. The democratic transitions of the mid-1970s brought with them large institutional changes in the judicial system. It took a decade for the courts to justify a more active role in society.

The semi-peripheral countries of Central and Eastern Europe underwent democratic transitions in the late 1980s. During the Communist period, and even though the situation varied from country to country, there was very little room for the rule of law or independent judiciary. Probably for this reason, the judicialization of politics through judicial review became a central issue early in the transition period. The Russian case is particularly telling in this respect because the autocratic traits of Russian political culture antedate 1917 and have fostered a deep-seated resistance against a strong independent judiciary. In the late 1980s, the *glasnost* media started reporting extensively on such a phenomenon as the "telephone law" in which party officials would telephone a judge and "advise" him on what the outcome of a particular case ought to be (Thomas 1995: 425). In 1989, the Soviet Committee on Constitutional Supervision was established. The Committee had the power to declare as invalid laws, presidential decrees and other normative instruments (Kitchin 1995: 443). In the two years of its existence, it struck down many laws and decrees. The political incongruence of this Committee was that it coexisted with the Soviet Constitution of 1977, the Brezhnev Constitution, which was utterly hostile to the idea of the judicialization of politics. Indeed, the same incongruence continued after the coup of August 1991, when the Soviet Constitutional Committee was replaced by the Russian Constitutional Court. This court had increased powers of judicial review, and its first chairman, Valery Zvorkin, made it clear that the court's dual mission was to create the rule of law and to prevent the relapse into totalitarianism (Kitchin 1995: 446). The not unexpected clashes between the Court and President Yeltsin led to its suspension, and to a new Constitution with a revised regime of judicial review that same year.[5]

Other countries in the former communist Europe have been successful in instituting judicial review through the establishment of Constitutional Courts. The most remarkable example is probably Hungary where the Constitutional

Court – established when the parliament adopted a highly revised version of the old socialist constitution in October 1989 – has played a crucial role in shaping the political system of the country and has become the most credible institution of the new democratic regime in light of its advanced human rights jurisprudence (Zifzak 1996: 1).

Aside from the Constitutional Court and judicial review, the other major focus of the rule of law and judicial reform in Central and Eastern Europe has been the creation of a legal framework and a judicial system suited to promoting and consolidating the sweeping transition from an administrative-command economy to a market economy. The assumption – a distinctly Western law and modernization assumption – is that privatization of the immense state sector and the consequent massive expansion of contractual relations will both presuppose and induce an increasing reliance on law and judicial institutions (Hendley 1995: 41). Without this, there will be neither stability nor predictability, which are the prerequisites of a healthy economic environment based on the market and the private sector. These concerns have been paramount in the international assistance provided to Central and Eastern Europe by the World Bank, the USAID, and various American foundations. In the early 1990s, the USAID announced its intention to invest more resources in democracy and rule of law programmes in the region, particularly in view of the fact that the countries under consideration were "advanced developing countries," that is to say, semi-peripheral countries (USAID 1994: 2).

Though the programmes are still going on, the most recent assessments of the legal and judicial reforms in this region, and particularly in its most important country, Russia, are now less enthusiastic than before. For instance, Hendley concedes that her hypothesis, that the combination of privatization and political differentiation in Post-Soviet Russia might serve as a catalyst for a profound change in Russian legal culture, was overly optimistic. According to Hendley, the Soviet past weighs too heavily on the Russian present; managers do not believe in the enforceability of contracts through legal means and try to achieve the basic purpose of contracts (ensuring their supplies) by other means (Hendley 1995: 63). Under these circumstances, the distrust of law and legal institutions cannot be remedied with quick-fix reform: "The patron-client networks that characterized the prior system [the authoritarian policies of the ruling Communist Party] may be more easily taken over by private law enforcers, namely the mafia, than by formal legal institutions" (Hendley 1995: 48).[6]

I turn now to some semi-peripheral countries of Latin America. Rule of law and judicial programmes in Latin America, as much as in Central Eastern

Europe, have a strong international component. They are a domain of high-intensity globalization in which the USA plays the leading role, followed at a distance by some countries of the European Union. In some Latin American countries more than in others, there are strong internal energies driving the reforms, at times in tandem with the globalizing pressures, at times in collision with them. There are also strong internal resistances to reform. In the countries that were ruled until the 1980s by an authoritarian regime – such as Argentina, Chile, Brazil, El Salvador and Honduras – the internal impulse for judicial reform in the democratic transition focused more on the independence of the judiciary, due process guarantees and judicial review, and far less on access to justice.

During the dictatorship, judges – generally viewed in Latin America as a conservative body who systematically favored the propertied classes and the rulers of the day – were either sympathetic to the military *juntas* (as in Argentina) or easily neutralized by them (as in Brazil) (Osiel 1995). This was even the case of the Chilean judicial system, which had a reputation for conservatism but also for probity and seriousness. The activism of the Chilean judicial system against the democratic socialist measures of Salvador Allende in the early 1970s, which closely resembled the activism of the US Supreme Court against the New Deal, became a landmark of conservative judicial protagonism in Latin America. For this reason, the truth commissions that were established to investigate the violations of human rights and the crimes perpetrated by the *juntas*, such as those in Argentina, Chile, El Salvador and Honduras, recommended thorough judicial reforms (Popkin and Roht-Arriaza 1995). Indeed, the first test for the new judicial system – which in most cases remained very much the same as the old one – was the trial of the dictators and the torturers at their orders. The test failed, either because of the political compromises between the outgoing and incoming political class (the cases of Brazil and Chile), or because the instability caused by the trials forced the government to retreat (the case of Argentina).

The other major focus of the judicialization of politics in the last decade in Latin America has been judicial review, that is, the power of the courts to declare a law, or other normative decree, null and void on the grounds that it violates the Constitution. In some countries, judicial review rests in the Supreme Court (Argentina and Brazil); in others it rests in Constitutional Courts (Colombia). The effective exercise of this power and its contribution to the consolidation of democracy varies widely from country to country.

At one extreme we may find the Argentinean Supreme Court. According to Carlos Nino, since its independence some 160 years ago, Argentina has lived under open and genuine democracy for a bit more than 20 years, and the Supreme Court has been, more than anything else, an impairment of the democratic process (Nino 1993: 317). By way of example, Nino mentions a long-standing judicial doctrine: the "doctrine of the *de facto* law," the doctrine that ascribes validity to the laws enacted by regimes that come to power by force. The vicissitudes of this doctrine in recent times show how far the political control of the judiciary by the government can go. One of the first measures of President Alfonsin, after he took office in 1983, was to send a draft law to Congress asking for the nullification of the so-called self-amnesty law, a law which the military had enacted right at the end of their period to cover the abuses of human rights committed under their rule. The nullification was unanimously approved by the Congress, the law was subsequently upheld by the Supreme Court, thus breaking away from the doctrine of the *de facto* law for the first time in more than a century. After taking office in 1991, President Menem, not happy about the Supreme Court, hastened to pass a law to increase the number of Supreme Court judges and fill the new positions with people loyal to his ideas (Stotzky and Nino 1993: 8; Nino 1993: 319).[7] In the same year, the Supreme Court took up the old doctrine with the positivist argument that the laws enacted by the Congress should be deemed valid regardless of the "affective or ideological evaluation" that can be made of military regimes. This leads Nino to the conclusion that "the Supreme Court, and in fact the judicial system as a whole, fell short during most of Argentina's history of realizing its responsibility as custodian of the democratic system" (1993: 321).

At the other extreme, we might consider the Colombian Constitutional Court created by the Constitution of 1991. The Colombian Constitution has the broadest system of constitutional control. At the request of any citizen, it grants to the lower courts the power to suspend a decision or measure by any public or private authority on the basis of its being unconstitutional, and the sentence may be reviewed on appeal by the Constitutional Court (*tutela* actions). Judicial review is vested in the Constitutional Court, which has had some high-profile interventions in the fields of human rights and cultural diversity established by the Constitution, and has even nullified two government decrees declaring the state of exception (Villegas 1993; 1996; 1997). In an interview, the President of the Court confided that the Court was walking a tight rope, since the government, unhappy about the show of judicial independence, and having the majority in Congress, could at any moment propose the revision of the Constitution to abolish the Court or reduce its review powers.[8]

262   Globalizing Institutions

The high-profile interventions or omissions of the highest courts in Latin America have been very controversial and often on a collision course with the executive or the legislature. Their contribution to the consolidation of democracy is ambiguous and cannot be established in general. This protagonism of the judicial system has, however, been upset by a kind of negative protagonism: the increased and ever more publicized dissatisfaction of the citizenry with the inefficiency, slowness, inaccessibility, elitism, arrogant corporatism, and even corruption, of the judicial system in its everyday functioning. Moreover, the Latin American judicial system seems to be very timid in bringing corruption charges against government officials. Cases of corruption are reported daily in the mass media, but very little judicial investigation takes place. In Brazil, President Collor de Mello, who was impeached by the Congress on corruption charges, was acquitted in court. In this regard, and for reasons mentioned below, Colombia seems to be a partial exception. The office of the Attorney-General (*Fiscalia*) has been conducting a high-profile battle against political corruption, particularly relating to organized crime and drug trafficking. Ministers and other high ranking party officials have been arrested, and almost half of the members of parliament were, for a time, under investigation (known as the process of the 8000).

The most notorious feature of the focus on the rule of law in the developing world from the mid-1980s onwards is the high-intensity globalization character of the reformist pressure on the judicial system. In Latin America, the institutions that exert this pressure are the USAID, the World Bank, the Inter-American Development Bank, the US Justice Department, the Ford Foundation and the European Union (collectively or through some of its members). I cannot go into great detail here about the multiple features of this pressure, so I will limit myself to a brief comment on some of them.

As far as the USAID is concerned, since the early 1990s, support for the rule of law has become a major component of its assistance programmes. Though USAID investments in law programmes date back to the 1960s – the first wave of "law and development" – the current resurgence of activities in this area began in the mid-1980s with the USAID Administration of Justice programme in Latin America. Latin America was the testing ground for the law programmes that, since the 1990s, have spread to Asia, Africa, Eastern Europe and the newly independent countries (USAID 1994: VII). The USAID distinguishes four generations of law programmes since the early 1960s. The first generation focused on legal education and law reform; the second, on basic-needs legal aid; the third, on court reform. The current fourth generation is the most ambitious and political in the Agency's terms, because it encompasses all the concerns of the three previous generations of programmes and broadens their scope, while including them in the design and implementation of country democracy programmes (USAID 1994: 4). In the latest generation, unlike in the previous periods, assistance is conceived as political and not merely as technical. The objective is to promote democracy, even against the resistance of the host country. In the latter case, resistance must be overcome through coalition and constituency-building strategies to forge elite commitment to law reform (USAID 1994: VIII). In the Agency's jargon, such strategies "facilitate host country demand."[9] In an assessment of six rule of law programmes, four of them in Latin America, the Agency concedes that this strategy was successful only in one of them: Colombia.[10]

The ROL programmes are wide-ranging and involve the following strategies: coalition and constituency-building; structural legal reform; access creation; and legal system strengthening. A closer look at the deployment of these strategies shows that, from country to country, they vary in scope and emphasis. Considering some of the semi-peripheral Latin American countries – Uruguay, Argentina and Colombia – the involvement in Colombia far exceeds that in the other two countries, both in time and resources. While the programme in Argentina extends over the period of 1989-93, and in Uruguay 1990-93, in Colombia it spans 1986-99. The funding provided for Uruguay amounts to less than 1 million dollars (850,000 dollars), for Argentina, 2 million, and for Colombia (1986-96), 38.7 million (USAID 1994: A-2). Moreover, while in Argentina and Uruguay the programmes have focused on judges and the regular court system, in Colombia they have concentrated on the Attorney-General's office (the *Fiscalia*), that is to say, on criminal investigation and prosecution.

While the USAID proclaims today the political character of its law and judicial reform programmes, the World Bank prefers to emphasize the need to foster the legal and judicial environment conducive to trade, financing, and investment, justifying its position with the Bank's charter, which defines the promotion of economic development as the Bank's principal mandate, and does not include political reform.[11] This mandate is very broad indeed: "it encompasses everything from writing or revising commercial codes, bankruptcy statutes and company laws, through overhauling regulatory agencies and teaching justice ministry officials how to draft legislation that fosters private investment" (Messick 1998: 2). The increasing interest of the World Bank in court reform is thus justified because "experience has shown that such reform cannot be ignored in the process of economic development or adjustment" (Shihata 1995: 14).

The Bank's intervention in this area is worldwide and may be very wide-ranging in scope. In Laos, for instance, it has addressed the country's legal system as a whole because, since it had embarked on a complete change of its economic and social system, the country "needed a parallel overhaul of its legal system" (Shihata 1995: 14). In Latin America, the Bank has provided, among others, grants or loans for legal and judicial reform in Venezuela (1992, 30 million dollars),[12] in Bolivia (1995, 11 million dollars), in Ecuador (1996, 10.7 million dollars) and Peru (1997, 22.5 million dollars).

The Inter-American Development Bank is a new global actor in this field of judicial reform, defining it since 1995 as an important new area. The first loans were made in that year: Costa Rica, 11.2 million dollars; and Colombia, 9.4 million dollars, once again targeted to the *Fiscalia* and the fight against drug trafficking. In 1996, the most important loans were made to El Salvador, 22.2 million dollars; Honduras, 7.2 million dollars; and Bolivia, 12 million dollars. Still in 1996, Paraguay received a loan of 22 million dollars "to support the strengthening of the climate of legal certainty and predictability to allow economic and social development and reinforce the rule of law." In 1997, Peru received a loan of 20 million dollars to develop alternative dispute settlement mechanisms.[13]

Outside Latin America the concern with the rule of law and judicial reform is also very much present. In peripheral countries, such as Mozambique or Cambodia, and in spite of the abysmal social problems that afflict their populations, this concern is often part and parcel of painful and fragile democratic transitions after years, or even decades, of civil war and dictatorship.[14] The problematic nature of these transitions is further compounded by the hardships imposed on popular classes by the neo-liberal economic recipes that usually accompany such transitions. In these countries the rule of law/court reforms tend to be extreme instances of high-intensity globalization, in that the reforms are mainly driven by donor countries, international assistance agencies, and international financial institutions. They define the priorities, impose the orientation and sequencing of the reforms and, of course, provide the resources to bring them about.

Concerning the semi-peripheral countries the situation is very different. In many of them, the interest in rule of law and court reform runs very high, but internal developments, rather than globalizing pressures, seem to explain it. In some countries the judicial system is assuming a more prominent role and consequently becoming more controversial and inviting debate on the expansion of the judicial power and the judicialization of politics. In Africa, South Africa is a particularly interesting case. As Heinz Klug has pointed out, having emerged from a long period of authoritarianism and apartheid,

South Africa has shown a striking faith in the judicial system to mediate in the construction of a post-apartheid political order (1996). The Constitutional Court, established under the "interim" constitution of 1993, was assigned the role of reviewing the final 1996 Constitution enacted by the Constitutional Assembly. The court performed that role in very concrete terms, nullifying some of the provisions of the document initially submitted to it by the Assembly, and the latter subsequently made the changes according to the court's ruling. The South African, as well as the Russian, Hungarian and Colombian cases, show the extent to which constitutional courts and judiciary review, in general, have contributed towards the judicialization of politics during the last decade. In the South African case, argues Heinz Klug, the faith in the judiciary to uphold the new democratic order "is particularly striking, given the past failure of the judiciary to uphold basic principles of justice in the face of apartheid policies and laws" (1996: 2).

Two other semi-peripheral countries, both in Asia, present interesting trends towards a greater political protagonism on the part of the judicial system. In India, the judicial system has been in recent years right at the centre of the political debate, pressed or encouraged by a strong public opinion against political corruption. The indictment of the former Prime Minister, P. V. Narasimha Rao, on forgery charges, and of many other politicians and high state officials on corruption charges, may well prove to be the test case of the courts' integrity and independence.[15] In South Korea, the judicial system has traditionally been an appendage of authoritarian government: first Japan's colonial rulers, then a succession of military rulers. Moreover, corruption in the judicial system has been pervasive all along. Today, however, in tandem with the slow ongoing democratization process, the judicial system has begun to assert its independence, starting with a set of proposals put forward by the chief justice of the Supreme Court, Yun Kwan, soon after his confirmation in 1993, which have sparked public attention and political debate (Hoon 1993). Since then, two former presidents have been convicted in corruption cases, and the Constitutional Court has become an important arbiter of the pace and extent of the transition to democracy (Yang, 1998:170)

State Weakness and the Judicialization of Politics

In the next two sections I shall analyze the sociological and political meaning of the rising interest in courts and of the rule of law/judicial reform movement across the globe. I will answer two questions: what type of state form is both presupposed and produced by the expansion of judicial power? What are the prospects for democracy? In this section I will try to answer the first question.

My working hypothesis is that there is a close link between legal and judicial reform on one side, and the state, both as political system and as an administrative apparatus, on the other. What this means is that the question of judicial reform, though being a judicial question, is, above all, a political question. By the same token, the judicialization of politics entails the politicization of the judiciary. The way this phenomenon is occurring all over the world is, however, very diverse.

In core countries, the rising protagonism of courts, particularly in continental Europe, is, above all, the symptom of a failure of the state as a democratic state. This failure is the result of the public perception of a loss of transparency, accountability and participation in government. Judicial activism against political corruption and the expanded judicial review of the separation of powers and state competences are the responses to such perception. It should be borne in mind that, in the case of corruption, the mass media and civic organizations have performed a decisive role in pressing the judicial system to act. Though the judicial system is considered to be, in general, a reactive institution – that is to say, it waits for citizens to request its services – the prosecutors, who are part of the system, are supposed to be proactive and initiate crime investigation. But the truth of the matter is that, in most countries, prosecutors have acted only after reports from the media, indeed oftentimes limiting themselves to following leads offered by the media. The reasons why some cases are brought to the attention of the media and others not are often mysterious. According to Zaffaroni (1997: 10), behind the media attention are conflicts among powerful economic or political groups, in which the losers are publicly exposed.

To a lesser extent judicial activism is related to the perceived failure of the state as a welfare state. The moderate growth of litigation in the fields of administrative law, social and economic rights, torts, consumer and environmental protection, and occupational health and safety has been prompted by a growing distrust of the state, a loss of confidence in the capacity or willingness of the state either to act positively to implement the rights and policies that guarantee the well-being of citizens, or to protect them against the wrong-doing of powerful private actors. In this respect, the European countries in the post-war period offered a sharp contrast with the USA. Stronger and more developed welfare states provided efficient protection and reduced the impact on citizens whenever protection failed, thus making litigation unnecessary, or keeping it at much lower levels than in the USA. Current legal and judicial changes in Europe, which as I mentioned above, some see as the Americanization of Europe, are, in part, a direct effect of the crisis of the welfare state.

The double failure of the democratic and welfare features of the state, which has been associated with the legislature and the executive, has induced a dislocation of the legitimacy core of the state from the legislature and the executive to the judiciary. The extent of this dislocation, and its virtuality to avert a crisis of legitimacy of the state as a whole, is an open question. But the very fact that this dislocation has occurred is, in and of itself, remarkable and intriguing. After all, the judicial system is part of the state and, as such, should be regarded as part of the problem, rather than part of the solution. On the other hand, as I have already mentioned, the increasing protagonism of courts has also drawn attention to their own inefficiency, particularly in areas in which there is potential high judicial demand on the part of the citizens. That courts can be easily put on the defensive, and that the promises they make may exceed by far what they deliver, adds another element of perplexity to the current dislocation of legitimacy. But the most disturbing element is probably that, by such dislocation, democratic legitimacy may henceforth lie in the only non-elected branch of government.

Since it is far from obvious that a more central role should be assigned to courts, we must ask ourselves why this has happened. In Europe, the independence of the courts has been premised upon their social insulation and political neutralization. In late nineteenth century, Europe was immersed in unprecedented social disorganization and conflict generated by the capitalist revolution, raising new problems that were bundled together in a new umbrella, the social question: explosive urbanization and the sub-human housing conditions; rampant anomie, crime and prostitution; degraded health and life conditions of uprooted peasants; industrial child labour and malnutrition. The judicial system stood aloof from all this turmoil, quietly defending property rights and adjudicating contractual obligations among individuals, mostly members of the bourgeoisie.

In our century, collective conflicts, if certainly not solved, were institutionalized via the class compromises promoted by social democracy and leading to the welfare state. The political cleavages remained deep, particularly in the context of the cold war, but this underlying consensus became the basis of governability, which consisted of transforming social problems into rights effectively enforced. Since courts were kept away from all this political process, probably precisely for this reason, their independence was not tampered with. For the last two decades, the economic and social basis of the class compromises underlying the welfare state have been eroding and with them the nature of the democratic political obligation. Resentful and distrustful citizens have been claiming redress for the violation of their rights, and the punishment of an all too promiscuous intimacy between state officials and politicians on the one side, and the corporate world on the other. The independence of the judiciary, once premised upon its low profile and passivity, has become the necessary condition of the public pressure on it to become more active and high-profile. The contrast between Europe and the USA should be pointed out again in this context. Granted that it is very difficult to compare patterns of judicial independence, it is unquestionable that political control over the judiciary, particularly as concerns the higher courts, has been greater in the USA than in Europe: courts in the USA are more politically controlled and more active; courts in Europe are less politically controlled and less active. It shouldn't be surprising if the increased protagonism of courts in Europe were to be met by attempts to tighten the political grip on them. In Italy, at least, there are some signs that this may occur.

The phenomenon may be transient but it points to a new state form. In fact, we seem to be heading toward a post-welfare state form – the core countries version of the weak state consensus. It will remain a regulatory and interventionist state, strong enough to produce its weakness efficiently, opening the space for partial replacement of social rights with contractual relations among citizens, corporations, NGOs and the state itself. Because the direct provision of welfare services will diminish, more intermediaries will be at stake and, consequently, the provision will become more controversial. This would explain why the downsizing of the welfare administrative sector may lead to the upsizing of the judicial system, a phenomenon that is indeed already occurring as witnessed, for instance, in the recent explosion of the numbers of judges or courts in some countries.[16] Because they act in individual, not collective, disputes, and because they are ambiguous, given the relative unpredictability of their rulings, courts tend to depoliticize public life.[17]

By criminalizing certain previously accepted political behavior – I mean the fight against corruption – the judicial system contributes to regulating the turbulence and bouts of state anomie that tend to occur in periods of transition from one state form to another. On the other hand, by becoming more active in the area of administrative law and the protection of rights, courts contribute to diffusing the conflict that may arise in the process of dismantling the welfare state. The judicial system thus injects legitimacy into the democratic social pact of a state enfeebled by the erosion of the

Law and Democracy 269

conditions that had hitherto sustained it. This judicialization of politics is not without problems: caught in the dilemma of having all the independence to act but no powers to enforce, the promise of court activism may soon prove to exceed, by far, its delivery. When that occurs – if it occurs – courts will cease to be part of the solution to become precisely part of the problem.

In semi-peripheral countries, the political nature of the growing focus on the rule of law and the judicial system is more complex, and its impact on the form of the state is more ambiguous. Some of them have recently emerged from long-term dictatorships of various sorts and the high profile of courts is part and parcel of the democratic transition. Very often such judicial protagonism is mainly due to the activism of the constitutional courts. Their role is a regime-building role, as defined by the boundaries among the various branches of government, allocating competencies among central, regional and local authorities (South Africa, Hungary, Portugal). The ambiguous, relatively unpredictable, and piecemeal character of the courts' intervention is particularly functional whenever the political forces have not been able to reach a political compromise. In such cases, the Constitution acknowledges the differences, rather than settling them. It is up to the Constitutional Court to arbitrate the differences, often by political experiment through trial and error.

Two main contrasts must be noticed between trends in core countries and trends in semi-peripheral countries. On the one hand, while in core countries the reforms under way seem to respond to internal dynamics, even if conditioned by global trends, in some semi-peripheral countries of Central and Eastern Europe and Latin America, the reforms are being conducted under high-intensity globalizing pressure, a pressure dominated by American institutions and American legal models. On the other hand, while in core countries the focus is mainly on courts, since the rule of law is taken for granted and legal reform is an established political process, in most semi-peripheral countries the focus is much broader, contemplating the rule of law and legal reform, as well as judicial reform.

In my view, both contrasts are explained by the more far-reaching political reforms deemed necessary in the semi-peripheral countries. What is really at stake here is the creation of the post-structural adjustment state. Most semi-peripheral countries have been ruled for the past forty years, for shorter or longer periods, by authoritarian regimes and strong interventionist states. The Communist states of Central and Eastern Europe ruled an administrative-command economy; the developmentalist states of Latin America and Asia based their rule on a strong nationalized economic sector, and on a tight, mostly protectionist, regulation of the economy as a whole.

Neither the Communist nor the developmentalist states were welfare states, but both developed schemes of social protection in health and social security, far more advanced in the Communist states than in the developmentalist states. In different ways, the neo-liberal consensus presiding over the expansion of global market capitalism contributed to the downfall of both state forms. They were to be replaced by weak states, acting as facilitators of the new model of development based on the reliance of markets and the private sector.

In the Communist states, and in view of their total collapse, the building of the post-structural adjustment state is an all-encompassing task. It involves not just institution building of different kinds but also the building of a legal culture capable of sustaining the legal reforms called for by the new economic environment. In the developmentalist states the situation is very different, because although the democratic transitions changed the political regime, they did not, by themselves, change the state institutional structure significantly. These changes were to be carried out within the framework of the existing state. The neo-liberal dilemma in this regard became apparent in the early 1990s. It can be formulated as follows. Only a strong state can produce its own weakness efficiently, but once this weakness has been produced, it has spillover effects that go beyond the intended reach, to the point of endangering the performance of the tasks assigned to the state in the new model of development. The pathologies of state weakness became apparent in the early 1990s: massive tax evasions, widespread corruption, withering away of a public service culture, loss of control over the national territory, the emergence of mafias and paramilitary groups disputing the state monopoly of violence, abysmal mismanagement of development grants and loans, etc. In sum, the weak state cannot control its own weakness.

In recent years the World Bank has started to lament the fact that the state has become too weak to perform the new, but equally central, role assigned to it by the neo-liberal development model. In one of its reports, the Bank emphasizes that the state cannot be just the facilitator of market economy: it must also be its regulator (Rowat 1995: 17). Significantly, the Bank's World Development Report of 1997 is titled *The State in a Changing World*, and is dedicated to rethinking the state, refocusing on its effectiveness and on reinvigorating its institutional capability. The priority the Bank now gives to the rule of law, and legal and judicial reforms, stems from the need to restore the regulatory capacity of the state in new terms: the post-developmentalist state. The state continues, of course, to be involved in development, but because the state has ceased to be the very engine of development, social transformation is not a political problem any more: it is merely the economic and technical problem of bringing about a better life for all citizens. The rule of law and the judicial system are thus conceived of as principles of social ordering, as instruments of a depoliticized conception of social transformation.

The depoliticization of social transformation may, however, prove to be a very problematic endeavor. Concurrent with it is the dramatic growth of poverty and social inequality across the globe, as well as the gradual erosion of the fragile safety nets once provided by the welfare state, no matter how incomplete or embryonic. To address this issue with a combination of liberal democracy, rule of law and judicial activism seems utterly insufficient. Contrary to European experience, where democracy has always flourished at the cost of economic liberalism, in both peripheral and semi-peripheral countries today, democracy is offered as the political counterpart of economic liberalism. Not surprisingly, a press release on building democracy by the USAID states as being one of the major problems to be addressed by its programmes: "misperceptions about democracy and free-market capitalism" (USAID 1996).

Contrary to the experience in core countries, democracy is being promoted by the USAID and the international financial institutions as the socially more acceptable version of a weak state. As we have already seen above, the rule of law and judicial reform programmes are conceived by the USAID as political rather than technocratic in nature. Without ideological competition, the hegemonic political globalization can thus engender depoliticization without having to compromise the benefits of presenting itself as political.

The Prospects for Democracy

In this section I will try to give an answer to the question of the prospects for democracy deriving from the global reliance on the rule of law and judicial activism. Two cautionary notes: First, in a world increasingly dominated by globalized forms of power and of unequal exchanges, the prospects for democracy will heavily depend on the possibility of democratizing global interactions and social relations. Democracy has always been conceived as a national political form, congruent both with the national economy and the national culture. Consequently, democratic theory assumed, in David Held's formulation, "A 'symmetrical' and 'congruent' relationship between political decision-makers and the recipients of political decisions" (1993: 25). Hence, political accountability, transparency, protection and participation have always been basically national problems. This symmetry and congruence have been shattered by economic and cultural globalization. As long as symmetry and congruence are not reestablished at a global level, national democracy will be an endangered species.

The second cautionary note is that the prospects for democracy cannot be identified without specifying what we mean by democracy. There are different models of democracy. Even liberal democracy may be defined differently. I shall distinguish between two ideal types of democracy, which, in order to avoid prejudgments, I shall call Democracy I and Democracy II. Both subscribe to the basic features of democracy stated in the Introduction, but, while Democracy I ranks them according to their capacity to deliver governability, and gives priority to the value of freedom over the value of equality, Democracy II ranks them according to their capacity to empower citizens and achieve social justice, thus seeking a dynamic equilibrium between freedom and equality. Both forms of democracy conceive the national societies as open societies, but, while for Democracy I, such "openness" is premised upon free markets and the neo-liberal economic globalization, for Democracy II the fate of the open society is linked to the outcomes, risks and opportunities emerging from the conflict between hegemonic globalization (transnational greed) and counter-hegemonic globalization (transnational solidarity). While Democracy I accepts world capitalism as the final and highest criterion of modern social life, and consequently accepts the precedence of capitalism whenever the latter feels threatened by democratic "disfunctions," Democracy II conceives of itself, rather than capitalism, as the final and highest criterion of modern social life, and therefore sees itself as taking precedence over capitalism whenever threatened by it.

Taking Democracy I as our model, to ask about the prospects for democracy as deriving from legal and court reforms amounts to asking about the contribution of the latter to strengthen the capacity of the emerging state form to bring about the compatibility between economic liberalization and political liberalization – that is to say, between capitalism and democracy. The overarching liberal consensus referred to in the Introduction presupposes such compatibility. However, in light of the recent past, the compatibility between capitalism and democracy has become an open question. In their systematic comparison of a series of semi-peripheral countries, some of which are undergoing democratic transition and/or structural adjustment, Haggard and Kaufman conclude that, even if there is support for the compatibility assumption, there are, nonetheless, important tensions between capitalism and democracy, particularly when the former produces highly unequal distributions of assets and income, abrupt social dislocations and, above all, severe rural inequalities (Haggard and Kaufman 1992: 342). The effects of these distributional conflicts on democratic stability remain an open question. In fact, this impact is mediated by a complex set of factors, such as the economic performance in itself, the political institutions, the organization of civil society, and the capacity of the state to sustain order, etc. The role of law and the judicial system, in this context, is twofold.

First, it may increase the stability and predictability of economic transactions, promote social peace, and improve the administrative capacity of the state. In this case, the rule of law and the courts contribute directly towards economic performance, and indirectly towards democratic stability. The second role consists in dispersing the social conflicts emerging from social dislocations and the distributive inequalities produced by global capitalism. As the rule of law transforms social problems into rights, and courts transform collective conflicts into individual disputes, they tend to discourage collective action and organization. Moreover, the judicial rhythm, the relative unpredictability of judicial decisions and even the judicial inefficiency, if not too high, may have a cooling effect on social contestation, lowering social expectations without, however, nullifying them altogether. By all these mechanisms, the rule of law and courts promote governability by preventing the overload of the political system and expanding the boundaries of public toleration, particularly in those countries in which the rule of law and the independent courts are part and parcel of recent democratic transitions.

This analysis so far fails to consider the effects of the performance of these roles upon the judicial system itself. The prevention of political overload may lead to judicial overload. The latter is being anticipated by the agencies in charge of the global court reform, and to prevent it they are increasingly including models of alternative dispute resolution (ADR) in their reform projects.

Democracy I is by far the dominant conception of democracy today. It is also the conception that is being globalized in the hegemonic programmes of political liberalization across the globe. It is in fact an instrumental conception, a means to stabilize economic liberalization and prevent the complete decay of state institutions and the usual "pathologies" that go with it. Its weakness lies in not guaranteeing its own survival in the case of a conflict with economic liberalization. But short of complete collapse, Democracy I may be contracted in different ways in order to accommodate the political needs of global capitalism. Many semi-peripheral countries, not to mention the peripheral ones, live under different versions of contracted or restricted democracy. In these situations, the rule of law and the judicial system perform ambiguous, and often contradictory roles. On the one side, the high-profile interventions of courts function as symbolic amplifiers of the democratic rule in that they dramatize the democratic competition among the political elites or factions, or among state institutions or branches of government. This symbolic amplification of democracy within the inner circle of the political system is usually the other side of the contraction of democracy in the outer circle of the political system, that is, in the relations between citizens and their organizations on the one side, and the state and the political class on the other. Such contraction manifests itself in many different ways: as a deficit of representation; as a deficit of participation; and very often as the emergence of violent and corrupt political actions. Rather than being a countervailing force, the rule of law and the judicial system may reproduce such contraction by reinforcing the distinction between enfranchised and disenfranchised citizens.

But on the other hand, the judicial system may find itself in the front line of the struggle between democratic and anti-democratic forces. According to The Andean Commission of Jurists, in Colombia, 290 judges and judicial officials were assassinated between 1978 and 1991. They were investigating or trying cases involving individuals or organizations that felt powerful enough to attack the system head on, rather than using it to their benefit, for instance, by manipulating procedural guarantees and legal loopholes.[18] Short of such a violent intrusion, the contraction of democracy may impinge upon the judicial system in various other forms. The most common one is judicial reform itself, as a way of tailoring the activity of the courts to the coercive needs of the state, or as way of securing the non-interference of the courts in the areas in which the state operates in a distinctly authoritarian way. As an illustration, in Colombia, one of the most successful judicial innovations according to the USAID has been the creation of the, so-called, Public Order Courts to fight organized crime and terrorism. But these courts, staffed by faceless judges and operating under special procedural rules, violate basic due process guarantees, and their activity has been targeted mainly against poor peasants caught in the middle of the struggle among *terratenientes*, drug dealers, the military, paramilitary groups and guerrilla groups.

Democracy II is a counter-hegemonic conception of democracy. In its perspective, Democracy I is seen as an incomplete conception of democracy, rather than a wrong one. Democracy II accepts, therefore, Democracy I as a starting point. Its difference from Democracy I is that it does not believe that the compatibility of world capitalism with democracy can be sustained forever, while maintaining that, in the case of collision between democracy and capitalism, democracy must prevail. The core idea of Democracy II is that global capitalism inflicts systematic harm upon the majority of the populations of the globe, as well as upon nature and the environment. Only unified opposition to global capitalism can reduce, if not eliminate, such harm. Democratic can be said of any peaceful, but not necessarily legal, struggle that seeks to reduce systematic harm by empowering the populations systematically affected by it. Democracy II is, therefore, less procedural and more substantive than Democracy I, and its focus is less on governability than on citizen empowerment and social justice.

The criteria for the rule of law and the judicial system to meet the demands of Democracy II are, thus, much more stringent than those applying to Democracy I. A number of complex issues must be addressed in this regard. Here I mention briefly four of them. The first one concerns the political orientation of judicial activism. Judicial activism or protagonism is not in itself a good or bad thing for Democracy II. It must be evaluated in terms of its substantive merits. For instance, up until recently the best known instances of court activism were politically conservative, if not reactionary. Just think of the German courts in the Weimar Republic and their scandalous double standards, punishing extreme right and extreme left violence; the rulings of the US Supreme Court against New Deal legislation; and the opposition of the Chilean Supreme Court to the democratic socialist measures of Salvador Allende. More recently, Italian prosecutors benefitted from special procedural laws that had been approved by the political elites to expedite criminal prosecution of the leftist organization known as the Red Brigades. In Portugal, the first high-profile judicial intervention in the post-1974 democratic period was the indictment of an extreme left organization known as the FPs 25. The punishment of violent political organizations is as much of an asset for Democracy II as it is for Democracy I. But it is an unconditional asset only to the extent that the extreme right and the extreme left are treated equally. This, however, has rarely been the case.

The second issue refers to the ways the judicial system addresses the large-scale, collective or structural conflicts. Structural conflicts are the social sites of systematic harm produced either directly or indirectly by global capitalism in its interactions with local, regional or national societies. Their symptoms or manifestations may be very diverse. The massive occurrence of disputes among individuals or organizations is one of them, as, for instance, the exponential growth of consumer bankruptcy cases, consumer or environmental protection cases, or even tort liability cases. The usual responses to judicial overload caused by these types of litigation have been restriction of demand, routinization or simplification of procedure, diversion to alternative dispute mechanisms, etc. In the perspective of Democracy II, courts may have here a democratic contribution only if, rather than trivializing such disputes, they make the connection between individual disputes and the underlying structural conflicts. This will involve a far-reaching post-liberal reform in substantive law as well as in procedural law and court organization: class actions; broad standing; proactive judicial syste;, greater lay participation on the part of citizens and NGOs; radical politics of individual and collective rights; and progressive multiculturalism, etc. None of this will be possible without a vast reform of legal education. In sum, in order to meet the criteria of Democracy II the judicial system must see itself as part of a political coalition that takes democracy seriously and gives it precedence over markets and property.

This leads me to the third issue, which concerns the access to law and justice. Contrary to the recommendations of the World Bank, from the perspective of Democracy II it is imperative to repoliticize the question of the access to law and justice by questioning not only the pool of citizens, grassroots movements, and NGOs that must have access, but also the kind of law and justice to which they struggle for access.

I mentioned above that one of the common manifestations of structural conflicts is the massive proliferation of individual disputes in a given area of social life. As common, however, is the opposite manifestation: the systematic suppression of individual disputes, or their resolution by extrajudicial violent means. By way of example I mention the capital/labour conflict. Such indicators as the growth of structural unemployment in many countries, the declining share of salary incomes in the national income, and the proliferation of the so-called atypical work and of jobs so badly paid that the workers stay below the poverty line, show that the structural conflict between capital and labour on a global scale is intensifying rather than diminishing. Nevertheless, in many core and semi-peripheral countries labour litigation has been sharply declining for the last decade. The increased vulnerability of workers and labour unions in the post-Fordist era has acted as a deterrent to resorting to courts to defend labour rights.

Whenever the political and social conditions are such that structural conflicts suppress rather than provoke judicial disputes, access to law and justice according to Democracy II involves the active promotion of disputes. In other words it must address the suppressed demand of justice. In this case, a post-liberal judicial system must be socially constructed, as much as a mechanism of dispute settlement as a mechanism of dispute creation.

To the extent that the sustainability of democracy at the local and national level will increasingly depend on the democratization of international and transnational political relations, it is conceivable that the democratic potential of the judicial system will increasingly depend on the emergence of forms of international justice more adequate to confront the systematic harm produced by structural conflicts at the level at which it is produced – the global level. One may think of institutions similar to the European Court of Justice, but premised, rather, on the principle of democracy first, and capitalism (markets and property) second, and not the opposite, as is the case of the European Court.

The ideal-typical counter-position of Democracy I and Democracy II is useful only to identify clearly two possible and contrasting political roles to be performed by the courts in democratic societies. In reality the social and political processes are much messier. Partial versions of both types of democracy may be coexisting side by side, supported by different social groups, or articulate, interpenetrate or fuse in complex, hybrid political constellations. Thus, in real social processes, the political role of courts is inherently ambiguous, undetermined, open-ended and, above all, in itself an object of social struggle. Different political groups will struggle to control the nature, orientation or interpretation of court rulings. The attempt by dominant groups to keep the judicial activism within the boundaries of Democracy I – restricting it to promote governability and facilitate economic transactions – will be met with resistance by subordinate groups trying to expand judicial activism into the areas of citizens' empowerment and social justice. The relative strength of these groups will dictate the overall political profile of the courts' roles.

The scale, time frame and context of political struggles also condition the nature of judicial intervention. Taken in isolation at a given point in time, an individual court ruling cannot be said to promote (or hinder) unequivocally either Democracy I or Democracy II. Let us take the example of judicial rulings against political corruption. It is today consensual that political corruption is detrimental to Democracy I. On the one hand, by transforming rights into favors and by engendering inefficiency and unpredictability in public administration, it erodes the confidence in the state, thereby bringing about ungovernability (Della Porta and Vannucci 1997: 114). On the other hand, by undermining the conditions of market competitions, elevating costs, and having a negative impact on investment, political corruption is an impairment to an efficient and open market economy (Ades and Di Tella 1997: 98). A few court rulings against political corruption do not necessarily contribute to the end of corruption. They may even function, by their sporadic nature, as a cover up, whitewashing and legitimizing the political system that goes on producing political corruption in a systematic fashion.

278 *Globalizing Institutions*

In a time dominated by media politics and by politics as spectacle, the courts' intervention in high-profile cases – usually, the cases involving powerful, high-profile individuals – performs a symbolic function which we could call the judicial carnivalization of politics: a "ceremony" through which, for a brief period, the powerful are treated as ordinary citizens like any one of us. On the contrary, a systematic judicial campaign against political corruption, particularly if complemented by a high-profile, aggressive judicial intervention in the public sphere, specially in the mass media, will, as has happened in Italy, contribute decisively to eradicate corruption, thus strengthening Democracy I.[19]

The global focus on the role of law and the judicial system is part and parcel of the hegemonic type of democracy – Democracy I – and, as such, it is a form of hegemonic globalization. However, to the extent that subordinate groups across the globe manage to intensify social struggles in such a way as to inscribe the goal of Democracy II in the political agenda, and resort, for that purpose among other means, to the intervention of courts, the latter will operate as a form of counterhegemonic globalization. The reason why, nowadays, this possibility seems remote lies in the fact that the political forces engaged in struggles geared to Democracy II have not yet been willing, or able, to identify the full democratic potential of the indeterminacy and ambiguity of the judicial activism within the confines of Democracy I. Such unwillingness or incapacity occurs both because high-profile judicial activism is, in most countries, a novelty at best and, as such, an unfamiliar political tool, and also because in pro-Democracy II social struggles, the role of courts tends to be much less central, its political weight being premised upon complex articulations with many other forms of political action. The constitutional status of the judicial system and its institutional insulation does not facilitate the emergence of constellations of political action in which resorting to courts is part of a broader political strategy. Depending on the circumstances, such an encompassing political strategy may indeed dictate either the intensive use of courts or, on the contrary, the systematic avoidance of courts. Among the circumstances, we can list the political content of the laws to be implemented, and the degree of freedom of the judges to interpret them; the patterns of training and recruitment of judges and prosecutors; the vulnerability of courts to political patronage, or to corruption, etc.

From another perspective, the determination of the hegemonic or counter-hegemonic character of judicial activism is subjected to the same difficulties discussed above in identifying and distinguishing traits of Democracy I and of Democracy II in concrete political processes. Assuming that hegemonic liberal globalization involves a total priority of freedom over equality, whose social cost is the promotion of unprecedented exclusionary policies, we can establish, as a kind of rule of thumb, that the counter-hegemonic value of court activism is premised upon the latter's capacity to block the race to the bottom across the globe. Such capacity is to be tested and exercised against powerful actors (protection of labour, minority, women's, consumer, sexual orientation and environmental rights), against the state (protection of citizens against illegal, discretionary or otherwise unpredictable acts of public administration) or against political power in a broad sense (punishment of abuse of power and of political corruption).

Conclusion

The focus for the last decade on the rule of law and the judicial system across the globe is a major transnational political phenomenon of our time. Sometimes a product of internal dynamics, sometimes a product of high-intensity globalization pressure, more often than not, a product of a combination of both, this trend, known as judicialization of politics, or as an expansion of judicial power, is intimately related to the construction of a new state form, which can be characterized as post-welfare (in core countries) or post-developmentalist (in semi-peripheral countries). This is an efficient weak state suited to complement the efficient regulation of social and economic life by markets and the private sector. This new model of development, seemingly enjoying a global consensus (how strong or well informed this consensus is remains an open question) is premised upon the idea that social transformation has ceased to be a political issue. The rule of law and the judicial system appear to be the ideal instruments of a depoliticized conception of social transformation.

Concomitantly, democracy has been promoted as the political regime best suited to guarantee the stability, governability and social legitimacy of an efficient weak state, as well as a depoliticized capitalist social transformation. The rule of law and the courts have been called upon to be the main pillars of such a democratic project.

This hegemonic project, the ideal-type of which I have designated as Democracy I, is based on the assumption that capitalism and democracy are compatible and even interdependent. Such an assumption has been highly problematic in the past, and nothing has changed in the last decade to make it less problematic now. Nothing has changed in the recent past to eliminate or even reduce, in the framework of this democratic project, the precedence of capitalism over democracy, particularly now that capitalism is global and democracy continues to be national. It is highly improbable that, against past experience, the rule of law and courts will sustain democracy against capitalism.

The vulnerability of this democratic project is twofold. First, democratic stability is dependent upon not letting social inequalities go too far. Yet, they have actually been increasing dramatically for the past decade. It is quite an open question, mediated by many political factors, when such dramatic increase will reach the breaking point beyond which turbulence will take over democratic stability. Second, a liberal democratic public sphere presupposes the rule-based equality of all citizens and the equal accountability of the government towards them. Under the neo-liberal model of development, powerful social agents are emerging in command of such an economic and political leverage that they can easily circumvent the laws, or change them to suit their interests. The principle of equality is thereby manipulated beyond recognition. On the other hand, the same development model makes the nation states tightly accountable to global capitalist enterprises, at the same time that it forces them, or allows them, to be more and more vaguely accountable to national individual citizens. The combination of these two trends may contribute to turn capitalist democratic societies into ever shrinking islands of democratic public life in a sea of societal fascisms.[20]

Both vulnerabilities of democracy I project are the product of, or are compounded by, structural conflicts and therefore can only be effectively neutralized by political action addressed to the democratic settlement of such conflicts. Under Democracy I, the rule of law has done little to address structural conflicts, when in fact it has not exacerbated them, while the judicial system, by its very liberal institutional design, has in general stayed away from such conflicts. In this respect, the political role of courts is determined as much by the disputes that are selected to be processed by them, as by the disputes that are suppressed or selected out. Thus perceived, the political role of courts is rather disquieting, for courts, by their actions or omissions, tend to hide or negate the very existence of systematic harm; or else, that not being at all possible, they tend to divide those who might otherwise unite to fight against such harm.

The analysis of recent judicial experience shows that the rule of law and the judicial system are a central component of Democracy I and crucial to sustain it, short of a situation of incompatibility *vis-à-vis* the accumulated needs of global capitalism. It seems, therefore, that democracy can only be effectively defended in such a situation if the assumption of the taken-for-granted compatibility between capitalism and democracy is rejected as an assumption, and if democracy is conceptualized as taking precedence over capitalism, should a situation of incompatibility arise. This is the project I have called Democracy II. In this project, the rule of law and the judicial system are as important as in Democracy I. They are, however, less central because they must be conceived as part of a much broader set of participatory institutions and social movements, pluralistically organized and networking around a simple, but crucial, principle: democracy first, capitalism second.

Notes

*   I would like to thank Jane Jenson, Harry Arthurs, Erik Olin Wright, Mauricio Garcia Villegas, Gabriel Gomez, Cesar Rodriguez, Luis Carlos Arenas, David Trubek, Allen Hunter, and David Nelken for their comments on earlier versions of this paper. Many thanks to my research assistant João Paulo Dias and, last but not least, to Maria Irene Ramalho for her invaluable editorial comments.
1.   The current debate on the autonomy and jurisdiction of the new permanent international criminal court under the initiative of the UN is illustrative of the tensions and constraints confronting the internationalization of the judicial system.
2.   On the concept of core, semi-peripheral and peripheral states in the world system, see Wallerstein (1974).
3.   Elsewhere, I deal in great detail with these factors. See Santos (1995: 270-274).
4.   For this description I rely heavily on Nelken (1996). On the political impact of corruption in Italy, see Della Porta and Di Tella (1997). On corruption in Europe, see Della Porta and Meny (1997). On the economics and politics of corruption in general, see Heywood (1997).
5.   The Russian Constitutional Court was suspended for more than a year. It resumed its activities in March 1995, and it was immediately thrust into the public spotlight. According to Pomeranz (1996), one of the most controversial cases that the Constitutional Court has dealt with since its 1995 reinstatement has been the Chechen case, which revolved around President Yeltsin's decision to send federal troops into the Chechen Republic without first seeking legislative consent. For Pomeranz, this controversial case on the division of powers represented the opportunity for the new Constitutional Court to dispel the activist image that it had acquired during the previous period, before suspension.
6.   See also Granin (1998).
7.   With the same intention of keeping the judicial system under political control, several judges of the Constitutional Court of Peru were dismissed by the Government in 1997 (Pastor 1998: 22).
8.   The interview was given to the author on September 10, 1996, as part of a research project under way on the landscape of justices in Colombia.
9.   One cannot help tracing in this "new" strategy the same imperialistic posture that led, in a very recent past, the USAID and the USA government to collaborate with military *juntas*, when they were not directly involved in their coming to power.
10.   Other evaluations of the rule of law and judicial reform movement in Latin America mention Chile and Costa Rica as successful cases, and Mexico and Argentina as failures. See Carothers (1998: 101).

11. The USAID sees itself as an experimental risk-taking innovator in developing approaches, with modest funding, that can then be taken over by other donors willing to make more substantial investments (USAID 1994).

12. The total investment of Venezuela in judicial reform, including funds provided by the Inter-American Development Bank, amounts to 120 million dollars. According to recent official data, of the 23,379 detained in Venezuelan prisons, only 7,945 have been convicted. These and other similarly disquieting data have led the President of the Judicial Council to consider that judicial and legal reform is a question "of survival of democracy."

13. From 1992 to 1997, the World Bank and the Inter-American Development Bank distributed 300 million dollars in loans and grants in 25 countries (Messick 1998: 1). The European Bank for Reconstruction and Development, the European Union, and some European countries through their agencies for international cooperation (most prominently, the GTZ, Deutsche Gesellschaft für Technische Zuzammenarbeit) have also been active in funding judicial reform and rule of law projects.

14. On Cambodia, see Lorenz (1995). The Khmer Rouge literally liquidated the judicial system as a whole. Only one judge with legal training remained in the country after that. In the case of Mozambique, after centuries of colonialism and thirty years of war, the few able lawyers of the country are justices of the Supreme Court or practice law in Maputo. In the rest of the country, the judicial system, in the liberal modern sense, hardly exists. The Danish international aid agency (DANIDA) and the Portuguese government have recently provided the funds to rebuild (or rather to build anew) the judicial system.

15. The cover story, entitled "Steely Resolve", in *India Today*, October 31, 1996 is dedicated to the courts' determination to uphold accountability at all costs: "A judicial *coup d'état*? Hardly. The growing assertiveness of the higher judiciary over the past year in meting out corruption in public life has caused near hysteria amongst politicians" (20).

16. On the Portuguese case, see Santos *et al.* (1996)

17. The activism of courts in the USA may have something to do with the extent to which real political cleavages have been smoothed out in this country.

18. Colombia is probably the only country in the world with a philanthropic organization devoted to providing welfare assistance for the widows and children of assassinated judges. This philanthropic organization (FASOL) is an interesting case of internationalist judicial solidarity, in that it is funded in part by German judges, who contribute to it a day's salary per year. In such a situation of contracted democracy, one may well wonder where the protection function of the judicial system lies when the system cannot even protect itself.

19. In Italy, the judges helped to open up the political system allowing for the emergence of new opposition parties but, at the same time, they also contributed to a new wave of populism, a "virtual democracy," using the media to appeal directly to the people.

20. On the concept of societal fascism and the different forms it takes, see Santos (1998).

References

Ades, Alberto and Di Tella, Rafael 1997, 'The New Economics of Corruption: A Survey and Some New Results,' in Heywood (ed.), pp.80-99.

Carothers, Thomas 1998, 'The Rule of Law Revival,' *Foreign Affairs* 77: 95-106.

Della Porta, Donatella and Meny, Yves 1997, *Democracy and Corruption in Europe*, London Printer.

Della Porta, Donatella and Vannucci, Alberto 1997, 'The Perverse Effects of Political Corruption,' in Heywood (ed.), op. cit. pp.100-122.

Galanter, Marc 1992, 'Law Abounding: Legalization Around the North Atlantic,' *The Modern Law Review* 55: 1-24.

Granin, Vadim 1998, 'Vestiges of an Ideology: The Soviet Legacy and its Effect on Russian Legal Reform,' *Parker School Journal of East European Law*, 4, 2: 183-206.

Haggard, Stephen and Kaufman, Robert R. 1992, *The Political Economy of Democratic Transitions*, Princeton: Princeton University Press.

Held, David (ed.) 1993, *Prospects for Democracy*, Stanford: Stanford University Press.

Held, David 1993, 'Democracy: From City-States to a Cosmopolitan Order?,' in Held (ed.), pp. 13-52.

Hendley, Kathryn 1995, 'The Spillover Effects of Privatization on Russian Legal Culture,' *Transnational Law and Contemporary Problems* 5: 40-64.

Heywood, Paul (ed.) 1997, *Political Corruption*, Oxford: Blackwell.

Hoon, Shim Jae 1993, 'Judging the Judges,' *Far Eastern Economic Review*, December 9, 28-30.

Kitchin, William 1995, 'Legal Reform and the Expansion of Judicial Power in Russia,' in Tate and Vallinder (eds.), pp. 441-459.

Klug, Heinz 1996, *Constitutionalism, Democratization and Constitution-making for a New South Africa*, LL.M. dissertation, University of Wisconsin-Madison Law School.

Lorenz, F. M. 1995, 'Democratic Reform and the Rule of Law in Cambodia,' *Washington State Bar News*, February, 26-30.

Messick, Richard 1999, 'Judicial Reform and Econmic Devlopment: a survey of Issues,' *The World Bank Research Observer*, 14, 1: 117-136.

Nelken, David 1996, 'The Judges and Political Corruption in Italy,' *Journal of Law and Society* 23: 95-112.

Nino, Carlos S. 1993, 'On the Exercise of Judicial Review in Argentina,' in Stotzky (ed.), pp. 309-335.

Osiel, Mark J. 1995, 'Dialogue with Dictators: Judicial Resistance in Argentina and Brazil,' *Law and Social Inquiry* 20: 481-560.

Pastor, Ricardo 1998, 'La Reforma de la Justicia Peruana,' paper presented to the *Workshop on Judicial Reform*, Oñati: International Institute of Sociology of Law.

Pomeranz, William 1996, 'Judicial Review and the Russian Constitutional Court: The Chechen Case,' Manuscript.

Popkin, Margaret and Roht-Arriaza, Naomi 1995, 'Truth as Justice: Investigatory Commission in Latin America,' *Law and Social Inquiry* 20: 79-115.

Rosenberg, Gerald 1991, *The Hollow Hope: Can Courts bring about Social Change?*, University of Chicago Press.

Rowat, Malcom 1995, 'Judicial Reform in Latin America and the Caribbean: Operational Implications for the Bank,' in Rowat *et al.*, pp. 16-18.

Rowat, Malcom, Malik, Walled, and Dakolias, Maria (eds.) 1995, *Judicial Reform in Latin America and the Caribbean*, Washington: The World Bank.

Santos, Boaventura de Sousa 1995, *Toward a New Common Sense: Law Science and Politics in the Paradigmatic Transition*, New York: Routledge.

--------- 1998, *Reinventar a Democracia*, Lisbon: Gradiva.

Santos, Boaventura de Sousa, Marques, Maria M.L., Pedroso, João and Ferreira, Pedro 1996, *Os Tribunais nas Sociedades Contemporâneas: o Caso Portugues*, Oporto, Afrontamento.

Shapiro, Martin 1993, 'The Globalization of Law,' *Global Legal Studies Journal* 1: 37-64.

Shihata, Ibrahim F.J. 1995, 'Legal Framework for Development: The World Bank's Role in Legal and Judicial Reform,' in Rowat *et al.* (eds.), pp. 13-15.

Thomas, Cheryl A. 1995, 'The Attempt to Institute Judicial Review in the Former USSR,' in Tate and Vallinder (eds.), pp. 421-440.

USAID 1994, *Weighing In on the Scales of Justice: Strategic Approaches for Donor-Supported Rule of Law Programs*, USAID Program and Operations Assessment Report no.7, Washington, DC.

USAID 1996, 'USAID's Strategies for Sustainable Development: Building Democracy,' Website release.

Villegas, Mauricio G. 1993, *La Eficacia Simbolica del Derecho. Examen de Situationes Colombianas*, Bogota: Ediciones Uniandes.

Villegas, Mauricio G. 1996, 'Valores Constitucionales y Necesidades Politicas: Comentarios sobre la Eficacia Judicial del la Constitucion Colombiana,' Paper presented at the Annual Meeting of the Law and Society Association, Glasgow.

Villegas, Mauricio G. 1997, 'Normalidad y Anormalidad Constitucional en Colombia: 1957-1996,' in *Analisis Sociojuridico de la Justicia en Colombia*, Bogota: Cijus-Universidad de los Andes, Chapter 4.

Wallerstein, Immanuel 1974, *The Modern World-System I: Capitalist Agriculture and the Origins of the European World-Economy in the Sixteenth Century*, New York: Academic Press.

World Bank 1997, *World Development Report 1997*, Nova Iorque: Oxford University Press.

Yang, Kun 1998, 'The Constitutional Court in the Context of Democratization: The Case of South Korea,' *Verfassung und Recht in Ubersee*, 31: 160-170.

Zaffaroni, Eugenio R. 1997, 'Globalización y Sistema Penal en America Latina: de la seguridad nacional a la urbana,' paper presented at the *Summer Course on Globalization and Legal Cultures*, Oñati: International Institute of Sociology of Law.

Zifzak, Spencer 1996, 'Hungary's Remarkable, Radical, Constitutional Court,' *Journal of Constitutional Law in Eastern and Central Europe* 3: 1-56.